# The Law of Obligation
# Central and Southeast I

*The Law of Obligations in Central and Southeast Europe* examines the new codifications, reforms, and other recent developments in Central and Southeast Europe which have significantly modernized the law of obligations in the last two decades, focusing particularly on the legal systems of Poland, Czech Republic, Slovak Republic, Hungary, Slovenia, Croatia, Serbia, and Turkey.

With chapters authored by prominent academics and promising young legal scholars, this book discusses the results of the modernizations and describes the legislative reforms of the law of obligations that are underway or are discussed and advocated for in the countries of Central and Southeast Europe. Divergences of the new civil codes and other legislative acts from earlier legal solutions are identified and the rationale behind these departures is analysed, as well as the introduction of the new legal institutes in the law of obligations in these parts of the world. The Introduction provides a concise country-by-country overview of the recodification, modernization, and reform of the law of obligations in Central and Southeast Europe. In Part I, chapters discuss the process of recodification in the Slovak Republic, Czech Republic, Poland, and Hungary, with focus on the main novelties in their contract and tort law. The chapters in Part II then discuss several, more specific legal institutes of the law of obligations, and other recent developments and contemporary challenges to the law of obligations in the Czech Republic, Slovenia, Croatia, Serbia, and Turkey.

This book is of interest to legal scholars in the field of private law, as well as to students, practitioners, members of law reform bodies, and civil servants in Central and Southeast Europe, and beyond.

**Zvonimir Slakoper** is a full professor of civil law and the Head of the Department of Civil Law at the University of Rijeka, Croatia, Faculty of Law, and a full professor of commercial law at the University of Zagreb, Croatia, Faculty of Economics and Business. His expertise covers the law of obligations, especially banking contracts, and company law, and he has written, co-authored, and edited several books, including university textbooks, and many journal articles in these fields.

**Ivan Tot** is an assistant professor of commercial law in the Faculty of Economics and Business at the University of Zagreb, Croatia, and a co-chair of the European Law Institute Croatian Hub. His research mainly focuses on the law of obligations, banking law, and European contract law.

# The Law of Obligations in Central and Southeast Europe

## Recodification and Recent Developments

Edited by
**Zvonimir Slakoper and Ivan Tot**

LONDON AND NEW YORK

First published 2022
by Routledge
2 Park Square, Milton Park, Abingdon, Oxon OX14 4RN

and by Routledge
605 Third Avenue, New York, NY 10158

*Routledge is an imprint of the Taylor & Francis Group, an informa business*

*British Library Cataloguing-in-Publication Data*
A catalogue record for this book is available from the British Library

*Library of Congress Cataloging-in-Publication Data*
Names: Slakoper, Zvonimir, editor. | Tot, Ivan, 1983– editor.
Title: The law of obligations in Central and Southeast Europe : recodification and recent developments / edited by Zvonimir Slakoper and Ivan Tot.
Description: Milton Park, Abingdon, Oxon ; New York, NY : Routledge, 2021. | Includes bibliographical references and index.
Identifiers: LCCN 2021002536 | ISBN 9780367512743 (hardback) | ISBN 9781003080565 (ebook)
Subjects: LCSH: Obligations (Law)—Europe, Central. | Obligations (Law)—Balkan Peninsula.
Classification: LCC KJC1495 .L39 2021 | DDC 346.4302—dc23
LC record available at https://lccn.loc.gov/2021002536

ISBN: 978-0-367-51274-3 (hbk)
ISBN: 978-1-032-02895-8 (pbk)
ISBN: 978-1-003-08056-5 (ebk)

Typeset in Bembo
by Apex CoVantage, LLC

# Contents

# Foreword

It is an honour for me to write the foreword to this volume which includes several chapters that are based on the early drafts presented at the Zagreb International Conference on the Law of Obligations. The number of papers presented was overwhelming and shows the vitality that the topic has in the region of Central and Southeast Europe. This is an evident success for which the accolades go to the organizers and editors, my dear colleagues, Zvonimir Slakoper and Ivan Tot, and the other members of the organization.

As Chair of the Special Interest Group (SIG) on 'Global Private Law' of the European Law Institute, an expert group that I coordinate together with my colleague Anne McNaughton (ANU College of Law), I was invited to be a member of the conference's Scientific Committee, but also to preside over the inaugural session and to hold a SIG meeting within the framework of the conference. I can thus bear witness about the high interest of the papers presented in it. Also, as a European lawyer, it is just natural that one expresses his gratitude to the organizers for having launched such an important initiative. Zagreb, due to its geographical location and the talent of its legal community, is naturally a point of meeting for the legal experts of Central and Southeast Europe, and now also a confluence point for those interested in the law of obligations in Europe more generally. The fact that this first conference    for a second one has already been announced – was structured around thematic axes in which national law issues were juxtaposed to others from a European perspective favoured the attraction of specialists from diverse places and turned the conference into an original European kaleidoscope. Valuable bridges between national developments and EU law have been built at the same time.

The chapters included in the present volume will not only be of interest to the reader from Croatia or other jurisdictions from the very region, but also legal comparatists, students of European law generally, and any lawyer who wants to stay informed on the latest developments in the law of obligations at EU level as well. In places like Croatia, Hungary, etc., one can find modern recodifications of private law, which also often solve legal issues that torment lawyers from more archaic jurisdictions. To this regard, the volume's first part collects papers on the key legal concepts in the Slovak private law recodification; the new statutory regimes on tort liability in Poland, the Czech Republic, and Hungary; the limits to will autonomy in the new private law codifications in the region, as a possible model for Polish law; or the classic topic of contractual breach, seen through the prism of the new Hungarian law, by one of its best specialists. And along with this, issues like set-off, unjust enrichment, real estate transactions, or the impact of constitutional case law in private law, which are dealt with in the second part of the volume, are all issues of true interest from a European perspective as well.

In summary, this work constitutes a valuable window through which to, in some cases, gain access, and at any case look in-depth at a new and dynamic set of legal systems, which are unfortunately little known beyond their borders but which have much to offer to the European private law scholar in general and the legal comparatist in particular. By publishing these chapters in English and making them available to a broader readership, the editors and contributors valuably add to a wider debate on which Central and European lawyers have much more to say than what is sometimes assumed from afar.

*Albert Ruda-González*
Associate Professor of Private Law. Dean
University of Girona, Faculty of Law

# Preface

In the last two decades, the law of obligations in many Central and Southeast European countries was significantly modernized either through adoptions of the new civil codes or through the extensive reforms of the existing civil codes and other legislative acts. In several Central and Southeast European countries, legislative reform of the law of obligations is underway or is being discussed. This book includes discussions on the recodification process, specific legal institutes, and recent developments of the law of obligations in Central and Southeast Europe, with a primary focus on the legal systems of Poland, Czech Republic, Slovak Republic, Hungary, Slovenia, Croatia, Serbia, and Turkey.

This book is one of the several planned volumes that grew out of a conference dedicated to the law of obligations, organized by the Department of Law at the University of Zagreb, Faculty of Economics and Business (FEB Zagreb), and held in Zagreb in December 2019 under the title 'Zagreb International Conference on the Law of Obligations'. One of the five topics of the conference was devoted to the new codifications of the law of obligations in Central and Southeast Europe. Several of the chapters contained in this volume are based on the early drafts presented at the conference under this topic.

As heads of the conference scientific and organizing committees, we are grateful to our partners who supported the Department of Law at FEB Zagreb in the organization of the conference: the UNCITRAL Secretariat and the ELI Global Private Law SIG. We would also like to thank members of the conference scientific and organizing committees and all the conference participants and speakers.

As editors of this volume, we would like to thank the authors who contributed the chapters that appear in this volume and also to Albert Ruda-González who generously agreed to write the foreword to this book. We are grateful to everyone at Routledge who supported this project and contributed to the production process, particularly to Siobhán Poole, Emma Morley and Henry Strang, as well as to everyone at Apex CoVantage, particularly to our project manager Christopher Mathews and our copyeditor Caroline Lalley. We are especially indebted to Siobhán Poole for believing in the project at its proposal and supporting us ever since.

*Zvonimir Slakoper* and *Ivan Tot*

# Abbreviations

| | |
|---|---|
| ABGB | Austrian General Civil Code (*Allgemeines bürgerliches Gesetzbuch*) |
| ADCC | Academic Draft of the Civil Code (Poland) |
| AYM | Constitutional Court of the Republic of Turkey (*Anayasa Mahkemesi*) |
| BGB | German Civil Code (*Bürgerliches Gesetzbuch*) |
| *BGBl* | *Bundesgesetzblatt* (Official Gazette of the Federal Republic of Germany) |
| BGer | Federal Supreme Court of Switzerland (*Bundesgericht*) |
| BGH | Federal Court of Justice of Germany (*Bundesgerichtshof*) |
| *BKR* | *Zeitschrift für Bank- und Kapitalmarktrecht* (Germany) |
| BW | Dutch Civil Code (*Burgerlijk Wetboek*) |
| CCiv | French Civil Code (*Code Civil*) |
| CCQ | Civil Code of Quebec (*Code civil du Québec*) |
| CESL | Common European Sales Law |
| *CILW* | *Computer and Internet Lawyer* (United States) |
| CISG | United Nations Convention on Contracts for the International Sale of Goods |
| CK | Lithuanian Civil Code (*Civilinis kodeksas*) |
| CL | Latvian Civil Code (*Civillikums*) |
| Cod | Civ Italian Civil Code (*Codice Civile*) |
| CUP | Cambridge University Press |
| DCFR | Draft Common Frame of Reference |
| *DNotZ* | *Deutsche Notar-Zeitschrift* (Germany) |
| DV | *Darzhaven Vestnik* (Official Gazette of the Republic of Bulgaria) |
| *DzU* | *Dziennik Ustaw* (Official Gazette of the Republic of Poland) |
| *EBLR* | *European Business Law Review* |
| ECB | European Central Bank |
| ECJ | Court of Justice (at the Court of Justice of the European Union) |

| | |
|---|---|
| *ELTE LJ* | *ELTE Law Journal* (Hungary) |
| *ERCL* | *European Review of Contract Law* |
| *ERPL* | *European Review of Private Law* |
| *EuCML* | *Journal of European Consumer and Market Law* |
| *FZ* | *Fletorja Zyrtare* (Official Gazette of the Republic of Albania) |
| *GZK* | *Gazeta Zyrtare/Službeni list* (Official Gazette of the Republic of Kosovo) |
| HGB | German Commercial Code (*Handelsgesetzbuch*) |
| HMK | Turkish Code of Civil Procedure (*Hukuk Muhakemeleri Kanunu*) |
| *Hrv Prav Rev* | *Hrvatska pravna revija* (Croatia) |
| HUP | Harvard University Press |
| ÎCCJ | Romanian High Court of Cassation and Justice (*Înalta Curte de Casaţie şi Justitie*) |
| IYUK | Turkish Administrative Jurisdiction Procedures Law (*İdari Yargılama Usulleri Kanunu*) |
| *Jb OstR* | *Jahrbuch für Ostrecht* (Germany) |
| *JCP* | *Journal of Consumer Policy* |
| *JdS* | *Journal des Sociétés* (France) |
| *JETL* | *Journal of European Tort Law* |
| *JLS* | *Journal of Legal Studies* (United States) |
| *JORF* | *Journal Officiel de la République Française* (Official Journal of the French Republic) |
| *Juridica Intl* | *Juridica International* (Estonia) |
| *Just Rev* | *Justičná revue* (Slovak Republic) |
| *JZ* | *Juristenzeitung* (Germany) |
| KC | Polish Civil Code (*Kodeks cywilny*) |
| KKPC | Polish Civil Law Codification Commission (*Komisja Kodyfikacyjna Prawa Cywilnego*) |
| *Kwart Prawa Prywat* | *Kwartalnik Prawa Prywatnego* (Poland) |
| LAT | Supreme Court of the Republic of Lithuania (*Lietuvos Aukščiausiasis Teismas*) |
| LG | regional courts in Germany (*Landgericht*) |
| LV | *Latvijas Vēstnesis* (Official Gazette of the Republic of Latvia) |
| *MJ* | *Magyar Jog* (Hungary) |
| *MJECL* | *Maastricht Journal of European and Comparative Law* |
| MK | *Magyar Közlöny* (Official Gazette of Hungary) |
| MLEC | UNCITRAL Model Law on Electronic Commerce |
| MO | *Monitorul Oficial* (Official Gazette of Romania) |
| NCC | New Romanian Civil Code (*Noul Codul civil al României*) |
| *NJW* | *Neue Juristische Wochenschrift* (Germany) |
| NN | *Narodne novine* (Official Gazette of the Republic of Croatia) |

| | |
|---|---|
| NOZ | New Czech Civil Code (*Nový Občanský zákoník*) |
| NSČR | Supreme Court of the Czech Republic (*Nejvyšší soud České republiky*) |
| NS SR | Supreme Court of the Slovak Republic (*Najvyšší súd Slovenskej republiky*) |
| NS SSR | Supreme Court of the Slovak Socialist Republic (*Najvyšší súd Slovenskej socialistickej republiky*) |
| ObZ | Slovak Commercial Code (*Obchodný zákonník*) |
| OblZ | Slovenian Obligations Code (*Obligacijski zakonik*) |
| OGH | Austrian Supreme Court of Justice (*Oberster Gerichtshof*) |
| OJ | *Official Journal of the European Union* |
| OLG | higher regional courts in Germany (*Oberlandesgericht*) |
| OR | Swiss Code of Obligations (*Obligationenrecht*) |
| OstEurR | *Osteuropa Recht* (Germany) |
| OUP | Oxford University Press |
| OZ | Slovak Civil Code (*Občiansky zákonník*) |
| *Panst Prawo* | *Państwo i Prawo* (Poland) |
| PECL | Principles of European Contract Law |
| PETL | Principles of European Tort Law |
| *PP* | *Pravna praksa* (Slovenia) |
| *Prav Letop* | *Pravni letopis* (Slovenia) |
| *Prav Obzor* | *Právny obzor* (Slovak Republic) |
| *Prav Praxe* | *Právní praxe* (Czech Republic) |
| *Prav Rozhl* | *Právní rozhledy* (Czech Republic) |
| *Prz Leg* | *Przegląd Legislacyjny* (Poland) |
| *Prz Prawa Handl* | *Przegląd Prawa Handlowego* (Poland) |
| *Prz Ustaw Gosp* | *Przegląd Ustawodawstwa Gospodarczego* (Poland) |
| Ptk | Hungarian Civil Code (*Polgári Törvénykönyv*) |
| *RG* | *Türkiye Cumhuriyeti Resmî Gazete* (Official Gazette of the Republic of Turkey) |
| RK | Supreme Court of the Republic of Estonia (*Riigikohus*) |
| *RT* | *Riigi Teataja* (Official Gazette of the Republic of Estonia) |
| *Ruch Praw Ekonom Socjol* | *Ruch Prawniczy, Ekonomiczny i Socjologiczny* (Poland) |
| *Sb* | *Sbírka zákonů* (Official Gazette of the Czech Republic) |
| SELP | Sellier European Law Publishers |
| *SG RS* | *Službeni glasnik Republike Srbije* (Official Gazette of the Republic of Serbia) |
| *SG RSrp* | *Službeni glasnik Republike Srpske* (Official Gazette of the Republic of Srpska) |
| *SL CG* | *Službeni list Crne Gore* (Official Gazette of Montenegro) |

| | |
|---|---|
| *SL FNRJ* | *Službeni list Federativne Narodne Republike Jugoslavije* (Official Gazette of the Federal People's Republic of Yugoslavia) |
| *SL RBiH* | *Službeni list Republike Bosne i Hercegovine* (Official Gazette of the Republic of Bosnia and Herzegovina) |
| *SL SCG* | *Službeni list Srbije i Crne Gore* (Official Gazette of Serbia and Montenegro) |
| *SL SFRJ* | *Službeni list Socijalističke Federativne Republike Jugoslavije* (Official Gazette of the Socialist Federal Republic of Yugoslavia) |
| *SL SRJ* | *Službeni list Savezne Republike Jugoslavije* (Official Gazette of the Federal Republic of Yugoslavia) |
| SN | Supreme Court of the Republic of Poland (*Sąd Najwyższy*) |
| *SN FBiH* | *Službene novine Federacije Bosne i Hercegovine* (Official Gazette of the Federation of Bosnia and Herzegovina) |
| SPZ | Slovenian Property Law Code (*Stvarnopravni zakonik*) |
| *Stud Cywilis* | *Studia Cywilistyczne* (Poland) |
| *Stud Juridica* | *Studia Juridica* (Poland) |
| *Stud Prawn* | *Studia prawnicze* (Poland) |
| *SV RM* | *Službeni vesnik na Republika Makedonija* (Official Gazette of the Republic of Macedonia) |
| TBK | Turkish Code of Obligations (*Türk Borçlar Kanunu*) |
| TFEU | Treaty on the Functioning of the European Union |
| TMK | Turkish Civil Code (*Türk Medenî Kanunu*) |
| *Transform Prawa Prywat* | *Transformacje Prawa Prywatnego* (Poland) |
| TsÜS | Estonian General Part of the Civil Code Act (*Tsiviilseadustiku üldosa seadus*) |
| TZ | Bulgarian Commercial Act (*Targovski zakon*) |
| UCC | Uniform Commercial Code |
| ULFC | The Hague Convention relating to a Uniform Law on the Formation of Contracts for the International Sale of Goods |
| ULIS | The Hague Convention relating to a Uniform Law on the International Sale of Goods |
| *UL RS* | *Uradni list Republike Slovenije* (Official Gazette of the Republic of Slovenia) |
| UNCITRAL | United Nations Commission on International Trade Law |
| UNIDROIT | International Institute for the Unification of Private Law |
| UPICC | UNIDROIT Principles of International Commercial Contracts |

| USRH | Constitutional Court of the Republic of Croatia (*Ustavni sud Republike Hrvatske*) |
| VÕS | Estonian Law of Obligations Act (*Võlaõigusseadus*) |
| VSL | High Court of Ljubljana (*Višje sodišče v Ljubljani*) |
| VSRH | Supreme Court of the Republic of Croatia (*Vrhovni sud Republike Hrvatske*) |
| VTSRH | High Commercial Court of the Republic of Croatia (*Visoki trgovački sud Republike Hrvatske*) |
| *VuR* | *Verbraucher und Recht* (Germany) |
| *WGO* | *WGO-Monatshefte für Osteuropäisches Recht* (Germany) |
| *WiRO* | *Wirtschaft und Recht in Osteuropa* (Germany) |
| YZOO | Yugoslav Obligations Act of 1978 |
| *Zb* | *Zbierka zákonov* (Official Gazette of the Czechoslovak Socialist Republic, Slovak edition) |
| *Zbornik PFR* | *Zbornik Pravnog fakulteta Sveučilišta u Rijeci* (Croatia) |
| ZEPEP | Slovenian Electronic Business and Electronic Signature Act (*Zakon o elektronskom poslovanju in elektronskem podpisu*) |
| ZET | Croatian Electronic Commerce Act (*Zakon o elektroničkoj trgovini*) |
| *ZeuP* | *Zeitschrift für Europäisches Privatrecht* (Germany) |
| ZGB | Swiss Civil Code (*Zivilgesetzbuch*) |
| *ZIP* | *Zeitschrift für Wirtschaftsrecht* (Germany) |
| ZOO | Croatian Obligations Act (*Zakon o obveznim odnosima*) |
| ZPO | German Code of Civil Procedure (*Zivilprozessordnung*) |
| ZVDSP | Croatian Act on Ownership and Other Real Rights (*Zakon o vlasništvu i drugim stvarnim pravima*) |
| *Zz* | *Zbierka zákonov* (Official Gazette of the Slovak Republic) |
| ZZD | Bulgarian Obligations and Contracts Act (*Zakon za zadŭlzheniyata i dogovorite*) |
| ZZK | Slovenian Land Register Act (*Zakon o zemljiški knjigi*) |
| *Žin* | *Valstybės žinios* (Official Gazette of the Republic of Lithuania) |

# Contributors

**Ewa Bagińska** is a full professor of civil law and the Head of the Department of Civil Law at the University of Gdańsk, Faculty of Law and Administration. Her expertise covers civil law, especially tort law, and consumer protection law, and she has widely published in these areas as well as in the areas of comparative civil liability law, medical law, and insurance law. She is a member of the European Group on Tort Law and Co-Chair of the European Law Institute Polish Hub.

**David Borlinič Gačnik** is a judicial trainee at the High Court in Maribor, and a PhD student in civil law at the University of Maribor, Faculty of Law. In his research, he is primarily focused on civil law, especially property law and contract law.

**Jiří Handlar** is an assistant professor of civil law at the Masaryk University in Brno, Faculty of Law, and a judge at the Regional Court in Brno. In his research, he is primarily focused on civil law, especially contract law, and has widely published in these areas.

**Marek Ivančo** is an assistant professor of civil law at the Comenius University in Bratislava, Faculty of Law. In his research, he is primarily focused on the procedural issues of civil law and has published widely in this field.

**Jure Jakšić** is a senior judicial consultant at the District Court of Maribor, and a PhD student in EU law at the University of Maribor, Faculty of Law. In his research, he is primarily focused on EU law and civil law.

**Orhan Emre Konuralp** is an assistant professor of civil procedure and enforcement and bankruptcy law at the Istanbul Aydın University, Faculty of Law. Previously he was a research assistant at the Bilkent University in Ankara, Faculty of Law, and a postdoctoral researcher at the Swiss Institute of Comparative Law in Lausanne. His research mainly focuses on civil procedure law, enforcement law, and bankruptcy law.

**Attila Menyhárd** is a full professor of civil law and the Head of the Department of Civil Law at the Eötvös Loránd University in Budapest, Faculty of Law. His expertise, research, and teaching activities cover the whole range of civil law, particularly property law, contract law, tort law, and succession law, as well as commercial law, company law, and comparative and European private law. He is the Head of the New Civil Code Advisory Board to the Supreme Court and a member of UNIDROIT Governing Council.

**Dorota Miler** is an academic assistant at the University of Augsburg, Faculty of Law. Her research mainly focuses on comparative private law (in particular, the general part of private law, law of obligations, and succession law) and the international private law.

**Damjan Možina** is a full professor of civil and commercial law at the University of Ljubljana, Faculty of Law. He studied law in Ljubljana and Berlin (Humboldt). His research areas include contract and tort law, general civil law, European private law, and the law of state liability.

**Zvonimir Slakoper** is a full professor of civil law and the Head of the Department of Civil Law at the University of Rijeka, Faculty of Law, and a full professor of commercial law at the University of Zagreb, Faculty of Economics and Business. His expertise covers law of obligations, especially banking contracts, and company law, and he has written, co-authored, and edited several books, including university textbooks, and many journal articles in these fields.

**Marko Stilinović** is a research assistant and a PhD student in civil law at the University of Zagreb, Faculty of Law. In his research, he is mainly focused on civil and inheritance law.

**Marek Števček** is a professor of civil law and the Head of the Department of Civil Law at the Comenius University in Bratislava, Faculty of Law. He is the Rector of the Comenius University in Bratislava, and the Chairman of the Commission for the Recodification of Private Law. He has written, co-authored, and edited many books and journal articles in the fields of civil substantive and procedural law.

**Ivan Tot** is an assistant professor of commercial law at the University of Zagreb, Faculty of Economics and Business. His research mainly focuses on the law of obligations, banking law, and European contract law. He is a co-chair of the European Law Institute Croatian Hub.

**Ana Vargek Stilinović** is a counsellor at the Croatian National Bank, and a PhD student in European Law at the University of Zagreb, Faculty of Law. Her expertise covers consumer protection, banking supervision, and legal aspects of monetary policy.

**Paulina Wyszyńska-Ślufińska** is an assistant professor of civil law at the University of Gdańsk, Faculty of Law and Administration, and a licensed attorney (Bar Association in Gdańsk). Her research mainly focuses on civil law, especially tort law, and insurance law.

# 1 Recodification and recent developments in the law of obligations in Central and Southeast Europe

*Zvonimir Slakoper and Ivan Tot*

## 1 Introduction

In the last twenty years, the law of obligations in many European countries was significantly modernized, while in several the legislative reform of the law of obligations is either underway or is being actively discussed and advocated. The new 'wave of reforms'[1] of the law of obligations has covered not only the countries with a longstanding tradition of civil law codification but is also spreading throughout Central and Southeast Europe. So far, the twenty-first century in this part of Europe truly is the 'recodification era',[2] with several countries replacing their civil codes with the new ones, and other planning to substantially rewrite them, while many countries with uncodified civil law being underway to enact a civil code for the first time in modern history. The reform of the law of obligations is a significant part of both the recodification and codification efforts. Even in those countries where these processes are not existent, the law of obligations was recently reformed.

Under the umbrella of 'Central and Southeast Europe', the following groups of countries are covered here: (i) the three Baltic states: Estonia, Latvia, and Lithuania; (ii) the four Visegrád Group states: Poland, Czech Republic, Slovakia, and Hungary; (iii) the seven states of the former Yugoslavia: Slovenia, Croatia, Bosnia and Herzegovina, Serbia, Montenegro, Kosovo, and North Macedonia; and (iv) the remaining three Southeast European states: Romania, Bulgaria, and Albania. Turkey, which belongs to Southeast Europe only partly, is also discussed within the fourth group.

---

1 Reiner Schulze, 'Changes in the Law of Obligations in Europe' in Reiner Schulze and Fryderyk Zoll (eds), *The Law of Obligations in Europe: A New Wave of Codifications* (SELP 2013) 3.

2 Julio César Rivera, 'The Scope and Structure of Civil Codes: Relations with Commercial Law, Family Law, Consumer Law and Private International Law: A Comparative Approach' in Julio César Rivera (ed), *The Scope and Structure of Civil Codes* (Springer 2013) 17. See also Péter Cserne, 'The Recodification of Private Law in Central and Eastern Europe' in Pierre Larouche and Péter Cserne (eds), *National Legal Systems and Globalization: New Role, Continuing Relevance* (Springer 2013) 45ff; Ewoud Hondius, 'Recodification of Private Law in Central and Eastern Europe and in the Netherlands' [2014] (1) *ELTE LJ* 51.

This introductory chapter aims to provide a concise country-by-country overview of the recodification, modernization, and reform of the law of obligations in Central and Southeast Europe, as well as to present the issues which are analysed more thoroughly in the following chapters. In the final remarks to this chapter, some common features of the law of obligations in Central and Southeast Europe are identified.

## 2  The law of obligations in the Baltic states

After regaining their independence in the Baltic Revolution of 1991, Estonia, Latvia, and Lithuania were among the first of the post-socialist European countries to endeavour to recodify their civil law. The period during which they were part of the Soviet Union was viewed in all three states as a period of discontinuity with their earlier civil law, thus all three states decided to abolish the socialist civil codes adopted during the Soviet occupation. Yet, the process of recodification occurred differently in the three Baltic states.[3]

### *2.1  Estonia*

Estonia opted to proceed with a step-by-step codification of its civil law, instead of enacting the earlier draft civil code from 1940.[4] Between 1993 and 2001, five separate laws were enacted which function together as one civil law codification and govern the general part of civil law, property law, family law, the law of succession, and the law of obligations. The Law of Obligations Act (*Võlaõigusseadus,*[5] VÕS) was adopted in 2001 and entered into force on 1 July 2002. On the same day, the revised version of the General Part of the Civil Code Act (*Tsiviilseadustiku üldosa seadus,*[6] TsÜS), adopted in 2002, also entered into force.

TsÜS was drafted primarily under the influence of the German and Swiss law, with several notable concepts, such as the rules on mistake and fraud, developed based on UPICC and PECL.[7] VÕS is based on the comparative study of the German BGB, Swiss OR, and Dutch BW, with influences from

---

3 Cserne (n 2) 54; Norbert Reich, 'Transformation of Contract Law and Civil Justice in the New EU Member Countries: The Example of the Baltic States, Hungary and Poland' (2004) 23 *Penn State Intl L Rev* 587, 594–95.

4 Cserne (n 2) 54–55; Reich (n 3) 595. For a historical overview see Irene Kull, 'Codification of Private Law in Estonia' in Julio César Rivera (ed), *The Scope and Structure of Civil Codes* (Springer 2013) 134–39.

5 *RT* I 2001, 81, 487, as later amended.

6 *RT* I 2002, 35, 216, as later amended.

7 Kull, 'Codification' (n 4) 142. See also Paul Varul, 'Legal Policy Decisions and Choices in the Creation of New Private Law in Estonia' [2000] *Juridica Intl* 104, 111–12.

PECL and UPICC.[8] Also, various other jurisdictions have been taken into account,[9] as well as CISG and several other international conventions.[10]

The monistic concept was adopted in VÕS, thus the regulation of commercial transactions, as well as consumer transactions, is not found in separate codes.[11] VÕS consists of a general part which governs the general principles of the law of obligations and the rules of general contract law[12] and a special part which includes regulation of the specific types of contracts and the extra-contractual obligations.[13] The modern contract types, such as financial leasing, factoring, and franchising, are also regulated within the special part.[14] The EU directives are transposed in the provisions of VÕS, not in separate laws.[15]

## 2.2 Latvia

Latvia is the only Baltic state that had a civil code in force before the Soviet occupation. After regaining its independence, Latvia re-enacted in 1993 its old Civil Code of 1937 (*Civillikums*,[16] CL) which was significantly influenced by the BGB.[17] The law of obligations is governed by Part IV of the reinstated CL which regulates the general part of the law of obligations, specific contracts, and extra-contractual obligations.[18] Amendments to the CL in 2006, 2009, and 2013, related *inter alia* to the introduction of the concept of moral damages, the introduction of the prerequisite of the foreseeability of damage in contractual liability, and restriction of the application of contractual penalties, are seen as a significant modernization of the Latvian contract law.[19]

---

8  Varul, 'Legal Policy' (n 7) 114; Irene Kull, 'Reform of Contract Law in Estonia: Influences of Harmonisation of European Private Law' [2008] *Juridica Intl* 122, 127–28.
9  These include the German HGB and the Czech Commercial Code, as well as the civil codes of Italy, Russia, Louisiana, Quebec, and Japan, and the private law sources of the Scandinavian countries. See Villu Kõve, 'Applicable Law in the Light of Modern Law of Obligations and Bases for the Preparation of the Law of Obligations Act' [2001] *Juridica Intl* 30, 36; Kull, 'Codification' (n 4) 143; Varul, 'Legal Policy' (n 7) 114.
10  See Kõve (n 9) 36; Kull, 'Reform' (n 8) 128.
11  Kull, 'Codification' (n 4) 142, 146; Kull, 'Reform' (n 8) 124.
12  For the limitations of freedom of contract in the Estonian law see Miler, ch 4.
13  Kull, 'Codification' (n 4) 142–43; Varul, 'Legal Policy' (n 7) 113–14; Paul Varul, 'The Creation of New Estonian Private Law' (2008) 16 *ERPL* 95, 105–6.
14  Kull, 'Codification' (n 4) 143; Kõve (n 9) 36.
15  See Kull, 'Reform' (n 8) 126–27; Varul, 'Legal Policy' (n 7) 114.
16  *Valdības Vēstnesis* 41 of 20 February 1937, as later amended.
17  Cserne (n 2) 55; Kalvis Torgāns, 'European Initiatives (PECL, DCFR) and Modernisation of Latvian Civil Law' [2008] *Juridica Intl* 137.
18  Kaspar Balodis, 'The Latvian Law of Obligations: The Current Situation and Perspectives' [2013] *Juridica Intl* 69, 70; Linda Damane and others, 'Private Law' in Tanel Kerkmäe and others (eds), *The Law of the Baltic States* (Springer 2017) 291ff.
19  Balodis (n 18) 70–71; Damane and others (n 18) 296.

CISG was not used as an inspiration for Latvian contract law.[20] Similarly, the solutions of PECL, DCFR, and UPICC are only debated in academia, whereas the government is 'quite reserved' to proposals based on soft law.[21]

A considerable part of contract law is regulated outside of the CL in various separate laws. Apart from special regulations for transport and insurance contracts,[22] several types of commercial law contracts are regulated in the Commercial Code,[23] including financial leasing, factoring, and franchising. Consumer contract law is partly found in the Consumer Protection Act,[24] but the EU directives are mostly transposed through special legislation.[25] There are no recent plans for recodification.[26]

## 2.3 Lithuania

Before the Soviet occupation, a draft Lithuanian Civil Code was prepared in 1940 but was never enacted.[27] After Lithuania regained its independence, a decision was made to abolish the socialist Civil Code of 1964 and to prepare a comprehensive new civil law codification.[28] The new Civil Code (*Civilinis kodeksas*,[29] CK) was enacted in 2000 and came into force in 2001. The structure of the CK follows the German pandectistic approach.[30] The law of obligations is found in Book VI of the CK which includes the general part of the law of obligations and special part governing contract law, tort law, the law on quasi-contracts, and the law of statutory civil obligations.[31] Book I of the CK is also of special importance for the law of obligations as the general rules on legal transactions and their validity are found there.[32] The special part in Book VI includes regulation of fifty-three specific contract types, including financial leasing, factoring, and franchising.[33]

---

20  Kalvis Torgāns, 'Latvian Contract Law and the EU' [2001] *Juridica Intl* 38, 39.

21  Torgāns, 'European Initiatives' (n 17) 138–39.

22  Damane and others (n 18) 298; Torgāns, 'Latvian Contract Law' (n 20) 39.

23  *Komerclikums*, *LV* 158/160 of 4 May 2000, as later amended.

24  *Patērētāju tiesību aizsardzības likums*, *LV* 104/105 of 1 April 1999, as later amended.

25  See Damane and others (n 18) 298; Torgāns, 'Latvian Contract Law' (n 20) 39. See also Reich (n 3) 595, 602–3, 609–11.

26  cf Balodis (n 18) 73–74.

27  Reich (n 3) 594.

28  See Valentinas Mikelenas, 'The Influence of Instruments of Harmonisation of Private Law upon the Reform of Civil Law in Lithuania' [2008] *Juridica Intl* 143, 143–45. For a history of the private law in Lithuania see Simona Selelionyté-Drukteiniené, Vaidas Jurkevičius, and Thomas Kadner Graziano, 'The Impact of the Comparative Method on Lithuanian Private Law' (2013) 21 *ERPL* 959, 961–67.

29  Act VIII-1864 of 18 July 2000, *Žin* 2000, 74–2262, as later amended.

30  Laurynas Didžiulis, *Contract Law in Lithuania* (Wolters Kluwer 2019) para 13.

31  ibid para 17; Valentinas Mikelenas, 'The Main Features of the New Lithuanian Contract Law System Based on the Civil Code of 2000' [2005] *Juridica Intl* 42, 43.

32  Mikelenas, 'The Main Features' (n 31) 43. For limitations of freedom of contract in the Lithuanian law see Miler, ch 4.

33  Mikelenas, 'The Main Features' (n 31) 43.

The CK contains rules that apply both to general civil and commercial contracts, and 'calibrated rules' governing the commercial contracts.[34] Another explicitly recognized category is consumer contracts for which the CK sets forth special rules relating to their formation, content, and performance.[35] The EU directives were mostly incorporated into the CK, rather than transposed into special legislation.[36]

The CK was drafted primarily under the influence of the CCQ and BW,[37] while several other foreign legal sources were also taken into consideration.[38] In contract law, the German influence is visible *inter alia* in the concept of a legal transaction and the fact that there is no requirement of causa or consideration.[39] The regulation of extra-contractual obligations primarily has attributes of the French legal family, as witnessed by the general *neminem laedere* rule, the *non-cumul* principle, the general concept of quasi-contracts, and the division of unjustified enrichment remedy in *condictio indebiti* and *actio de in rem verso*.[40] The regulation of restitution independently from unjustified enrichment system, and the enabling of disgorgement based on damages, are described as common law influences.[41]

The regulation of contract law in the CK was most significantly influenced by UPICC, with many UPICC rules directly incorporated into CK, especially relating to the formation of contracts and the quality of performance.[42] PECL was also used as a general source of inspiration.[43] Following the enactment of the CK, the Supreme Court of Lithuania started much more frequently to refer to UPICC and PECL in its decisions, while in several cases reference to PETL was also given.[44]

## 3 The law of obligations in the Visegrád Group states

Of the four Visegrád Group states, new civil codes were recently enacted in Hungary and the Czech Republic, while considerable efforts towards recodification

---

34 Didžiulis (n 30) paras 20, 62.
35 Mikelenas, 'The Main Features' (n 31) 45.
36 Mikelenas, 'The Influence' (n 28) 144–45; Valentinas Mikelenas, 'Unification and Harmonisation of Law at the Turn of the Millennium: The Lithuanian Experience' (2000) 5 *Unif L Rev* 243, 254.
37 Didžiulis (n 30) para 52; Cserne (n 2) 55.
38 Including Cod Civ, CCiv, BGB, ZGB, OR, CL, the civil codes of Russia and Japan, and the Swedish civil law. See Selelionyté-Drukteiniené, Jurkevičius, and Kadner Graziano (n 28) 974; Didžiulis (n 30) para 52; Mikelenas, 'Unification' (n 36) 249–51; Cserne (n 2) 55.
39 Didžiulis (n 30) para 13.
40 ibid.
41 ibid.
42 See Mikelenas, 'The Main Features' (n 31) 43, 47, 50; Mikelenas, 'The Influence' (n 28) 146–47; Mikelenas, 'Unification' (n 36) 251–53; Didžiulis (n 30) para 52; Selelionyté-Drukteiniené, Jurkevičius, and Kadner Graziano (n 28) 975–76.
43 Selelionyté-Drukteiniené, Jurkevičius, and Kadner Graziano (n 28) 976. See also Didžiulis (n 30) para 52; Mikelenas, 'The Main Features' (n 31) 43.
44 See Selelionyté-Drukteiniené, Jurkevičius, and Kadner Graziano (n 28) 983–86.

were made in the last two decades in Poland and the Slovak Republic, where the earlier civil codes are still in force.

### 3.1 Poland

The process of civil law codification was on the agenda in Poland as early as the first half of the twentieth century. One of the results of this early codification effort was the Polish Code of Obligations of 1933 which is still considered as one of the most important achievements of the Polish legislation.[45] Largely the result of a comprehensive comparative analysis, the Code has taken inspiration from the German, Austrian, French, Russian, Hungarian, and Swiss law of obligations, as well as from the Franco-Italian Draft Code of Obligations and Contracts of 1927.[46] The commercial law relations were regulated separately in the Commercial Code of 1934,[47] primarily under the influence of the German law model.[48]

The dualism was abandoned with the Polish Civil Code of 1964 (*Kodeks cywilny*,[49] KC).[50] The Code of Obligations of 1933 was almost entirely taken over into the KC, with one of the main modifications being the employment of a more abstract and technical legislative style typical for the German legislation.[51] The German influence on the KC is also visible in its pandectistic structure.[52] The general provisions applicable to all types of legal transactions are found in the first book, while the third book of KC includes regulation of the general part of the law of obligations, torts, unjustified enrichment, specific contracts, and *negotiorum gestio*.[53]

The KC is described as 'surrealistic',[54] since it had not brought radical discontinuation of the Polish civil law, despite being enacted under the socialist

45  Fryderyk Zoll, 'A Civil Code Outside of Reality: The Polish Codification of the Year 1964, Its Origin, Development and Future' in Wen-Yeu Wang (ed), *Codification in International Perspective: Selected Papers from the 2nd IACL Thematic Conference* (Springer 2014) 128.
46  ibid 127–28. See also Rafał Mańko, 'Unification of Private Law in Europe from the Perspective of the Polish Legal Culture' (2008) 11 *Yearb Pol Eur Stud* 109, 116; Jerzy Rajski, 'European Initiatives and Reform of Civil Law in Poland' [2008] *Juridica Intl* 151.
47  Michal Romanowski, 'Position of the Law of Obligations in Polish Law in the Context of a Reform of the European Law of Obligations' in Reiner Schulze and Fryderyk Zoll (eds), *The Law of Obligations in Europe: A New Wave of Codifications* (SELP 2013) 72.
48  Mańko (n 46) 116.
49  Act of 23 April 1964 – Civil Code (*Ustawa z dnia 23 kwietnia 1964 r – Kodeks cywilny*, DzU 1964, 16, 93), as later amended.
50  Romanowski (n 47) 72.
51  Zoll, 'A Civil Code Outside of Reality' (n 45) 130.
52  With the notable exception of family law being a part of a special code. Adam Brzozowski, 'Civil Law (Law of Contracts, Property and Obligations)' in Stanislaw Frankowski (ed), *Introduction to Polish Law* (Kluwer Law International 2005) 38; Mańko (n 56) 119–20.
53  See Romanowski (n 47) 66–70. See also Brzozowski (n 52) 42, 70ff.
54  Zoll, 'A Civil Code Outside of Reality' (n 45) 133.

regime.[55] Thus, the transition to the market economy in the 1990s only required the elimination of typical socialist remnants from the KC, and Poland entered into the new political and economic reality with a still sufficiently modern civil code.

After the first stage of reform in 1990, in the following twenty years amendments were adopted to several areas of the KC.[56] The reforms have taken into consideration the solutions adopted in OR, BW, CCQ, and civil codes of Italy, Lithuania, Hungary, Slovakia, and the Czech Republic.[57] Rules inspired by CISG, UPICC, and PECL were introduced as well.[58] Consumer contract law was also regulated within the KC, but many of the EU consumer directives were transposed into special laws.[59] Relating to specific contracts, one of the amendments has also incorporated the regulation of the financial leasing into KC.[60] Relating to tort law, recent amendments have reformed the public authority liability for illegal conduct, prescription of tort claims, and non-pecuniary damages to relatives in wrongful death cases.[61]

A highly debated issue in the Polish legal doctrine is whether a new civil code is needed to achieve a more coherent system of private law, or the modernization should continue to be carried out within the current KC.[62] In 1996, the Civil Law Codification Commission (KKPC) was appointed by the government, and among the results of its work are the 'Green Book' on the 'optimal vision' of the Polish civil law, and a draft of a General Part of the Civil Code, published in 2008 and later revised.[63] Although the KKPC was resolved of its duties in 2015, its work is continued in the Polish academia as part of the Academic Draft Civil Code (ADCC) project.[64] Foreign sources used in the preparation of the General Part of the ADCC are not explicitly identified, but it seems that the drafters have taken into consideration the provisions of BGB, ZGB, BW, CCQ, ABGB, CCiv, CK, as well as the Civil Code of Russian

---

55  See ibid; Cserne (n 2) 56.

56  Brzozowski (n 52) 38–40.

57  Romanowski (n 47) 73.

58  Rajski (n 46) 153.

59  See Brzozowski (n 52) 73–74; Romanowski (n 47) 91; Rajski (n 46) 152–53. See also Jan Rudnicki, 'Remarks Regarding the Influence of European Legislation upon Codification of Civil Law' (2017) 71 *Stud Juridica* 207.

60  See Wojciech J Katner, 'Leasing in the Polish Civil Code' (2011) 16 *Unif L Rev* 401.

61  See Bagińska and Wyszyńska-Ślufińska, ch 3, text to n 66. See also Ewa Bagińska, 'Developments in Personal Injury Law in Poland: Shaping the Compensatory Function of Tort Law' (2015) 8 *J Civ L Stud* 309.

62  Cserne (n 2) 55–56; Zoll, 'A Civil Code Outside of Reality' (n 45) 133–34. See also Miler, ch 4, n 4.

63  See Piotr Machnikowski, 'Poland' in Petr Lavický and Jan Hurdík (eds), *Private Law Reform* (Masaryk University 2014) 197ff; Fryderyk Zoll, 'Contract Law in the Draft of the New Polish Civil Code: Formation of Contract, Performance and Non-Performance of Obligations' in Reiner Schulze and Fryderyk Zoll (eds), *The Law of Obligations in Europe: A New Wave of Codifications* (SELP 2013) 93ff. See also Bagińska and Wyszyńska-Ślufińska, ch 3, text to nn 67–70.

64  See 'Akademicki Projekt Kodeksu Cywilnego' <www.projektkc.uj.edu.pl/> accessed 15 June 2020.

Federation and the Civil Code of Ukraine, while DCFR was also used as a source of inspiration for several provisions.[65]

These recent recodification efforts are discussed in more detail in two of the following chapters in this volume. The chapter by Ewa Bagińska and Paulina Wyszyńska-Ślufińska shows that there is a justified need to modernize the Polish tort law system and suggests the possible directions of its further development.[66] The chapter by Dorota Miler gives a critical analysis of both the current rules of KC on freedom of contract and its limitations and the solutions proposed in the General Part of the ADCC.[67]

### 3.2  Czech Republic

In contrast to Polish private law, the private law in former Czechoslovakia was significantly 'deformed by socialism'.[68] The law of obligations was not a part of the Czechoslovak Civil Code of 1964,[69] as it was replaced with mandatory rules of the Economic Code of 1964[70] that have fully suppressed the party autonomy.[71] Therefore, an extensive reform was needed to adapt the Czechoslovakian private law to the needs of the market economy after the Velvet Revolution, and it was carried out in 1991 with an amendment that affected around 80% of the text of the original code.[72] The Commercial Code was adopted the same year,[73] and it included regulation of commercial contracts. In the following twenty years, both codes were amended more than fifty times.[74] Following an unsuccessful attempt at recodification in the mid-'90s, the efforts towards recodification made after 2000 were fruitful and have led to the enactment of the new Civil Code.[75]

---

65  See Miler, ch 4, text to nn 124–25.

66  See ch 3.

67  See ch 4.

68  Cserne (n 2) 57. For a general overview of the development of the Czech law of obligations see Luboš Tichý, 'Czech and European Law of Obligations at a Turning Point' in Reiner Schulze and Fryderyk Zoll (eds), *The Law of Obligations in Europe: A New Wave of Codifications* (SELP 2013) 29–31. See also David Elischer, Ondřej Frinta, and Monika Pauknerová, 'Recodification of Private Law in the Czech Republic' in Julio César Rivera (ed), *The Scope and Structure of Civil Codes* (Springer 2013) 106, 111–14; Josef Fiala and Jan Hurdík, *Contract Law in the Czech Republic* (2nd edn, Wolters Kluwer 2020) paras 10–11.

69  Act 40/1964, Civil Code (*Zákon 40/1964 Sb, Občanský zákoník*), as later amended.

70  Act 109/1964 (*Zákon 109/1964 Sb, Hospodářský zákoník*), as later amended.

71  Tichý (n 68) 30.

72  Act 509/1991 (*Zákon 509/1991 Sb, Zákon, kterým se mění, doplňuje a upravuje občanský zákoník*). See Števček and Ivančo, ch 2, text to nn 2–3.

73  Act 513/1991 (*Zákon 509/1991 Sb, Obchodní zákoník*), as later amended.

74  Tichý (n 68) 31.

75  For an overview of the recodification process see e.g. Elischer, Frinta, and Pauknerová (n 68) 111, 128–29.

With the new Civil Code (*Občanský zákoník*,[76] NOZ), which was enacted in 2012 and came into force on 1 January 2014, the previous dualist model of codification was abandoned. The structure of the NOZ follows the pandectistic approach.[77] General provisions on obligations are found in Part I of the NOZ, while general provisions on contracts are found in Part IV of the NOZ which governs the law of obligations under the heading of relative property rights. The general part of contract law is followed by the regulation of specific contracts, and the obligations arising out of torts, unlawful enrichment, and *negotiorum gestio*. General contract law applies both to civil law and commercial law contracts, but there are also special rules for commercial contracts.[78] Consumer contract law is mostly integrated within the general provisions on obligations, but several of the EU consumer law directives remained transposed in separate laws.[79]

In drafting the NOZ, the most significant influence on the entire NOZ was of the Czech Draft Civil Code of 1937 which was an updated version of the Austrian ABGB.[80] Examples of transplants from foreign sources are the structure of the regulations of the sales contract borrowed from the Swiss OR, and the influence of the German BGB and Italian Cod Civ on the regulation of the process of contracting a sales contract.[81] The provisions on the assignment of a contract are also considered to be inspired by the Italian Cod Civ,[82] while the different regulation for the lease and usufructuary lease contracts was impacted by the BGB.[83] The influence of BGB is also found in several provisions regulating the tort liability.[84] A notable common law influence is the introduction of the institute of trust.[85] Apart from instances of the reception of the foreign codes, many contract law provisions were inspired by the solutions found in international conventions and soft law instruments. Some of the examples are the influence of CISG on the rules on formation of contracts, the influence of *Code Européen des Contrats* on the rules on pre-contractual liability, and the influence of UPICC on the rules on change of circumstances.[86] The regulation

---

76  Act 89/2012, Civil Code (*Zákon* 89/2012 *Sb, Občanský zákoník*), as later amended.
77  Tichý (n 68) 32.
78  Fiala and Hurdík (n 68) para 8.
79  See Elischer, Frinta, and Pauknerová (n 68) 123–25. For the Czech consumer contract law see Stephan Heidenhain, 'Harmonisation of the Czech Consumer Rights in the New Civil Code' [2014] (2) *ELTE LJ* 41.
80  Tichý (n 68) 32. For other influences on the NOZ see Elischer, Frinta, and Pauknerová (n 68) 129.
81  Tichý (n 68) 32, 38.
82  Bohumil Dvořák, 'Assignment of a Contract in the New Czech Civil Code' [2014] (2) *ELTE LJ* 123; Milan Hulmák, 'Czech Republic' in Petr Lavický and Jan Hurdík (eds), *Private Law Reform* (Masaryk University 2014) 139.
83  Petr Bohata, 'Neues Privatrecht in der Tschechischen Republik – Revolution oder Normalität?' (2012) 58 (2) *OstEurR* 2, 14.
84  See in this volume Bagińska and Wyszyńska-Ślufińska, ch 3, text to nn 24–25.
85  Fiala and Hurdík (n 68) para 16.
86  Tichý (n 68) 32–33, 40; Hulmák (n 82) 140.

of the healthcare services contract was influenced by DCFR.[87] In tort law, the principle of *neminem laedere* is considered to be directly inspired by PETL.[88]

Three of the chapters in this volume are exploring the novelties of the NOZ. The dualistic system of contractual and non-contractual liability is discussed in the chapter by Ewa Bagińska and Paulina Wyszyńska-Ślufińska.[89] The limitations of freedom of contract are analysed in the chapter by Dorota Miler.[90] Different approaches of various legal systems to the ascertainment of a claim as a requirement for set-off are evaluated in the chapter by Jiří Handlar who critically analyses the unclear position of NOZ on this matter.[91]

### 3.3 Slovak Republic

Before the enactment of the first Czechoslovak Civil Code in 1950, the Slovak legal system was based on the Hungarian custom law.[92] After 1950, the Slovak and Czech legal systems shared the same history of private law under the socialist regime, and of the comprehensive reforms in 1991. After the dissolution of the Czechoslovak Republic in 1993, the independent Slovak Republic retained the dualist model of codification created in 1991 with the extensive amendments to the Civil Code of 1964 (*Občiansky zákonník*,[93] OZ) and the then adopted Commercial Code (*Obchodný zákonník*,[94] ObZ). Both codes are still in force.

The law of obligations is mostly found in the OZ which contains provisions on contracts, torts, unjustified enrichment, *negotiorum gestio*, public tender, and public promise, as well as in the ObZ which contains provisions on commercial contracts, commercial public tender, and promise of indemnity.[95] Regulation of twenty specific contract types is included in the OZ, while twenty-six contract types are regulated by the ObZ.[96] There is no systematic approach to transposition of the EU directives, thus several of the consumer law directives were implemented in the OZ, several in the Consumer Protection Act of 2007, while others were transposed through special statutes.[97]

---

87  Tichý (n 68) 32, 40.
88  Jiri Hrádek, 'Regulation of Liability for Damage in the New Czech Civil Code' [2014] (2) *ELTE LJ* 223, 224.
89  See ch 3, text to nn 16–30.
90  See ch 4, text to nn 142–45, 158–68, 192–94, 201–2.
91  See ch 6, text to nn 30–37.
92  Monika Jurčová, 'The Influence of Harmonisation on Civil Law in the Slovak Republic' [2008] *Juridica Intl* 166, 167; Josef Fiala, Jan Hurdík, and Katarína Kirstová, *Contract Law in the Slovak Republic* (3rd edn, Wolters Kluwer 2017) paras 2, 10.
93  Act 40/1964, Civil Code (*Zákon 40/1964 Zb, Občiansky zákonník*), as later amended.
94  Act 513/1991, Commercial Code (*Zákon 513/1991 Zb, Obchodný zákonník*), as later amended.
95  Fiala, Hurdík, and Kirstová (n 92) paras 13–14, 19.
96  Jurčová (n 92) 167.
97  See ibid 168–69.

The recodification efforts began in the mid-'90s, but they have resulted only with several unsuccessful attempts at creating the new Slovak Civil Code.[98] However, in 2018 a comprehensive amendment to the OZ was prepared and is yet to be enacted. It provides for a substantive modernization of the Slovak law of obligations, which due to the extent of the proposed changes can be considered as a recodification.[99] Although the amendment will not be repealing the entire ObZ, the heavily criticized dualistic system is going to be replaced with a monistic model of regulation of civil and commercial transactions in the OZ. Significant changes to several institutes of general contract law are proposed, as well as the regulation of several new contract types, including financial leasing and franchising.

In this volume, the current state of recodification of the Slovak law of obligations is discussed in the chapter by Marek Števček and Marek Ivančo who also provide an overview of the main institutional novelties that will be a part of the revised OZ after the current bill is enacted.[100]

### 3.4 Hungary

Following the transformation from socialist to market economy in 1990, Hungary decided in 1998 to start preparing a modern civil code that would replace the Hungarian Civil Code of 1959,[101] adopted in the socialist regime, and amended more than 150 times since its enactment.[102] The new Hungarian Civil Code of 2013 (*Polgári törvénykönyv*,[103] Ptk) entered into force on 13 March 2014. The CCQ and BW were used as an inspiration, but the Ptk is not exclusively based on any foreign model.[104] Contract law in the Ptk is influenced by solutions of CISG, but also of the UPICC, PECL, and DCFR.[105] Several of the EU private law directives were integrated into the Ptk, while others were transposed through separate acts.[106]

The regulation of the law of obligations in Book VI of Ptk begins with general rules applicable to any obligation, including to the legal declarations

---

98  Cserne (n 2) 58; Jurčová (n 92) 170. See also Anton Dulak, 'Slovakia' in Petr Lavický and Jan Hurdík (eds), *Private Law Reform* (Masaryk University 2014) 257ff.

99  See Števček and Ivančo, ch 2.

100  See ch 2.

101  Act IV of 1959 on the Civil Code (*1959 évi IV törvény a Polgári Törvénykönyvről*), MK 1959/82 (VIII 11), as later amended.

102  Cserne (n 2) 63; Lajos Vékás, 'Civil Code of 2013' in Attila Harmathy (ed), *Introduction to Hungarian law* (2nd edn, Wolters Kluwer 2019) § 1.

103  Act V of 2013 on the Civil Code (*2013 évi V törvény a Polgári Törvénykönyvről*), MK 2013/31 (II 26), as later amended.

104  Vékás (n 102) § 4.

105  Cserne (n 2); Vékás (n 102) § 4; András Kisfaludi, 'The Influence of Harmonisation of Private Law on the Development of the Civil Law in Hungary' [2008] *Juridica Intl* 130, 134–36.

106  Vékás (n 102) § 3; Ádám Fuglinszky, 'Some Structural Questions on the Relationship between Contractual and Extracontractual Liability in the New Hungarian Civil Code' in Attila Menyhárd and Emőd Veress (eds), *New Civil Codes in Hungary and Romania* (Springer 2017) 108.

in property, family, and succession law.[107] They are followed with the general rules of contract law, and the regulation of specific contracts, tort law, securities, unjustified enrichment, and *negotiorum gestio*. The monistic approach is adopted in contract law, with the Ptk containing exceptional rules for consumer contracts.[108] The modern contract types are regulated as well, including financial leasing, factoring, and franchising.[109] Trusts are also introduced, and the adopted model is similar to express trusts in the common law.[110] One of the novelties is also the introduction of the general regulation on the transfer of rights and contracts.[111]

The new Ptk has abolished the unified system of contractual and tort liability adopted in the previous code.[112] The presumed fault-based liability for breach of contract was replaced with a strict liability regime, the foreseeability clause was adopted from CISG, while an explicit *non-cumul* rule was also introduced.[113] The regulation of extra-contractual liability was influenced by the French law, and among several novelties of the new Hungarian tort law, the non-pecuniary damages were replaced by the institute of *solatium doloris*.[114]

The unjustified enrichment system of the previous code was not significantly changed in the new Ptk.[115] The relationship of unjustified enrichment to contracts and torts is one of the most sensitive issues in the Hungarian court practice which is very restrictive in the application of unjustified enrichment.[116] Claims for restitution of performances provided based on an invalid contract are covered by specific rules of Ptk, while the rules of unjustified enrichment are to be applied only supplementary.[117]

In this volume, the liability for breach of contract and the *non-cumul* system is comprehensively analysed in the chapter by Attila Menyhárd in which the Ptk rules on exclusion and limitation clauses, liquidated damages clauses, and penalty clauses are also discussed.[118] The introduction of a *solatium doloris*, as

107 Vékás (n 102) § 6.
108 ibid § 5.
109 Attila Menyhárd, 'Contracts' in Attila Harmathy (ed), *Introduction to Hungarian law* (2nd edn, Wolters Kluwer 2019) § 13.
110 Balázs Tőkey, 'New Particular Agreements in the New Hungarian Civil Code' in Attila Menyhárd and Emőd Veress (eds), *New Civil Codes in Hungary and Romania* (Springer 2017) 141–44.
111 András Kisfaludi, 'Transfer of Property, Claims, Rights and Contracts in the New Hungarian Civil Code' [2014] (2) *ELTE LJ* 109.
112 Attila Menyhárd, 'Basic Questions of Tort Law from a Hungarian Perspective' in Helmut Koziol (ed), *Basic Questions of Tort Law from a Comparative Perspective* (Jan Sramek Verlag 2015) 281.
113 Fuglinszky, 'Some Structural Questions' (n 106) 107ff; Menyhárd, 'Basic Questions of Tort Law' (n 112) 281ff.
114 Ádám Fuglinszky, 'Risks and Side Effects: Five Questions on the "New" Hungarian Tort Law' [2014] (2) *ELTE LJ* 199, 200–1.
115 Attila Menyhárd, 'Unjustified Enrichment in the New Hungarian Civil Code' [2014] (2) *ELTE LJ* 233, 234ff.
116 ibid 242–43.
117 Menyhárd, 'Contracts' (n 109) § 5.
118 See ch 5.

well as other novelties of the Hungarian tort law, are discussed in the chapter by Ewa Bagińska and Paulina Wyszyńska-Ślufińska.[119] The limitations of freedom of contract in Ptk are analysed in the chapter by Dorota Miler.[120]

## 4 The law of obligations in the former Yugoslav states

In the former Socialist Federal Republic of Yugoslavia, in the absence of a civil code, private law was regulated in various statutes, some of which were federal, while the others were enacted in the constitutive republics, due to a convoluted division of legislative competences. The general part of the law of obligations and the regulation of contracts and other obligations in the area of trade in goods and services were under the competence of the federal government. Thus, the law of obligations, mostly untouched by socialist ideology, was primarily regulated in the federal Obligations Act of 1978 (YZOO).[121] Since it was considered as a modern codification of the law of obligations, after the dissolution of Yugoslavia, each of the former socialist states continued to apply YZOO and it also heavily impacted the later reforms of the law of obligations in the now seven sovereign states. Therefore, a brief introduction to YZOO is required before discussing the subsequent developments in the law of obligations in these states.

### 4.1 Yugoslav Obligations Act of 1978

YZOO was structured in four parts: (i) general part of the law of obligations, (ii) specific contracts, (iii) rules on interlocal conflict of laws, and (iv) interim and final provisions. Apart from the general rules on obligations, and the general part of contract law, Part I of the YZOO also included regulation of extra-contractual obligations: torts, unjustified enrichment, and *negotiorum gestio*, followed by the institute of the public promise of reward and general rules on securities which were joined together under the heading of unilateral declarations of will. The inclusion of the extra-contractual obligations into the general part of the law of obligations was a result of following the structure presented in the academic draft code by Mihailo Konstantinović on which YZOO was largely based.

In preparation of this academic draft code, the 'Sketch' (*Skica*),[122] a comparative method of study was used, thus the YZOO was heavily influenced by different foreign legislative models. Although the foreign sources that were taken into consideration are not explicitly stated in the draft, it is largely accepted

---

119 See ch 3, text to nn 31–46.
120 See ch 4, text to nn 140–41, 146–47, 162, 179, 185–86, 204.
121 *SL SFRJ* 29/1978, as later amended.
122 Mihailo Konstantinović, *Obligacije i ugovori: Skica za zakonik o obligacijama i ugovorima* (Pravni fakultet u Beogradu 1969).

that the main influences were the Swiss OR and the French CCiv.[123] Under the influence of the OR, the Sketch, and in turn YZOO, adopted the linguistic style of dividing the paragraphs into one-sentence subparagraphs.[124] The monistic approach to regulating civil and commercial contracts, the focus of YZOO on contracts, rather than on a general notion of a legal transaction, and structure of the specific contract types, are also adopted from the OR.[125] The French CCiv mainly had an impact in the field of tort law, with YZOO adopting the *neminem laedere* as a general principle, and also not making a strict distinction between wrongfulness and fault.[126] However, there were several instances of tort law rules adapted from the OR,[127] as there were also notable influences of French law in the area of contract law, such as the adoption of *la cause* as a condition of validity of contract.[128]

Another source of inspiration was the Italian Cod Civ,[129] notably for the rules on the changed circumstances.[130] The Austrian ABGB also had a significant impact on YZOO. Some of the instances of reception from the ABGB were the institute of *laesio enormis*, the regulation of the lease contract in the style of the Austrian *Bestandvertrag*,[131] and the adaptation of the prohibition of *ultra alterum tantum*.[132] YZOO had also incorporated the Yugoslav General Usages on the Sale of Goods of 1954,[133] which were not only a codification of trade usages but also a collection of rules adopted from the Swiss OR and the Austrian and German jurisprudence.[134] Thus, German law also influenced the YZOO, and one of the examples is the reception of the doctrine of

123 See Marko Baretić and Saša Nikšić, 'Legal Culture and Legal Transplants: Croatian National Report' in Jorge A Sánchez Cordero (ed), *Legal Culture and Legal Transplants* (International Academy of Comparative Law 2010) 190; Zvonimir Slakoper, 'Allgemeines Bürgerliches Gesetzbuch (ABGB) und kroatisches bürgerliches Recht' in Michael Geistlinger and others (eds), *200 Jahre ABGB – Ausstrahlungen: Die Bedeutung der Kodifikation für andere Staaten und andere Rechtskulturen* (MANZ Verlag 2011) 105; Tatjana Josipović, Igor Gliha, and Saša Nikšić, 'Croatia' in Petr Lavický and Jan Hurdík (eds), *Private Law Reform* (Masaryk University 2014) 116; Ana Vlahek and Klemen Podobnik, 'Slovenia: Chronology of Development of Private Law in Slovenia' in Petr Lavický and Jan Hurdík (eds), *Private Law Reform* (Masaryk University 2014) 305.
124 Baretić and Nikšić (n 123) 190.
125 ibid 190–91; Saša Nikšić, 'Nekoliko napomena o nomotehničkom standardu Zakona o obveznim odnosima' in Zvonimir Slakoper (ed), *Liber amicorum in honorem Vilim Gorenc* (Pravni fakultet Sveučilišta u Rijeci 2014) 188.
126 Baretić and Nikšić (n 123) 192; Josipović, Gliha, and Nikšić (n 123) 116.
127 Nikšić (n 125) 188.
128 Baretić and Nikšić (n 123) 191; Josipović, Gliha, and Nikšić (n 123) 117.
129 Slakoper (n 123) 105; Vlahek and Podobnik (n 123) 305.
130 Nikšić (n 125) 190.
131 Slakoper (n 123) 111.
132 Ivan Tot, 'Prestanak tijeka zateznih kamata kada njihov iznos dostigne iznos glavnice' (2020) 68 (6615) *Informator* 13, 13–15.
133 *Opšte uzanse za promet robom*, SL FNRJ 15/1954.
134 Baretić and Nikšić (n 123) 191.

*Dauerschuldverhältnisse* in the general rules on termination of continuing obligations in YZOO.[135]

YZOO owed its feature of modernity mainly to the fact that international conventions also played a significant role in drafting the YZOO. The Hague Uniform Sales Law (ULIS and ULFC) had largely impacted the YZOO rules on sales and formation of contracts.[136] They are the only sources explicitly referred to in the Sketch as those from which the rules of the Sketch were borrowed.[137] As they served as the basis for the CISG, the YZOO contained some of its solutions even before the CISG was adopted. Another example of borrowing from the international conventions is the incorporation of the UNIDROIT International Convention on Travel Contracts into the YZOO regulation of the organized travel contract and the intermediary travel contract.

The borrowings from different foreign jurisdictions, but even more the YZOO deviations from the Sketch, created in some instances problems that are still present and relevant since the YZOO had a significant impact on the law of obligations in the now seven sovereign states. One of such controversies in the law of Slovenia, Croatia, and Serbia, which originated from a deviation of the YZOO from the Sketch, is related to the duty to pay default interest in claims based on unjustified enrichment, an issue which is discussed in detail in this volume in the chapter by Damjan Možina.[138]

### 4.2 Slovenia

After Slovenia regained its independence in 1991,[139] the YZOO continued to be applied in its Slovene version.[140] It is still partly in force since the later reform of the Slovenian law of obligations had not repealed its provisions on the several types of banking contracts. The rest of the YZOO was supplanted with the new Obligations Code of 2001 (*Obligacijski zakonik*,[141] OblZ). However, the OblZ retained the structure of YZOO, as well as its substance. The contents of the OblZ are 'almost entirely copy-pasted',[142] and 'only minor and mostly cosmetic modifications' were made when adapting the YZOO into the OblZ.[143] OblZ is described as 'more a formal "slovenization" than an actual modernization of the law of obligations'.[144]

---

135 Ivan Tot, 'Prestanak trajnih obveznih odnosa' (2018) 39 *Zbornik PFR* 1171.
136 Nikšić (n 125) 190; Vlahek and Podobnik (n 123) 305.
137 Konstantinović (n 122) 7–8.
138 See ch 7.
139 For the history of private law in Slovenia see Vlahek and Podobnik (n 123) 283ff.
140 *Zakon o obligacijskih razmerjih*, SL SFRJ 29/1978, 39/1985, 45/1989, 57/1989, UL RS 88/1999, 83/2001, 30/2002, 87/2002.
141 UL RS 83/2001, 28/2006, 40/2007, 97/2007, 64/2016, 20/2018.
142 Vlahek and Podobnik (n 123) 309.
143 Damjan Možina and Ana Vlahek, *Contract Law in Slovenia* (Wolters Kluwer 2019) para 35.
144 ibid para 36.

The monistic approach of YZOO was retained, while the consumer contract law was left out to be regulated in the special consumer protection legislation.[145] In the General Part of the OblZ, rules on formation of contracts were partly amended under the influence of CISG.[146] PECL was not taken into consideration, and it is considered that 'an opportunity for modernisation as well as "Europeanisation" of contract law was missed'.[147] In the special part of the OblZ, donation, gratuitous lending, and partnership agreement were regulated as specific contracts, while financial leasing, franchising, and factoring were intentionally not regulated as to enable further evolution of these contract types in the business practice.[148]

One of the major controversies of the OblZ was the reintroduction of the prohibition of *ultra alterum tantum*, the legal rule of YZOO under which interest ceases to run when the amount of the interest reaches the amount of principal. Article 376 OblZ applied the rule to default interest that triggered a series of decisions of the Slovenian Constitutional Court and legislative interventions, and even an ECJ preliminary ruling,[149] with the final result being the enacting of an absolute prohibition of the accumulation of contractual interest in Art 382a OblZ.[150]

In addition to the chapter by Damjan Možina,[151] two more chapters in this volume include discussions on the Slovenian law of obligations, and in both, due to the existing similarities, Croatian law is also analysed. The chapter by Dorota Miler includes analysis of the principle of freedom of contract and its limitations in Slovenian and Croatian law.[152] The Slovenian and Croatian rules on the formality of real estate transactions are analysed in light of the challenges presented by blockchain-based smart contracts in the chapter by David Borlinič Gačnik and Jure Jakšić.[153]

### 4.3 Croatia

Despite the long history of the application of the Austrian ABGB in Croatia, even in the modern times,[154] and also the application of the French codes in

---

145  See Vlahek and Podobnik (n 123) 310–12; Damjan Možina, 'Harmonisation of Private Law in Europe and the Development of Private Law in Slovenia' [2008] *Juridica Intl* 173, 176–77.

146  Vlahek and Podobnik (n 123) 309; Možina (n 145) 178.

147  Možina (n 145) 178.

148  Možina and Vlahek (n 143) paras 35, 46.

149  Case C-256/15 *Drago Nemec v Republika Slovenija* [2015] ECLI:EU:C:2016:954.

150  See Damjan Možina, '*Ne ultra alterum tantum* in evropsko pravo' [2010] *Podjetje in delo* 497; Možina and Vlahek (n 143) para 37. See also Tot (n 132) 15–18.

151  See ch 7.

152  See ch 4.

153  See ch 9.

154  See Slakoper (n 123) 101ff, 108–11; Tatjana Josipović, 'Private Law Codification in the Republic of Croatia' in Wen-Yeu Wang (ed), *Codification in International Perspective: Selected Papers from the 2nd IACL Thematic Conference* (Springer 2014) 109–14.

parts of its territory,[155] Croatian private law system is based on the German pandectistic model. It is mainly codified in four separate statutes which regulate property law, family law, inheritance law, and the law of obligations.[156] The latter is found in the new Obligations Act of 2005 (*Zakon o obveznim odnosima*,[157] ZOO). There is no separate statute on the general part of civil law. However, certain provisions of the general part of the ZOO are considered to apply to the entire private law, not only to the law of obligations.[158]

ZOO has repealed the YZOO which was previously adopted as Croatian law[159] when Croatia regained its independence in 1991. Similar to Slovenian OblZ, almost the entire text of YZOO was incorporated in the new ZOO, albeit significantly reorganized and adjusted to the Croatian legal terminology. Thus, the Swiss influence on contract law and the French influence on tort law was also retained. Of the substantial changes that were made, the requirement of the *la cause* was abandoned in contract law, and the objective concept of non-pecuniary damage as an infringement of a personality right was adopted in tort law. Although various comparative sources were taken into consideration in drafting the ZOO, including ABGB, French CCiv, Italian Cod Civ, Slovenian OblZ, and the Civil Code of the Russian Federation of 1994, a significant shift towards the German BGB was made. Some of the examples of the provisions modelled after the BGB are found in the regulation of the gratuitous lending and civil law partnership agreement, as well as in dividing the previous regulation of the lease contract into lease and usufructuary lease as separate contract types. Inspiration was also taken from PECL which influenced the new regulation of *culpa in contrahendo*, as well as some of the changes made to the liability for breach of contract.

ZOO is divided into three parts: (i) general part, (ii) special part, and (iii) interim and final provisions. The first part is divided into seven chapters which, *inter alia*, govern the general principles of the law of obligations, sources, sorts and effects of obligations, and their modification and termination. The special part of the ZOO consists of two chapters. The chapter on contractual obligations includes the general part of contract law and the regulation of more than thirty specific contract types. The chapter on extra-contractual obligations governs torts, unjustified enrichment, and *negotiorum gestio*, and also includes provisions on the public promise of reward and securities.

The focus of ZOO is on the contract, rather than on a legal transaction, with Art 14(3) ZOO providing that the provisions on contracts are to be applied appropriately to other legal transactions. The monistic approach to contract law is visible in Art 14(1) ZOO which prescribes that the provisions governing

---

155  For the history of private law in Croatia see e.g. Baretić and Nikšić (n 123) 184–92.

156  See Josipović, Gliha, and Nikšić (n 123) 112–14.

157  *NN* 35/2005, 41/2008, 125/2011, 78/2015, 29/2018.

158  Slakoper (n 123) 105.

159  *Zakon o obveznim odnosima, SL SFRJ* 29/1978, 39/1985, 46/1985, 57/1989, *NN* 53/1991, 73/1991, 111/1993, 3/1994, 107/1995, 7/1996, 91/1996, 112/1999, 88/2001.

contracts are to be applied to all sorts of contracts unless explicitly regulated otherwise for commercial contracts. And there are several instances of provisions which apart from the general rule also provide modification for commercial contracts. ZOO is also generally to be applied to consumer contracts; however, special consumer contract law is regulated in separate consumer protection legislation, while in ZOO only a few adjustments of the general rules are made particularly for consumer contracts.

A significant feature of the ZOO of 2005 is that the German approach to transposition of EU directives was also adopted, and thus, for instance, the Consumer Sales and Guarantees Directive[160] and the Unfair Contract Terms Directive[161] were used to harmonize contract law in general, not only the consumer contract law. Several other directives were also transposed in ZOO, rather than in separate statutes.[162]

Although ZOO is generally considered to be a codification of the law of obligations, apart from consumer contract law being largely dealt with outside the ZOO, at the time the ZOO was drafted and enacted there already were numerous special statutes governing the subject matter of the law of obligations which were not codified in the ZOO. Moreover, following the enactment of ZOO, the trend of regulating specific contracts in separate statutes continued, and thus financial leasing and factoring were each regulated in separate statutes. The law of obligations was fragmented even further with the change in the approach to transposition of EU directives. Instead of being implemented in the ZOO, as their previous versions were, the new Late Payment Directive[163] and the new Package Travel Directive[164] were each transposed in separate statutes, while corresponding provisions in ZOO were repealed.

Thus, if the ZOO is to be considered as 'codification', then nowadays a trend of 'decodification' can be observed with severe consequences for the coherence of the system of the law of obligations. For instance, transposition of the Late Payment Directive into separate statute has led to the adoption of a subjective concept of default for commercial transactions, which deviates from the objective concept of default accepted in ZOO.[165] There is now a special

---

160  Directive 1999/44/EC of the European Parliament and of the Council of 25 May 1999 on certain aspects of the sale of consumer goods and associated guarantees [1999] *OJ* L171/12 (Consumer Sales and Guarantees Directive).

161  Council Directive 93/13/EEC of 5 April 1993 on unfair terms in consumer contracts [1993] *OJ* L95/29 (Unfair Contract Terms Directive).

162  See Baretić and Nikšić (n 123) 202–3.

163  Directive 2011/7/EU of the European Parliament and of the Council of 16 February 2011 on combating late payment in commercial transactions [2011] *OJ* L48/1.

164  Directive (EU) 2015/2302 of the European Parliament and of the Council of 25 November 2015 on package travel and linked travel arrangements, amending Regulation (EC) No 2006/2004 and Directive 2011/83/EU of the European Parliament and of the Council and repealing Council Directive 90/314/EEC [2015] *OJ* L326/1.

165  Ivan Tot, 'Kamate' in Zvonimir Slakoper (ed), *Bankovni i financijski ugovori* (Narodne novine 2017) 141–42.

regime of default interest reserved for commercial transactions in parallel to the general regime of default interest in ZOO, what brought new uncertainties in the already deficient regulation of interest inherited from YZOO.[166]

Relating to interest, in this volume a discussion on the concept of 'negative interest' from the standpoint of Croatian law is found in the chapter by Ana Vargek Stilinović and Marko Stilinović.[167]

### 4.4 Bosnia and Herzegovina

Due to the complex internal structure of Bosnia and Herzegovina as a highly decentralized *sui generis* federal system consisting of two autonomous entities (Federation of Bosnia and Herzegovina, and the Republic of Srpska) and a separate district (Brčko District), and the division of legislative competences between them, there is no legal uniformity in Bosnia and Herzegovina in private law matters. Thus, the law of obligations is also not codified on the state level. In each of the three constitutive parts, the YZOO is still in force, albeit on a different legal basis, and in three different versions.[168] Whereas in the Brčko District the YZOO is applied in its original version, in each of the two entities YZOO is applied as amended in the entities.[169] Some of the special statutes governing specific contracts are also at least doubled, as is the case e.g. with different statutes on financial leasing in the two entities. Consumer contract law is regulated outside the three versions of YZOO, in statute adopted at the state level in 2006, however, a separate statute on consumer protection is also applied in the Republic of Srpska.

There were several attempts to reform the law of obligations in Bosnia and Herzegovina. A new Obligations Act was drafted in 2003 but was not enacted by the entities.[170] In 2010, another draft was prepared and it was supposed to be applied at the state level; however, it was also withdrawn from the legislative procedure. The draft of 2010 heavily relied on YZOO. However, in several of the changes made, the draft was influenced by CISG, PECL, and UPICC, while also adjusting the YZOO with the EU private law directives. There are no current plans for reform of the law of obligations nor for drafting a civil

---

166  See ibid 93ff.

167  See ch 8.

168  See Darko Radić, 'Development of Civil Law in Bosnia and Herzegovina' in Ardian Nuni and others (eds), *Civil Law Forum for South East Europe*, vol 1 (Centre for SEELS 2012) 262ff; Meliha Povlakić, 'Culpa in contrahendo im bosnisch-herzegowinischen Recht' in Rudolf Welser (ed), *Haftung aus Verschulden beim Vertragsabschluss in Zentral- und Osteuropa* (Manz 2012) 129–31.

169  The version of YZOO applied in the Federation of Bosnia and Herzegovina is the Obligations Act (*Zakon o obligacionim odnosima*) SL SFRJ 29/1978, 39/1985, 45/1989, 57/1989, SL RBiH 2/1992, 13/1993, 13/1994, SN FBiH 29/2003, 42/2011, whereas the version of YZOO applied in the Republic of Srpska is the Obligations Act (*Zakon o obligacionim odnosima*) SL SFRJ 29/1978, 39/1985, 45/1989, 57/1989, SG RSrp 17/1993, 3/1996, 37/2001, 39/2003, 74/2004.

170  Radić (n 168) 270.

code, either at the state level or the level of constitutive parts of Bosnia and Herzegovina.

### 4.5 Serbia

In Serbia, YZOO is also still in effect, in its Serbian version and as amended in the last three decades, although not significantly.[171] In 2007, a codification committee was appointed with the task of preparing a civil code and its work was brought to end in 2015 when the Draft Civil Code of Republic of Serbia was published.[172] The primary source of inspiration was Swiss, French, and German law, but many other foreign sources were also taken into consideration, e.g. CCQ, NCC, Ptk, as well as the civil codes of Russian Federation, and Brazil. Contract law provisions were influenced by CISG and PECL, as well as by EU directives.

The Draft Civil Code is structured into five books: (i) general part, (ii) law of obligations, (iii) property law, (iv) family law, and (v) inheritance law. Many of the rules included in the first book and most of those found in the second book are based on YZOO, albeit with changes in structure.[173] Some of the novelties refer to the regulation of breach of contract under the influence of CISG, and regulation of contract types that were previously not regulated or were regulated partially in special statutes (e.g. donation, civil law partnership, franchising, financial leasing, and payment services contract). The monistic approach of YZOO in regulating commercial and civil law contracts is retained.[174] Consumer contract law is, however, mostly left to be regulated outside the Civil Code.[175] The Draft is yet to be enacted into a civil code.

### 4.6 Montenegro

Throughout the period in which Montenegro was in the state union with Serbia, the law of obligations continued to be governed by YZOO. After declaring its independence in 2006, Montenegro reformed its law of obligations in 2008 with the new Obligations Act (*Zakon o obligacionim odnosima*).[176]

---

171  Obligations Act (*Zakon o obligacionim odnosima*) *SL SFRJ* 29/1978, 39/1985, 45/1989, 57/1979, *SL SRJ* 31/1993, *SL SCG* 1/2003, *SG RS* 18/2020.

172  See Mateja Djurovic, 'Serbian Contract Law: Its Development and the New Serbian Civil Code' (2011) 7 *ERCL* 65; Dušan Nikolić, 'Codification of Civil Law in Serbia (Historical Experience and Current Projects)' in Monika Jurčová and others (eds), *Liber amicorum Ján Lazar* (Právnická Fakulta Trnavskej Univerzity v Trnave 2014) 443ff.

173  Djurovic (n 172) 71; Nikolić (n 172) 470.

174  Djurovic (n 172) 72.

175  See Christine Riefa and Mateja Durovic, 'Serbian Consumer Law: Out with the Old, in with the New' (2015) 22 *MJECL* 862.

176  *SL CG* 47/2008, 4/2011, 22/2017.

However, its structure and substance both largely correspond to the YZOO.[177] One of the novelties is the inclusion of regulation of some of the specific contracts that were previously found in separate statutes, such as the tenancy agreement and lease of business premises.[178] Although previously regulated with a separate statute in 2005, financial leasing was not included in the new Obligations Act. The institute of pre-contractual liability was modernized under the influence of PECL.[179] The Consumer Sales and Guarantees Directive and the Unfair Contract Terms Directive were implemented in the Obligations Act,[180] but consumer contract law is mostly regulated in special consumer protection legislation.[181]

At the end of 2017, a Civil Code Commission was appointed by the government with a task to prepare the Montenegrin Civil Code. There is no draft of the Civil Code yet, nor of its part on the law of obligations. From available information about the drafting process, it appears that commission is taking inspiration from the Hungarian Ptk, Polish KC, Czech NOZ, Romanian NCC, Lithuanian CK, Dutch BW, French CCiv, the Civil Code of Catalonia, the Civil Code of Russian Federation, and the civil law of Cyprus, as well as from UPICC, PECL, DCFR, and CESL.[182]

### 4.7 Kosovo

The YZOO was applied in Kosovo until 2012 when the new Obligations Act was enacted.[183] Its structure and substance are taken over from YZOO. In March 2015, a Civil Code Commission was appointed and entrusted with the preparation of the Civil Code, as part of the EU funded project. The result of the codification work is the Draft Civil Code of the Republic of Kosovo, published in November 2019.[184] Its provisions are organized in five books: general part, obligations, ownership and other real rights, family, and inheritance. According to the explanatory memorandum on the Draft Civil Code, the main sources of influence were the civil codes of Estonia, Germany, and Albania.

However, the second book on obligations predominantly incorporates the YZOO rules, to some extent influenced also by Croatian ZOO. Its structure is

---

177 Draginja Vuksanović and Velibor Korać, 'Development of Civil Law' in Ardian Nuni and others (eds), *Civil Law Forum for South East Europe*, vol 1 (Centre for SEELS 2012) 316.

178 ibid 317.

179 ibid 318.

180 ibid 317.

181 Zvezdan Čadjenović, 'Unfair Contract Terms in the Contract Law of Montenegro', in Ardian Nuni and others (eds), *Civil Law Forum for South East Europe*, vol 1 (Centre for SEELS 2012) 224.

182 The information on the state of codification is published at 'Komisija za izradu građanskog zakonika' <www.mpa.gov.me/rubrike/komisija_za_izradu_gradjanskog_zakonika> accessed 17 June 2020.

183 Law 04/L-077, Obligations Act (*Ligji* 04/L-077, *Ligj për marrëdhëniet e detyrimeve / Zakon* 04/L-077, *Zakon o obligacionim odnosima*), GZK 16/2012.

184 Available at 'Civil Code Project' <http://civilcode-kosovo.org/documents/> accessed 17 June 2020.

the same as in YZOO with the division of the law of obligations in a general part, which contains general contract law but also the regulation of extra-contractual obligations, and a special part governing specific contracts. Although financial leasing was regulated with a separate statute in 2009, its regulation is not included in the Draft Civil Code.

### 4.8 North Macedonia

After the dissolution of Yugoslavia, YZOO continued to be applied in North Macedonia until a new Obligations Act was enacted in 2001,[185] which is, however, adoption of YZOO. Of the later amendments, the most comprehensive was the one from 2008 which was aimed at harmonization of the law of obligations with the EU directives.[186] Consumer contract law is regulated mostly outside the Obligations Act, in special consumer protection legislation, and there are also special statutes governing contract law, such as the one regulating financial leasing.

In 2010, the Civil Code Commission was appointed and the work on drafting the Civil Code was initiated. The pandectistic approach is followed, and four working groups were tasked with preparing the general part of the code and the parts on property law, the law of obligations, and inheritance law, whereas a decision was made to leave family law regulated outside the code in a separate statute.[187] Consumer contract law will also not be included in the code and will remain governed by special consumer protection legislation.[188] The working groups are taking inspiration from the German BGB, French CCiv, and the civil codes of the Russian Federation, Greece, and Albania.[189] A draft of Book III on the law of obligations was prepared in 2013 and revised in 2015, and it largely follows the structure and substance of the Obligations Act. Thus, it is not expected that the future Civil Code would bring radical departures from the YZOO.

## 5 The law of obligations in Romania, Bulgaria, Albania, and Turkey

Of the four remaining Southeast European countries, the law of obligations was affected by recodification in Romania, Albania, and Turkey, whereas no significant reforms occurred in Bulgaria.

---

185 *Zakon za obligacionite odnosi*, SV RM 18/2001, 78/2001, 4/2002, 59/2002, 5/2003, 84/2008, 81/2009, 161/2009, 23/2013, 123/2013.
186 Neda Zdraveva, Nenad Gavrilović, and Marija Radevska, 'Drafing a Civil Code' in Ardian Nuni and others (eds), *Civil Law Forum for South East Europe*, vol 1 (Centre for SEELS 2012) 306ff.
187 Rodna Zivkovska and Tina Przeska, 'Codification of the Civil Law in the Republic of Macedonia' (2014) 68 *Zbornik radova Pravnog fakulteta u Nišu* 251, 255ff.
188 Jadranka Dabovic Anastasovska and Neda Zdraveva, 'Duty of Information Disclosure in the Conclusion of Consumer Contracts: Implementation of the EU Law Standards in the Republic of Macedonia' (2017) 8 (2) *Iustinianus Primus L Rev* 1, 2.
189 Zivkovska and Przeska (n 187) 257.

## 5.1 Romania

The new Civil Code (*Codul civil al României*,[190] NCC) was promulgated in 2009 and entered into force on 1 October 2011, replacing both the previous Civil Code and the Commercial Code, and thus transitioning the Romanian private law system into a monistic system.[191] The CCQ was the primary source of inspiration for the drafters of the NCC, which was also influenced by the French CCiv, Italian Cod Civ, Swiss ZGB and OR, German BGB, and the Civil Code of Brazil.[192] PECL were also taken into consideration,[193] and contract law was inspired also by CISG and UPICC.[194] The law of obligations is found in Book V of the NCC. Apart from removing the borders between civil and commercial law transactions, replacing the notion of a 'merchant' with a notion of a 'professional', and introducing regulation of several new contract types,[195] a significant novelty is also the introduction of a dualistic system of delictual and contractual liability which previously was not regulated in the Romanian law.[196] Consumer contract law is regulated outside the NCC in the consumer protection legislation.[197]

## 5.2 Bulgaria

The system of private law in Bulgaria is significantly fragmented.[198] Previous attempts to create a civil code were unsuccessful and there are no current plans for civil law codification.[199] The general regime of the law of obligations is found in the Obligations and Contracts Act of 1950 (*Zakon za zadŭlzheniyata i dogovorite*,[200] ZZD), while commercial transactions are regulated by Commercial Act (*Targovski zakon*,[201] TZ). Consumer contract law is part of various

---

190 Law 287 of 17 July 2009 on the Civil Code (*Lege 287 din 17 iulie 2009 privind Codul civil*), MO I 511, 2009, as later amended. For an overview of the recodification process see Christian Alunaru and Lucian Bojin, 'Romania' in Petr Lavický and Jan Hurdík (eds), *Private Law Reform* (Masaryk University 2014) 213ff.

191 Emőd Veress, 'The New Romanian Civil Code: Difficulties in the Transition towards a Monist Private Law' in Attila Menyhárd and Emőd Veress (eds), *New Civil Codes in Hungary and Romania* (Springer 2017) 28, 31ff.

192 Alunaru and Bojin (n 190) 232; Lucian Bojin, 'The Law of Obligations in Romania' in Reiner Schulze and Fryderyk Zoll (eds), *The Law of Obligations in Europe: A New Wave of Codifications* (SELP 2013) 378.

193 Alunaru and Bojin (n 190) 232; Bojin (n 192) 383.

194 See Alunaru and Bojin (n 190) 245–46; Bojin (n 192) 383.

195 Bojin (n 192) 378–80.

196 See Bagińska and Wyszyńska-Ślufińska, ch 3, text to nn 47–60.

197 Bojin (n 192) 379–80.

198 Cserne (n 2) 59; Christian Takoff, 'Private Law in Bulgaria' in Christa Jessel-Holst, Rainer Kulms, and Alexander Trunk (eds), *Private Law in Eastern Europe* (Mohr Siebeck 2010) 149ff.

199 Takoff (n 199) 165–68.

200 *DV* 275/1950, as later amended.

201 *DV* 48/1991, as later amended.

special consumer protection laws.[202] ZZD is significantly modelled after the Italian Cod Civ, with influences from German BGB.[203] The provisions of TZ, as well as Bulgarian commercial and company law in general, were drafted mainly under the influence of the German HGB.[204] Apart from harmonization with the EU law, which is perceived as a decisive factor of further fragmentation of Bulgarian private law, there were no major reforms of the law of obligations in recent years.

### 5.3 Albania

To support the transition to a market economy, in 1994 Albania replaced its previous socialist Civil Code of 1981 with the new Civil Code.[205] The main foreign influences in drafting the new Civil Code were Italian Cod Civ, Swiss ZGB and OR, French CCiv, and Dutch BW. Contract law was mostly influenced by Cod Civ, whereas tort law was modelled after the BW.[206] The new code consists of five books: (i) general part, (ii) ownership and property, (iii) inheritance, (iv) obligations, and (v) contracts. The fourth book includes general provisions and provisions on performance and remedies for non-performance, as well as provisions on torts, *negotiorum gestio*, *condictio indebiti*, and unjustified enrichment. The general part of contract law is regulated within the fifth book, as well as specific contracts, including franchising and financial leasing. Financial leasing was also regulated with a separate statute in 2005, as was factoring in 2006. Consumer contract law is mainly regulated outside the Civil Code in special consumer protection legislation.[207] Except for harmonization with the EU directives, recently there were no significant developments in the law of obligations.

### 5.4 Turkey

Recodification of civil law in Turkey in the twenty-first century has not severed the almost a century-old ties of the Turkish private law with the Swiss

---

202  Takoff (n 199) 161–64; Angel Shopov, 'Two Current Civil Law Issues of Consumer Protection: European and Bulgarian Aspects' (2015) 4 *EuCML* 44.

203  ibid.

204  Takoff (n 199) 150.

205  Law 7850 of 29 July 1994, Civil Code of the Republic of Albania (*Ligji* 7850, *datë* 29 7 1994, *Kodi Civil i Republikës së Shqipërisë*), FZ 11–14/1994, as later amended. See Gianmaria Ajani, 'Codification of Civil Law in Albania' in Georg Ginsburgs, Donald D Barry, and William B Simmons (eds), *The Revival of Private Law in Central and Eastern Europe* (Kluwer Law International 1996) 513ff.

206  ibid 524.

207  See Felicitas Parapatits, 'Albania: Reform of Consumer Protection Law' (2010) 18 *ERPL* 165; Mateja Djurovic, 'EU Consumer Law Outside the European Union: The Case of Albania' (2013) 36 *JCP* 269.

legal system.[208] Both the new Turkish Civil Code (*Türk Medenî Kanunu*,[209] TMK) and the new Turkish Code of Obligations (*Türk Borçlar Kanunu*,[210] TBK) retained its Swiss origin and influence. In the new TBK, there are only a few fundamental changes relating to contract law, concerning mostly the judicial control of standard terms and transfer of risk in sales law, while tort law was significantly revised, drawing inspiration from the Swiss Draft Project on the Revision and Unification of Civil Liability.[211]

One of the novelties of the new TBK is that it was also to be applied to claims arising from the liability of the state for its acts, which were previously governed by administrative law, not the civil law. This issue is discussed in this volume in the chapter by Orhan Emre Konuralp.[212]

## 6 Final remarks

This chapter aimed only for an overview of the recodification and reform of the law of obligations in Central and Southeast European countries, and not a comprehensive analysis. However, some common characteristics can be identified. Central and Southeast European private law systems are generally pandectistic systems, irrespective of historical influences of the civil codes that follow the institutions system. The dualist model of codification and regulation of legal transactions is mostly abolished (notably in the Czech Republic and Romania) or is soon to be abolished (e.g. in the Slovak Republic). It is still employed only where the recodification efforts are not present (e.g. Bulgaria) or their results were modest (e.g. Latvia). While the legal systems belonging to the Germanic legal family have mostly influenced contract law in Central and Southeast Europe, tort law, as well as extra-contractual obligations in general, is dominantly influenced by Romanic legal systems, particularly the French one (e.g. Lithuania, and legal systems based on the YZOO). Due to dominance of the monistic model of regulating legal transactions and influence of the CISG and UPICC in the recent reforms, the law of obligations is even more 'commercialized' and lines between civil and commercial law are continuing to be increasingly blurred. In most of Central and Southeast Europe, consumer contract law is rather regulated in special consumer protection legislation, than codified in a civil code or statute governing the law of obligations. Harmonization with EU private law is one of the key factors of fragmentation of private

---

208  For history of private law in Turkey see e.g. Arzu Oguz, 'The Role of Comparative Law in the Development of Turkish Civil Law' (2005) 17 *Pace Intl L Rev* 373.

209  Act 4721: Turkish Civil Code (4721 *sayılı Türk Medenî Kanunu*), *RG* 24607/2001, as later amended.

210  Act 6098: Turkish Code of Obligations (6098 *sayılı Türk Borçlar Kanunu*), *RG* 27836/2011, as later amended.

211  See Erdem Büyüksagis, 'The New Turkish Tort Law' (2012) 3 *JETL* 44; Christoph Müller and Olivier Riske, 'Cross-Fertilization between Swiss and Turkish Tort Laws' (2014) 22 *ERPL* 879.

212  See ch 10.

law (e. g. Croatia), and thus it is also creating incentives for recodification. Most of these issues are further explored in the following chapters of this book.


## Bibliography

Ajani G, 'Codification of Civil Law in Albania' in Ginsburgs G, Barry DD, and Simmons WB (eds), *The Revival of Private Law in Central and Eastern Europe* (Kluwer Law International 1996).

Alunaru C and Bojin L, 'Romania' in Lavický P and Hurdík J (eds), *Private Law Reform* (Masaryk University 2014).

Bagińska E, 'Developments in Personal Injury Law in Poland: Shaping the Compensatory Function of Tort Law' (2015) 8 *J Civ L Stud* 309.

Balodis K, 'The Latvian Law of Obligations: The Current Situation and Perspectives' [2013] *Juridica Intl* 69.

Baretić M and Nikšić S, 'Legal Culture and Legal Transplants: Croatian National Report' in Sánchez Cordero JA (ed), *Legal Culture and Legal Transplants* (International Academy of Comparative Law 2010).

Bohata P, 'Neues Privatrecht in der Tschechischen Republik – Revolution oder Normalität?' (2012) 58 (2) *OstEurR* 2 [https://doi.org/10.5771/0030-6444-2012-2-2].

Bojin L, 'The Law of Obligations in Romania' in Schulze R and Zoll F (eds), *The Law of Obligations in Europe: A New Wave of Codifications* (SELP 2013) [https://doi.org/10.1515/9783866539839.377].

Brzozowski A, 'Civil Law (Law of Contracts, Property and Obligations)' in Frankowski S (ed), *Introduction to Polish Law* (Kluwer Law International 2005).

Büyüksagis E, 'The New Turkish Tort Law' (2012) 3 *JETL* 44 [https://doi.org/10.1515/jetl-2012-0044].

Čadjenović D, 'Unfair Contract Terms in the Contract Law of Montenegro', in Nuni A and others (eds), *Civil Law Forum for South East Europe*, vol 1 (Centre for SEELS 2012).

Cserne P, 'The Recodification of Private Law in Central and Eastern Europe' in Larouche P and Cserne P (eds), *National Legal Systems and Globalization: New Role, Continuing Relevance* (Springer 2013) [https://doi.org/10.1007/978-90-6704-885-9_4].

Dabovic Anastasovska J and Zdraveva N, 'Duty of Information Disclosure in the Conclusion of Consumer Contracts: Implementation of the EU Law Standards in the Republic of Macedonia' (2017) 8 (2) *Iustinianus Primus L Rev* 1.

Damane L and others, 'Private Law' in Kerkmäe T and others (eds), *The Law of the Baltic States* (Springer 2017) [https://doi.org/10.1007/978-3-319-54478-6_6].

Didžiulis L, *Contract Law in Lithuania* (Wolters Kluwer 2019).

Djurovic M, 'Serbian Contract Law: Its Development and the New Serbian Civil Code' (2011) 7 *ERCL* 65 [https://doi.org/10.1515/ercl.2011.65].

——, 'EU Consumer Law Outside the European Union: The Case of Albania' (2013) 36 *JCP* 269.

Dulak A, 'Slovakia' in Lavický P and Hurdík J (eds), *Private Law Reform* (Masaryk University 2014).

Dvořák B, 'Assignment of a Contract in the New Czech Civil Code' [2014] (2) *ELTE LJ* 123.

Elischer D, Frinta O, and Pauknerová M, 'Recodification of Private Law in the Czech Republic' in Rivera JC (ed), *The Scope and Structure of Civil Codes* (Springer 2013) [https://doi.org/10.1007/978-94-007-7942-6_5].

Fiala J and Hurdík J, *Contract Law in the Czech Republic* (2nd edn, Wolters Kluwer 2020).

——, Hurdík J, and Kirstová K, *Contract Law in the Slovak Republic* (3rd edn, Wolters Kluwer 2017).

Fuglinszky A, 'Risks and Side Effects: Five Questions on the "New" Hungarian Tort Law' [2014] (2) *ELTE LJ* 199.

——, 'Some Structural Questions on the Relationship between Contractual and Extra-contractual Liability in the New Hungarian Civil Code' in Menyhárd A and Veress E (eds), *New Civil Codes in Hungary and Romania* (Springer 2017) [https://doi.org/10.1007/978-3-319-63327-5_9].

Heidenhain S, 'Harmonisation of the Czech Consumer Rights in the New Civil Code' [2014] (2) *ELTE LJ* 41.

Hondius E, 'Recodification of Private Law in Central and Eastern Europe and in the Netherlands' [2014] (1) *ELTE LJ* 51.

Hrádek J, 'Regulation of Liability for Damage in the New Czech Civil Code' [2014] (2) *ELTE LJ* 223.

Hulmák M, 'Czech Republic' in Lavický P and Hurdík J (eds), *Private Law Reform* (Masaryk University 2014).

Josipović T, Gliha I, and Nikšić S, 'Croatia' in Lavický P and Hurdík J (eds), *Private Law Reform* (Masaryk University 2014).

——, 'Private Law Codification in the Republic of Croatia' in Wang WY (ed), *Codification in International Perspective: Selected Papers from the 2nd IACL Thematic Conference* (Springer 2014) [https://doi.org/10.1007/978-3-319-03455-3_7].

Jurčová M, 'The Influence of Harmonisation on Civil Law in the Slovak Republic' [2008] *Juridica Intl* 166.

Katner WJ, 'Leasing in the Polish Civil Code' (2011) 16 *Unif L Rev* 401 [https://doi.org/10.1093/ulr/16.1-2.401].

Kisfaludi A, 'The Influence of Harmonisation of Private Law on the Development of the Civil Law in Hungary' [2008] *Juridica Intl* 130.

——, 'Transfer of Property, Claims, Rights and Contracts in the New Hungarian Civil Code' [2014] (2) *ELTE LJ* 109.

Konstantinović M, *Obligacije i ugovori: Skica za zakonik o obligacijama i ugovorima* (Pravni fakultet u Beogradu 1969).

Kõve V, 'Applicable Law in the Light of Modern Law of Obligations and Bases for the Preparation of the Law of Obligations Act' [2001] *Juridica Intl* 30.

Kull I, 'Reform of Contract Law in Estonia: Influences of Harmonisation of European Private Law' [2008] *Juridica Intl* 122.

——, 'Codification of Private Law in Estonia' in Rivera JC (ed), *The Scope and Structure of Civil Codes* (Springer 2013) [https://doi.org/10.1007/978-94-007-7942-6_6].

Machnikowski P, 'Poland' in Lavický P and Hurdík J (eds), *Private Law Reform* (Masaryk University 2014).

Mańko R, 'Unification of Private Law in Europe from the Perspective of the Polish Legal Culture' (2008) 11 *Yearb Pol Eur Stud* 109.

Menyhárd A, 'Unjustified Enrichment in the New Hungarian Civil Code' [2014] (2) *ELTE LJ* 233.

——, 'Basic Questions of Tort Law from a Hungarian Perspective' in Koziol H (ed), *Basic Questions of Tort Law from a Comparative Perspective* (Jan Sramek Verlag 2015) [https://doi.org/10.26530/oapen_574832].

——, 'Contracts' in Harmathy A (ed), *Introduction to Hungarian law* (2nd edn, Wolters Kluwer 2019).

Mikelenas V, 'Unification and Harmonisation of Law at the Turn of the Millennium: The Lithuanian Experience' (2000) 5 *Unif L Rev* 243 [https://doi.org/10.1093/ulr/5.2.243].

——, 'The Main Features of the New Lithuanian Contract Law System Based on the Civil Code of 2000' [2005] *Juridica Intl* 42.

——, 'The Influence of Instruments of Harmonisation of Private Law upon the Reform of Civil Law in Lithuania' [2008] *Juridica Intl* 143.

Možina D, 'Harmonisation of Private Law in Europe and the Development of Private Law in Slovenia' [2008] *Juridica Intl* 173.

——, '*Ne ultra alterum tantum* in evropsko pravo' [2010] *Podjetje in delo* 497.

—— and Vlahek A, *Contract Law in Slovenia* (Wolters Kluwer 2019).

Müller C and Riske O, 'Cross-Fertilization between Swiss and Turkish Tort Laws' (2014) 22 *ERPL* 879.

Nikolić D, 'Codification of Civil Law in Serbia (Historical Experience and Current Projects)' in Jurčová M and others (eds), *Liber amicorum Ján Lazar* (Právnická Fakulta Trnavskej Univerzity v Trnave 2014).

Nikšić S, 'Nekoliko napomena o nomotehničkom standardu Zakona o obveznim odnosima' in Slakoper Z (ed), *Liber amicorum in honorem Vilim Gorenc* (Pravni fakultet Sveučilišta u Rijeci 2014).

Oguz A, 'The Role of Comparative Law in the Development of Turkish Civil Law' (2005) 17 *Pace Intl L Rev* 373.

Parapatits F, 'Albania: Reform of Consumer Protection Law' (2010) 18 *ERPL* 165.

Povlakić M, 'Culpa in contrahendo im bosnisch-herzegowinischen Recht' in Welser R (ed), *Haftung aus Verschulden beim Vertragsabschluss in Zentral- und Osteuropa* (Manz 2012).

Radić D, 'Development of Civil Law in Bosnia and Herzegovina' in Nuni A and others (eds), *Civil Law Forum for South East Europe*, vol 1 (Centre for SEELS 2012).

Rajski J, 'European Initiatives and Reform of Civil Law in Poland' [2008] *Juridica Intl* 151.

Reich N, 'Transformation of Contract Law and Civil Justice in the New EU Member Countries: The Example of the Baltic States, Hungary and Poland' (2004) 23 *Penn State Intl L Rev* 587.

Riefa C and Durovic M, 'Serbian Consumer Law: Out with the Old, in with the New' (2015) 22 *MJECL* 862 [https://doi.org/10.1177/1023263X1502200605].

Rivera JC, 'The Scope and Structure of Civil Codes: Relations with Commercial Law, Family Law, Consumer Law and Private International Law: A Comparative Approach' in Rivera JC (ed), *The Scope and Structure of Civil Codes* (Springer 2013) [https://doi.org/10.1007/978-94-007-7942-6_1].

Romanowski M, 'Position of the Law of Obligations in Polish Law in the Context of a Reform of the European Law of Obligations' in Schulze R and Zoll F (eds), *The Law of Obligations in Europe: A New Wave of Codifications* (SELP 2013) [https://doi.org/10.1515/9783866539839.67].

Rudnicki J, 'Remarks Regarding the Influence of European Legislation upon Codification of Civil Law' (2017) 71 *Stud Juridica* 207 [https://doi.org/10.5604/01.3001.0010.5830].

Schulze R, 'Changes in the Law of Obligations in Europe' in Schulze R and Zoll F (eds), *The Law of Obligations in Europe: A New Wave of Codifications* (SELP 2013) [https://doi.org/10.1515/9783866539839.3].

Selelionyté-Drukteiniené S, Jurkevičius V, and Kadner Graziano T, 'The Impact of the Comparative Method on Lithuanian Private Law' (2013) 21 *ERPL* 959.

Shopov A, 'Two Current Civil Law Issues of Consumer Protection: European and Bulgarian Aspects' (2015) 4 *EuCML* 44.

Slakoper Z, 'Allgemeines Bürgerliches Gesetzbuch (ABGB) und kroatisches bürgerliches Recht' in Geistlinger M and others (eds), *200 Jahre ABGB – Ausstrahlungen: Die Bedeutung der Kodifikation für andere Staaten und andere Rechtskulturen* (MANZ Verlag 2011).

Takoff C, 'Private Law in Bulgaria' in Jessel-Holst C, Kulms R, and Trunk A (eds), *Private Law in Eastern Europe* (Mohr Siebeck 2010).

Tichý L, 'Czech and European Law of Obligations at a Turning Point' in Schulze R and Zoll F (eds), *The Law of Obligations in Europe: A New Wave of Codifications* (SELP 2013) [https://doi.org/10.1515/9783866539839.27].

Tőkey B, 'New Particular Agreements in the New Hungarian Civil Code' in Attila Menyhárd and Emőd Veress (eds), *New Civil Codes in Hungary and Romania* (Springer 2017) [https://doi.org/10.1007/978-3-319-63327-5_10].

Torgāns K, 'Latvian Contract Law and the EU' [2001] *Juridica Intl* 38.

——, 'European Initiatives (PECL, DCFR) and Modernisation of Latvian Civil Law' [2008] *Juridica Intl* 137.

Tot I, 'Kamate' in Slakoper Z (ed), *Bankovni i financijski ugovori* (Narodne novine 2017).

——, 'Prestanak trajnih obveznih odnosa' (2018) 39 *Zbornik PFR* 1171 [https://doi.org/10.30925/zpfsr.39.3.2].

——, 'Prestanak tijeka zateznih kamata kada njihov iznos dostigne iznos glavnice' (2020) 68 (6615) *Informator* 13.

Varul P, 'Legal Policy Decisions and Choices in the Creation of New Private Law in Estonia' [2000] *Juridica Intl* 104.

——, 'The Creation of New Estonian Private Law' (2008) 16 *ERPL* 95.

Vékás L, 'Civil Code of 2013' in Harmathy A (ed), *Introduction to Hungarian law* (2nd edn, Wolters Kluwer 2019).

Veress E, 'The New Romanian Civil Code: Difficulties in the Transition towards a Monist Private Law' in Menyhárd A and Veress E (eds), *New Civil Codes in Hungary and Romania* (Springer 2017) [https://doi.org/10.1007/978-3-319-63327-5_3].

Vlahek A and Podobnik K, 'Slovenia: Chronology of Development of Private Law in Slovenia' in Lavický P and Hurdík J (eds), *Private Law Reform* (Masaryk University 2014).

Vuksanović D and Korać V, 'Development of Civil Law' in Nuni A and others (eds), *Civil Law Forum for South East Europe*, vol 1 (Centre for SEELS 2012).

Zdraveva N, Gavrilović N, and Radevska M, 'Drafing a Civil Code' in Nuni A and others (eds), *Civil Law Forum for South East Europe*, vol 1 (Centre for SEELS 2012).

Zivkovska R and Przeska T, 'Codification of the Civil Law in the Republic of Macedonia' (2014) 68 *Zbornik radova Pravnog fakulteta u Nišu* 251 [https://doi.org/10.5937/zrpfni1468251z].

Zoll F, 'Contract Law in the Draft of the New Polish Civil Code: Formation of Contract, Performance and Non-Performance of Obligations' in Schulze R and Zoll F (eds), *The Law of Obligations in Europe: A New Wave of Codifications* (SELP 2013) [https://doi.org/10.1515/9783866539839.93].

——, 'A Civil Code Outside of Reality: The Polish Codification of the Year 1964, Its Origin, Development and Future' in Wang WY (ed), *Codification in International Perspective: Selected Papers from the 2nd IACL Thematic Conference* (Springer 2014) [https://doi.org/10.1007/978-3-319-03455-3_8].

# Part I

# Recodification of the law of obligations in Central and Southeast Europe

# 2 The conception and institutional novelties of recodification of private law in the Slovak Republic

*Marek Števček and Marek Ivančo*

## 1 Introduction

Recodification of private law in the Slovak Republic revolves primarily around the elementary Act 40/1964, Civil Code (*Občiansky zákonník*,[1] OZ), which has been in force for more than fifty-five years now. During this period, the OZ was amended almost seventy times, but only four amendments were adopted before 1989. The later amendments have mainly reflected the changes in social conditions and the introduction of the market economy that occurred after the Velvet Revolution in 1989.

The most extensive of the amendments, Act 509/1991,[2] was implemented after the Velvet Revolution. This Act has amended roughly 80% of the text of the original OZ but did not fully reflect on the issue of discontinuity with the previous forty-year social and economic development.[3] At the same time, the transition to a market economy created the need for a comprehensive amendment not only of the OZ but of the entire private law as such.

Since then, three recodification committees (with three different chairmen) have already been replaced and the recodification process has been in progress for almost thirty years now with still no definitive end on the horizon.

After 1989 and before 2018, there was a long period during which the recodification work had not been transposed into a relevant legislative text, except for only one case in 1998. That was the case of the Government Bill of 1998 amending the OZ, which has passed the inter-ministerial consultations, but the work did not continue in the new legislative period.

---

1 Act 40/1964, Civil Code (*Zákon 40/1964 Zb, Občiansky zákonník*), last amended by Act 394/2019 (*Zákon 394/2019 Zz*) of 28 October 2019.
2 Act amending and supplementing the Civil Code (*Zákon 509/1991 Zb, Zákon, ktorým sa mení, dopĺňa a upravuje Občiansky zákonník*).
3 Explanatory Memorandum to the Government Bill amending the OZ, pt A. Ministerstvo spravodlivosti Slovenskej republiky, 'Dôvodová správa' (Ministerstvo spravodlivosti Slovenskej republiky, 15 October 2018) <www.justice.gov.sk/Stranky/Ministerstvo/Aktuality-obcianskeho-zakonnika.aspx> accessed 6 May 2020 (Explanatory Memorandum).

One of the latest results of the recodification is the Government Bill of 2018 amending the Civil Code.[4] The Government Bill of 2018 was drawn up based on the Legislative Intent of the Civil Code.[5] This latest, most extensive amendment is, however, yet to be passed. This only underlines the fact that the authors aim to outline and break down the current topic. Nonetheless, one can reasonably expect the Government Bill of 2018 to be passed soon. Therefore, the chapter will mostly refer to this yet non-approved, but the most relevant version of the proposed amendment.

## 2 Civil code in Slovakia – *de lege lata* evaluation

Despite the efforts to adapt the basic civil legislation to the needs of the market economy through numerous amendments, much of important content is either still missing in OZ or has been regulated inadequately, and even contrary to the requirements and principles common in the European civil-law codifications. The reasons for the recodification have long been known and have been quite extensively described in the literature. Some of these, albeit overly cautious comments, come even before 1989,[6] but most of proposals reflect on the subsequent socio-political changes.[7]

In that sense, we can mention that the current text of the OZ still lacks the regulation of the *superficies solo cedit* principle (according to which any buildings or other objects which are located on the land and are firmly connected to the ground are inseparable from that land), as well as the institute of the so-called building right. Further, the regulation of personality rights is insufficient and the regulation of invalidity of legal acts with an emphasis on absolute invalidity is inadequate, etc.

Moreover, the actual legal regulation contained in the OZ is fragmented, unsystematic, and confusing.[8] After the amendment from 1989 and the abolition of the third, fourth, and fifth part of the OZ (regulating personal use, services, and rights and obligations from other legal acts), the second part of

---

4  Ministerstvo spravodlivosti Slovenskej republiky, 'Vládny návrh zákona, ktorým sa mení a dopĺňa zákon č 40/1964 Zb Občiansky zákonník' (Ministerstvo spravodlivosti Slovenskej republiky, 15 October 2018) <www.justice.gov.sk/Stranky/Ministerstvo/Aktuality-obcianskeho-zakonnika.aspx> accessed 6 May 2020 (Government Bill of 2018).

5  Komisia pre rekodifikáciu súkromného práva, 'Legislatívny zámer Občianskeho zákonníka' (Ministerstvo spravodlivosti Slovenskej republiky) <www.justice.gov.sk/Stranky/Nase-sluzby/Nase-projekty/Obciansky-zakonnik/Obciansky-zakonnik.aspx> accessed 15 February 2020 (Legislative Intent).

6  Ján Lazar, 'K stavu, problémom a perspektívam základnej občianskoprávnej úpravy' (1989) 72 *Prav Obzor* 388.

7  František Zoulík, 'Problematika rekodifikace soukromého práva v České republice' (1995) 43 *Prav Praxe* 126; Karol Plank, 'Koncepcia rekodifikácie občianskeho práva hmotného v Slovenskej republike' (1996) 48 (4) *Just Rev* 1; Ján Lazar, 'Východiská a koncepčné otázky návrhu slovenského Občianskeho zákonníka' (1997) 49 (12) *Just Rev* 16.

8  Legislative Intent (n 5) 11.

the OZ (rights *in rem*) is followed by the sixth part on tort liability and unjust enrichment, the seventh part on inheritance law, and the eighth part on the law of obligations. Another flood of amendments that followed, while bringing new content and refinements, has also further deepened the problem. Needless to say, the numerous amendments after 1989 were intended to provide only a temporary legislative fix. Yet, this temporary legislative fix has remained in place up to now.

The inconsistent and non-conceptual approach has also been reflected in the amendments intended to implement certain EU directives in the Slovak civil law. But the approach adopted by the European legislature itself has been fragmentary and incoherent,[9] which has been often criticized.[10] Thus, the general regulation of consumer contracts and the consumer contract on the right to use a building or part thereof is included among the general provisions of the OZ, which is considered non-systemic. Besides the regulation in OZ, there are also more than eight separate acts on consumer protection. In this sense, the flood of consumer legislation has led some authors in the second half of the twentieth century to refer to a 'crisis of the idea of codification',[11] or even to an 'age of decodification'.[12]

Nevertheless, there is a need for alignment with the current state of the European private law, which should consider developments in the harmonization of Member States' legal orders. In the words of Helmut Koziol:

> Therefore, as realists, we have to accept that the question is no longer whether we want harmonisation of law in the EU since it is already a fact which cannot be denied and we must come to terms with this development. Thus, what is on the agenda is not whether there should be a harmonisation of the law, but rather how harmonisation should take place.[13]

Furthermore, the current OZ of 1964 no longer meets the requirements of the modern twenty-first-century code.[14] Even after all the 'improvements' and

---

9 Reinhard Zimmerman, 'Codification: The Civilian Experience Reconsidered on the Eve of a Common European Sales Law' (2012) 8 *ERCL* 367, 386.

10 Hugh Collins, *The European Civil Code: The Way Forward* (CUP 2008) 2, 28ff.

11 Stefan Meder, 'Die Krise des Nationalstaates und ihre Folgen für das Kodifikationsprinzip' (2006) 61 *JZ* 477, 483.

12 Reinhard Zimmermann, 'Codification: History and Present Significance of an Idea' (1995) 3 *ERPL* 95, 105ff.

13 Helmut Koziol, 'Comparative Conclusions' in Helmut Koziol (ed), *Basic Questions of Tort Law from a Comparative Perspective* (Jan Sramek Verlag 2015) 689–90.

14 Ján Lazar, 'Základné aspekty kodifikácie slovenského Občianskeho zákonníka (úvodný referát)' in Ján Lazar (ed), *Návrh legislatívneho zámeru kodifikácie súkromného práva: Materiály z odbornej konferencie* (Ministerstvo spravodlivosti SR 2008) 27; Alexandra Kotrecová and Saskia Poláčková, 'Je možná rekodifikácia občianskeho práva hmotného bez rekodifikácie civilného práva procesného?' in *Dny práva – 2008 – Days of Law* (Masarykova univerzita v Brne 2008) 924ff.

'modernizations' in terms of content and systematic and formal aspects, the OZ seems to be very imperfect and incomplete legislative work. An example is its technical nature which, due to the numerous 'stickers', does not, after all, resemble a code. Unfortunately, there are provisions such as § 151me OZ, which was created by amending its § 151m, while § 151m OZ was created by amending § 151 OZ. Despite these statements, the reason concerning the modernity of the code seems to be the least discussed reason. Nevertheless, the modernization should be a feature that distinguishes the 'ordinary' amendment from the 'extraordinary' recodification. In this sense, recodification usually bears certain characteristics of a restatement since it is supposed to incorporate and consolidate the 'centuries' of legal achievements.[15] The 'ordinary' amendment does not necessarily need to involve modernization. The Government Bill of 2018 brings about a lot of novelties further described, to the extent that it indeed can be described as a recodification.

## 3  The conception of recodification of private law in Slovakia

The reflections and expert discussions regarding the actual shape of a new recodification in the Slovak Republic, as in other countries that were preparing a new codification of private law, were focused from its very beginning on two basic conceptual solutions:

a   the conception of a single or rather integrated civil code, the regulation of which integrates all basic private-law relations, including commercial obligations and consumer relations (monistic conception);
b   separate regulation of commercial law and civil law in two separate codes, with both the Commercial Code (*Obchodný zákonník*,[16] ObZ) and the OZ regulating contractual obligations (dualistic conception).[17]

The dualistic model of civil and commercial law (including contractual dualism) is mostly a matter of the nineteenth century, and in some countries, it has so far been maintained mainly due to historical traditions (Germany, Austria, France).[18] In Slovakia, a dualistic model has been applied since 1 January 1992. The recodification of private law under the dualistic conception is,

---

15  Bernhard Windscheid, 'Die geschichtliche Schule in der Rechtswissenschaft' in Paul Oertmann (ed), *Bernhard Windscheid: Gesammelte Reden und Abhandlungen* (Duncker & Humblot 1904) 75.
16  Act 513/1991, Commercial Code (*Zákon 513/1991 Zb, Obchodný zákonník*), last amended by Act 390/2019 (*Zákon 390/2019 Zz*) of 22 October 2019.
17  See Ján Lazar, 'K niektorým koncepčným otázkam rekodifikácie súkromného práva' (2001) 49 *Prav Praxe* 6, 6ff.
18  cf Franz Wieacker, *A History of Private Law in Europe* (Tony Weir tr, Clarendon Press 1995) 257ff; Zimmerman, 'Codification: The Civilian Experience Reconsidered' (n 9) 376ff.

however, no longer recommended by most of the leading European civil law scholars and, therefore, not even for the transition countries of Central and Eastern Europe.[19] It causes considerable difficulties.[20] This is observable, for example, with the mixed contracts concluded between entrepreneurs and non-entrepreneurs. In such relations, is civil or commercial law applicable to these contracts? Such issues are rather unknown in legal systems preferring monistic conception, where only a single contract law exists.

Based on the current developments in European countries, with particular reference to developments in neighbouring transition countries (Czech Republic, Hungary, Poland), and taking into account also Slovak experience of applying dualistic conception represented by the current OZ and the ObZ, the legislature is inclined to implement the monistic conception.[21]

However, unlike the civil codes based on the monistic conception, which have been conceived broadly, such as Czech, Dutch, Quebec, Russian, Italian, and Swiss civil code, the revised OZ will be based on a much narrower (modified) model of including civil and commercial obligations in a single code. It will exclude the provisions on companies, cooperatives, competition law, business register, intellectual property law, as well as the substantive regulation of individual labour law and private international law. Thus, the ObZ with the very restricted scope will still be retained, along with the Family Act, the Labour Code, the International Private and Procedural Law Act, as well as the special laws governing copyright and related rights, industrial and commercial rights belonging to intellectual property, etc. However, instead of two parallel systems of contract law, one in the OZ and the other in the ObZ (which are often duplicated and contradictory), there will only be a single and unified contract law system in the new private code.

As to the advantages of the monistic conception, it is assumed that if any particularities are regulated in the same code rather than being regulated in a completely different specific code, that such general legal regulation would simply be more effective and approachable for the addressed subjects of the legal norms. Subjects interpreting the legal norms would find all the relevant rules concentrated in one place, along with all applicable specific deviations.

First of all, this means that all the specific features of commercial contracts will remain unchanged, and they will be regulated in a factual, systematic, and totally clear and comprehensible way in the context and within the relevant contractual type, in a logical sequence from general to specific. For example,

---

19  This solution was recommended by various legal committees to the Slovak Republic during the international conference on recodification organized by the Council of Europe and the Ministry of Justice of the Slovak Republic in 1997. See Ján Lazar, *Otázky kodifikácie súkromného práva* (Iura edition 2006) 101.

20  cf Ján Lazar, 'Základné aspekty nového občianskeho a obchodného práva' [1993] 15 *Acta Facultatis Iuridicae Universitatis Comenianae* 77.

21  Legislative Intent (n 5) 13.

as regards the purchase contract, the specifics of the purchase of the company and the consumer purchase contract will follow the general provisions of the purchase contract. In this context, the idea of a wider 'commercialization of the civil code' appeared early in the article by Ján Lazar, who stated that this conception has become increasingly attractive recently, and numerous European civil law scholars consider the common regulation of basic civil and commercial law more in line with the pan-European integration processes than the traditional notion based on the maxim *lex specialis derogat legi generali* between the OZ and the ObZ.[22]

There are also other reasons supporting the monistic conception of a private law code. The trend in European countries that have adopted or are preparing new civil codes in the twentieth century and the beginning of the twenty-first century is clearly focused on a monistic conception. This has been the case with the Swiss, Italian, and Dutch Civil Code, but also the Civil Code of the Canadian province of Quebec. The transition countries of Central and Eastern Europe are also taking this path (e.g. Russia, Lithuania, Latvia, Estonia, and Romania). The same orientation has already been adopted by the civil codes in neighbouring countries (in the Czech Republic and Hungary). Even the states that have independently codified commercial law in the nineteenth century and in which dualism persists due to tradition, in the twenty-first century have already started implementing the reform measures. One such example is the adoption of the Austrian Undertaking Code, which replaced the Commercial Code in 2007.

Therefore, one might conclude that the recodification of private law in the Slovak Republic follows a monistic conception and especially the example of the recodification of private law in the Visegrád Four countries, e.g. in the Czech Republic, where a single code of private law (the new Civil Code[23]) was adopted.[24]

## 4 The current state of recodification and the institutional novelties it brings

As already mentioned, one of the latest results of the recodification effort is the Government Bill of 2018. The Commission on Recodification of Private Law had decided that the civil law shall be recast *per partes*, gradually, with the primary aim of first modifying those parts which can gain broad technical and political support quickly, whereas the topics that represent

---

22 Ján Lazar, 'Aktuálna úvaha o postavení občianskeho práva v česko-slovenskom systéme práva' (1993) 132 *Právnik* 1048.

23 Act 89/2012, Civil Code (*Zákon* 89/2012 *Sb, Občanský zákoník*), last amended by Act 33/2020 (*Zákon* 33/2020 *Sb*) of 21 January 2020 (NOZ).

24 Regina Hučková and Diana Treščáková, 'Monistická koncepcia rekodifikácie skromného práva verzus zmluvy uzatvárané pri obchodovaní' in *Dny práva – 2012 – Days of Law* (Masarykova univerzita v Brne 2013) 1148, 1152.

value issues and need deeper discussion would be recast only at a later stage. Even though modern codes are mostly enacted in their entirety, it is not that rare that the various parts are drafted and enacted in stages (e.g. in the Netherlands).[25] Moreover, *per partes* procedure does not conceptually preclude the notion of recodification *stricto sensu*. The Government Bill of 2018 provides for a vast revision of the current OZ which matches the notion of recodification as such.[26]

As explained by the Minister of Justice of the Slovak Republic, there were several reasons for adopting this approach: the inadequacy of the overall change in the private law system under Slovak conditions, the lack of clarity of the basic conceptual issues in the broader social context, as well as the lack of political will to push through such dramatic changes at once, even after the experience of the Czech Republic.[27]

In the current parliamentary term, the Ministry of Justice of the Slovak Republic will focus only on the reform of the law of obligations, while the recodification work will continue in the next parliamentary term by reforming the property rights and the law of succession.

The main objective of the reform of the law of obligations is the abolition of the dualism of the law of obligations in favour of the universal regulation stipulated in the OZ. This objective will be realized once the amendment to the OZ, which is currently in the Parliament, is approved.

In an attempt to mediate the broadest insight into the issue, the first half of this section deals with a mere general overview of the important institutional novelties being brought by the amendment to the OZ, while in the second half of this section the specific importance of recodification in the context of the prescription regime will be discussed.

## 4.1 A general overview of the institutional novelties

The legislature has expressed its desire to adapt the general provisions on legal transactions to the current trends.[28] Nonetheless, there are views expressing doubts about the correctness of certain proposed provisions of the OZ.[29] In order to improve the proposal of the reform of the law of obligations, critical feedback is an indispensable tool for the re-evaluation of the suitability and acceptability of the chosen solutions.

---

25  Zimmerman, 'Codification: The Civilian Experience Reconsidered' (n 9) 371.

26  See also the text before n 15 delineating the feature of modernity typical for a notion of recodification.

27  'Vieme, prečo sa nebude prijímať nový Občiansky zákonník' (*najpravo.sk*, 23 October 2018) <www.najpravo.sk/clanky/vieme-preco-sa-nebude-prijimat-novy-obciansky-zakonnik.html> accessed 1 February 2020.

28  Explanatory Memorandum (n 3).

29  cf Svetlana Ficová, Tamara Čipková, and Martin Hamřik, '55 let Graždanskomu kodeksu Slovackoj Respubliki' in Bronislav Mičislavovič Gongalo (ed), *Graždanskij kodeks Rossijskoj Federaciji: 25 let dejstvija* (Uraľskij gosudarstvennyj juridičeskij universitet 2019) 245ff.

## 4.1.1 Nullity of legal transactions

The Government Bill of 2018 emphasizes minimizing the scope of absolute nullity of legal transactions, which represents a serious interference with the contractual autonomy of private individuals. Instead, the relative invalidity or settlement of the parties' claims under a contract is preferred. This proposed solution was intended already at the very beginning of work on the new OZ after a thorough evaluation of all existing solutions in the Slovak Republic and abroad.[30]

The relative invalidity of a legal transaction is currently enshrined in § 40a OZ. It differs from the absolute nullity contained in § 39 OZ (which occurs directly by law) in a way that a legal transaction is considered to be valid despite having a legal defect until the invalidity is invoked by the beneficiary. Only the subjects who have not caused the invalidity themselves are eligible to invoke it. It is not possible to declare the invalidity of a legal transaction after the expiration of a three-year time limit from the date the invalid transaction was undertaken. This has been a major breakpoint. Whereas the relative invalidity has been limited by three years' period, the absolute nullity has not been limited at all. This fact has led to long-term uncertainty about the validity of legal transactions, which does not contribute to the stability of legal relations.[31]

Currently, the absolute nullity is a rule, whilst the relative invalidity is only an exception for a few cases, namely seven of them which are exhaustively enumerated in the OZ.[32] Thus, relative invalidity cannot be extended to other cases. However, the amendment to the OZ prefers relative nullity over absolute nullity. Under the current wording of § 267(1) ObZ, as well as in several foreign jurisdictions (e.g. § 586 of the Czech NOZ, and the interpretation of § 879 of the German BGB[33]), it is stipulated that absolute nullity will occur in cases where a public interest or public order is protected. Relative invalidity will occur if the standard protects a particular party, e.g. in the event of an error, fraud, or usury, or in the case of provisions on nominate contract types that protect one of the parties (e.g. protection of a sales representative). Nonetheless, this is not the case in the context of consumer protection, where the absolute nullity applies. The main reason for this adjustment is that absolute nullity constitutes a serious interference with the contractual autonomy of private individuals.

---

30  Lazar, *Otázky kodifikácie* (n 19) 117.
31  ibid.
32  This enumeration cannot be overcome by analogy, as flows from the case law. See NS SSR decision of 22 May 1985, Cpj 13/85, R 50/1985.
33  German Civil Code (*Bürgerliches Gesetzbuch*) in the version promulgated on 2 January 2002 (*BGBl* I 42, 2909; 2003 I 738), last amended by Article 1 of the Act of 21 December 2019 (*BGBl* I 3719).

*4.1.2   Standard contract terms*

The Government Bill of 2018 also regulates the contracting process (e.g. incorporation of business terms into a contract and control of the surprising clauses in standard contracts, which often caused problems in practice). It proposes to provide for two cumulative conditions for the effective incorporation of the terms and conditions into the contract (§ 71 of the revised OZ).

First, the contract must explicitly refer to the use of the terms incorporated. Typically, this will be a contractual clause expressly providing for the application of certain terms and conditions. Alternatively, in cases where an explicit reference would not be practicable, this condition may be fulfilled by visibly placing information on the use of the terms and conditions in the place where the contract is concluded. It can be warranty terms in the shop, where the purchase contracts are concluded, or in the workshop where the work contracts are concluded. In these cases, an explicit reference to the terms and conditions is not necessary. In the case of contracts concluded in writing, explicit reference will typically be possible and therefore required.

The second cumulative condition consists in the possibility for the contracting party to become acquainted with their content. This condition can typically be met e.g. by issuing business conditions on-site or by making them available on the website. Thus, unlike current regulation, it will not be necessary to prove that the terms and conditions were known to the party, since this demonstration is often not even possible in practice (e.g. it is typically not possible to prove that the warranty terms were familiar to the customer in the shop).

In the case of commercial terms and conditions normally used in the course of trade, it is sufficient that, given the circumstances and the position of the parties, it can be reasonably expected that they were known to the parties. By way of example, the familiarity of Incoterms can be assumed in the course of trade between traders and there is, therefore, no need to establish in particular that the parties have been given the opportunity to become acquainted with them.

Moreover, it has been proposed that deviating arrangements take precedence over the incorporated terms and conditions.

Further, the Government Bill of 2018 introduces the control of surprising provisions which is enshrined in § 74 of the revised OZ. The new regulation essentially follows the solution employed in § 305c BGB[34] and applies not only to the terms and conditions incorporated by reference but to any standardized contracts. In these cases, it is necessary to protect the party that did not prepare a standardized contract from the 'surprising' clauses that could not be

---

34   Under § 305c BGB, 'Provisions in standard business terms which in the circumstances, in particular with regard to the outward appearance of the contract, are so unusual that the other party to the contract with the user need not expect to encounter them, do not form part of the contract.'

reasonably expected in the standardized contract. This applies to both consumer and other relationships.

### 4.1.3 Voidability of the debtor's legal acts detrimental to creditor

The Government Bill of 2018 also brings a new regulation of voidability of the debtor's legal acts contained in §§ 838 to 852 of the revised OZ. The mechanism of voidability consists of the creditor's right to defend himself against the debtor who has the intention of curtailing the satisfaction of the creditor's enforceable claim (*in fraudem creditoris*). In practice, this institute was quite ineffective, and the new regulation reflects this and aims to introduce a functional institute for the protection of the creditors.

The reason for the new regulation can be attributed to a lot of inaccurate terms expressively used in the OZ, which have not been overcome by case law. One such polemical term is the 'enforceable claim',[35] which happens to be the elementary notion of the institute of voidability. The other quite unstable aspect is related to the question of whether the creditor is allowed to oppose and void any legal act of the debtor or only an act that was undertaken without relevant consideration.[36] The new legislation addresses these aspects and defines that the voidability might affect not only the debtor's legal act taken without the relevant consideration (§ 840 of the revised OZ) but also the legal act that debtor has intentionally taken to the detriment of the creditor provided that the other party knew or had to know the debtor's intention at the time the voidable legal act was taken (§ 839 of the revised OZ). In this context, a creditor may oppose and void in particular any legal transaction by which a debtor transferred his assets or a part thereof free of charge, any contract for deed entered into by a debtor, whose regular value is substantially higher than the transaction value, which a debtor has obtained or is to obtain, or, eventually, any legal act by which a debtor waives his right, forgives a debt of his debtor or refuses to accept a debtless inheritance. On the other hand, a creditor may not oppose and void a legal act without adequate consideration if it is a low-value occasional gift or any adequate performance of the debtor for the sake of public benefit, or if the debtor fulfils his obligation under the law (§ 840 of the revised OZ).

The proposal further distinguishes between the other party to the voidable legal act in general and the 'related person', which is a person stipulated in § 9 of the Act 7/2005,[37] and includes, in particular, a statutory body, senior

35 cf Marek Števček and others, *Občiansky zákonník I: § 1–450: Komentár* (CH Beck 2015) 318ff.
36 Ficová, Čipková, and Hamřik (n 29) 245ff.
37 Act 7/2005, on Bankruptcy and Restructuring (*Zákon 7/2005 Zz, Zákon o konkurze a reštrukturalizácii a o zmene a doplnení niektorých zákonov*), last amended by Act 390/2019 (*Zákon 390/2019 Zz*) of 22 October 2019.

officer, authorized representative, or member of the supervisory board of a legal person, a natural or legal person having a qualified share (at least 5% of the entity's registered capital or voting rights) of this legal person, or relatives of the natural persons affiliated with these legal persons. If the debtor has entered into a contract for deed or for the benefit of such a related person in the last three years with the intention of curtailing its creditor, and the related person knew or had to know about that intention at the time of the conclusion of the contract, it is possible to oppose and void such contract (§ 839 of the revised OZ). As regards a related person, unlike any other person, knowledge of the debtor's intention is always presumed. However, a related person retains the right to prove that, despite all due diligence, it could not have known the debtor's intention.

### 4.1.4 Introduction of new contract types

It is also desirable to mention that the Government Bill of 2018 also introduces the legal regulation of a few new contract types, which very often occur in practice, but their legal regulation has been missing so far. The introduction of these contract types into legal regulation will reduce transaction costs and simplify the ordinary course of things. These new contract types include, in particular, the leasing agreement, the service agreement, the electronic mediation service agreement, the franchise agreement, and the confidentiality agreement.

## 4.2 The specific importance of recodification in the context of the prescription regime

The duality of the prescription regime regulated by two different codes has caused many problems and uncertainties in practice. The legal certainty of private-law entities and the predictability of court decisions will be strengthened by uniform regulation and the refined concepts and institutes.

   Moreover, the recast text of the OZ introduces the possibility for parties to agree on a shorter or longer limitation period than would be provided for by law (§ 104 of the revised OZ). In the current version of the OZ, the parties are not allowed to agree on a different length of the limitation period. However, the proposed amendment allows for an agreement on a different length of the limitation period, provided that the agreed limitation period is not shorter than one year and longer than twenty years. At the same time, the agreement is precluded if it is detrimental to the consumer or if it relates to any of the exhaustively enumerated claims – a claim based on intentional infringement, a claim for compensation in respect of any personal injury and fatal accident, or a claim for non-material damage to secondary victims (§ 104 of the revised OZ).

As is usually the case with any recodification process, not all changes are unconditionally accepted either in the legal doctrine or practice. In that sense, the proposed wording of § 100 of the revised OZ regulating the prescription regime has also been criticized.[38] Under § 100 of the revised OZ, 'the right to claim performance from an obligation (claim) is subject to limitation'. This is a fundamental conceptual change compared to the current private law legislation, which is based on the premise that all property rights are barred by the statute of limitations except for ownership rights (§ 100(2) OZ). That provision, however, cannot be considered appropriate. Such a broad conception of the prescription excluding only property rights brings about a considerable number of not only interpretative but especially application problems. The conflict is based on the interpretation of the term 'property right' and runs into the criterion of legal certainty, which naturally requires a time limit on the enforceability of subjective rights.[39] In that sense, the current wording of § 100(2) OZ does not give a reliable answer to the limitation period of certain frequent subjective rights, which do not have the nature of property rights, but their (resulting) imprescriptibility is unacceptable.

The indicated deficit is partially compensated by case law, but this is certainly not an adequate and sufficient solution to such a fundamental issue. Positive law cannot give up its regulatory functions on fundamental issues while adverting to the gradual evolution of rational interpretation in decision-making practise. Especially if it is objectively feasible to express a basic private rule on the consequences related to the passage of time in another way that does not raise the doubts outlined.

In this respect, case law has already determined that even the rights, which do not typically fall under property rights, are subject to the prescription regime. These include in particular the right to claim the relative invalidity of a legal act,[40] the right of withdrawal,[41] the right to rent an apartment,[42] or the right to compensation for non-material damage in money,[43] etc. However, ambiguity materialized in the first sentence of § 100(2) OZ often led to unnecessary disputes since the courts themselves often did not fully reflect on the case law. Also, there were many disputable rights such as the right to terminate the contract, the right to refuse mutual performance, the right to set-off a claim,

---

38  This criticism was expressed in the contribution of Oľga Ovečková, 'Podstata a účel inštitútu premlčania *de lege lata* a *de lege ferenda*' (2019) 102 *Prav Obzor* 67. cf František Sedlačko and Marek Števček, 'K podstate a účelu premlčania v súkromnom práve' (2019) 102 *Prav Obzor* 346.

39  For the theoretical rationale of the prescription regime in modern European legal systems see Reinhard Zimmerman, 'Prescription' in Nils Jansen and Reinhard Zimmerman (eds), *Commentaries on European Contract Laws* (OUP 2018) 1829.

40  NS SSR decision of 22 May 1985, Cpj 13/85, R 50/1985.

41  NS SR decision of 7 June 1994, 1 Cdo 42/94, R 22/1995.

42  NS SR decision of 31 July 2009, 1 MCdo 8/2008, R 31/2010.

43  NS SR decision of 27 November 2012, 2 Cdo 194/2011, R 58/2014.

the right to exercise a pre-emptive right, or the right to fill in a blank promissory note.[44]

Following the aforementioned, the legislature proposes to amend the pertinent provision, whilst seemingly finding the inspiration in § 194(1) BGB, under which: 'The right to demand that another person does or refrains from an act (claim) is subject to limitation.' The wording of § 194(1) BGB was the source of inspiration also for the Lando Commission standing behind the PECL.[45] The text of Art 14:101 PECL reads as follows: 'A right to performance of an obligation (claim) is subject to prescription by the expiry of a period of time in accordance with these Principles.' Almost identical general limitation clause is also contained in the DCFR model rule III – 7:101.[46] Similar opinions are further presented in the foreign legal science[47] and were also included in CESL.[48] Regulation of the limitation period in CESL was presented in a separate eighth section, in Arts 178 to 186. The wording of Art 178 CESL reads as follows: 'A right to enforce performance of an obligation, and any right ancillary to such a right, is subject to prescription by the expiry of a period of time in accordance with this Chapter.'

It should, therefore, be noted that the proposed wording of § 100 of the revised OZ is not only consistent with the German concept within the meaning of § 194 BGB but also fully complies with the relevant provisions of the PECL, DCFR, and CESL. In a comparative view, attention can also be drawn to other modern European codifications, which are related to the proposed wording of § 100 of the revised OZ. Under Art 3:307 of the Dutch BW, 'A right of action to claim performance of a contractual obligation to give or do something becomes prescribed on the expiry of five years.' According to §

---

44  The Czech case law has concluded that the right to fill a blank promissory note is not subject to prescription. See decision of the High Court in Prague (*Vrchní soud v Praze*) of 18 October 2004, 9 Cmo 274/2004, R 71/2005 civ. However, this view is not accepted without reservation: cf Josef Kotásek, *Zákon směnečný a šekový* (Wolters Kluwer 2012) 104. The Slovak case law has not yet presented a definitive view on the prescription regime of a promissory note.

45  Zimmerman, 'Prescription' (n 39) 1834.

46  Though, we have to add that in spite of much common ground as regards the law of torts/delict, unjustified enrichment, or property law there are also many differences in detail. Not only due to that, 'it now appears to be widely acknowledged that the DCFR project was an overambitious aberration'. See Reinhard Zimmermann, 'Europäisches Privatrecht: Irrungen, Wirrungen' in *Begegnungen im Recht: Ringvorlesung der Bucerius Law School zu Ehren von Karsten Schmidt anlässlich seines 70. Geburtstages* (Mohr Siebeck 2011) 336.

47  Christian von Bar and Eric Clive (eds), *Principles, Definitions and Model Rules of European Private Law: Draft Common Frame of Reference (DCFR)*, vol 2 (OUP 2010) 1139. The authors of DCFR explained: 'Prescription is thus conceived as an institution of substantive law: because of the lapse of time the debtor is entitled to refuse performance. If the debtor does so, the creditor effectively loses the right to demand performance.' (ibid).

48  Commission, 'Proposal for a Regulation of the European Parliament and of the Council on a Common European Sales Law' COM (2011) 635 final (CESL). The main reason justifying the CESL was to improve the functioning of the internal market by facilitating cross-border trade. This was provided for by subjecting contracts to a uniform legal regime, which allows for businesses to lower their transaction costs. See Explanatory Memorandum to the CESL, s 1.

142(1) of the Estonian TsÜS, 'The right to require performance of an act or an imposition from another person (claim) expires within the term provided by law (limitation period).' According to Art 335 (1) of the Slovenian OblZ of 2001, 'The right to demand performance of the obligation to expire through statute-barring.' Under § 6:21 of the Hungarian Ptk of 2013, 'A statutory time limit for the exercise of the right or the enforcement of the claim shall be considered for the expiry of the said time limit if ordered by the relevant legislation expressly.' Reference may also be made to an interesting study by the Swiss Institute of Comparative Law which focuses on the statute of limitations in Germany, France, England, and Denmark.[49] In all of these cases, the prescription regime does not apply only to propriety rights, but to any subjective right, which does not fall necessarily under the propriety rights.

It has already been stated that not all changes brought within any recodification process are unconditionally accepted. Nevertheless, as provided in the previous lines, the Slovak legislature takes into account the foreign legal regulations relatively thoroughly.

The comparative argument cannot, in any event, suffice to reach a conclusion on the correctness and appropriateness of the proposed amendment of § 100 OZ or the appropriateness of the overall conception of prescription in private law. However, compliance with modern foreign regulations and, in particular, with essential European unification work has been a solid starting point.

To conclude this section, one could find appropriate to cite the core idea, which the legislature has always tried to follow whilst developing the amendment to the OZ: 'A prescription regime has to be as simple, straightforward and uniform as possible.'[50] We also add an apt quote from Europe's leading representative of legal science, Reinhard Zimmermann: 'A perfect prescription system does not exist.'[51] Nevertheless, we believe that the proposal of the revised OZ, not only as far as the prescription regime is concerned, might be close to the optimum defined as a synergy of the needs of legal practitioners and doctrinal solutions.

## 5  Conclusion

In connection with the expected reform of contract law introduced herein, we would like to express our firm conviction that legislature has conveyed a responsibly prepared amendment, which attempts not only to reduce the shortcomings of the current legal regulation but also to introduce the institutional novelties along with modern and effective rules.

---

49  Institut suisse de droit comparé, 'Gutachten zum Recht der Verjährung in Deutschland, Frankreich, England und Dänemark' (2011) Avis 10–225 <www.isdc.ch/en/services/online-legal-information> accessed 22 February 2020.
50  Bar and Clive (eds) (n 47) 1144.
51  Zimmerman, 'Prescription' (n 39) 1830.

No matter how perfect the idea behind the whole process is, it is always necessary to internally re-evaluate and criticize that idea in terms of new approaches. This is one of the basic prerequisites for intellectual progress and continuous improvement in science as such. Moreover, we can hardly expect the universal acceptance of any proposed rule. The idea that the professional public unanimously agrees on a particular solution is a utopian idea without undue exaggeration.

Nevertheless, the main source of inspiration for the preparation of the Government Bill of 2018 was the amendments of traditional codes in the neighbouring legal orders (and specifically, the German BGB and the Austrian ABGB) and all experience with recodification in the transforming countries of Central and Eastern Europe due to the common or similar legislative history (specifically e.g. the Czech NOZ, the Hungarian Ptk, and the Estonian Civil Code). Finally, international unification work (PECL, DCFR, and UPICC) has also played an important role.

This does not mean, however, that the recodification commission aimed to copy any code or to rely on a single model. The commission has learned from all negative experience gained when it was adhering to a particular model. Following the aforementioned, the legislature *expressis verbis* states that if there are provisions or entire institutes in the OZ, which meet modern methodological criteria and, in particular, have proven themselves to be effective and noncontradictory to the European standards, the legislature voices the desire to transpose such provisions even into the new or rather revised OZ.[52] However, as has already been pointed out, compliance, especially with the essential European unification work, has been a solid starting point. That is why we believe that recodification follows a proven and proper European approach and might solve many problems of the current Slovak private law.

## Bibliography

——, 'Vieme, prečo sa nebude prijímať nový Občiansky zákonník' (*najpravo.sk*, 23 October 2018) <www.najpravo.sk/clanky/vieme-preco-sa-nebude-prijimat-novy-obciansky-zakonnik.html> accessed 1 February 2020.

Bar C von and Clive E (eds), *Principles, Definitions and Model Rules of European Private Law: Draft Common Frame of Reference (DCFR)*, vol 2 (OUP 2010).

Collins H, *The European Civil Code: The Way Forward* (CUP 2008) [https://doi.org/10.1017/cbo9780511620010].

Ficová S, Čipková T, and Hamřik M, '55 let Graždanskomu kodeksu Slovackoj Respubliki' in Gongalo BM (ed), *Graždanskij kodeks Rossijskoj Federaciji: 25 let dejstvija* (Uraľskij gosudarstvennyj juridičeskij universitet 2019).

Hučková R and Treščáková D, 'Monistická koncepcia rekodifikácie súkromného práva verzus zmluvy uzatvárané pri obchodovaní' in *Dny práva-2012: Days of Law* (Masarykova univerzita v Brne 2013).

52 Legislative Intent (n 5) 20.

Institut suisse de droit comparé, 'Gutachten zum Recht der Verjährung in Deutschland, Frankreich, England und Dänemark' (2011) Avis 10-225 <www.isdc.ch/en/services/ online-legal-information> accessed 22 February 2020.

Komisia pre rekodifikáciu súkromného práva, 'Legislatívny zámer Občianskeho zákonníka' (*Ministerstvo spravodlivosti Slovenskej republiky*) <www.justice.gov.sk/Stranky/Nase-sluzby/Nase-projekty/Obciansky-zakonnik/Obciansky-zakonnik.aspx> accessed 15 February 2020.

Kotásek J, *Zákon směnečný a šekový* (Wolters Kluwer 2012).

Kotrecová A and Poláčková S, 'Je možná rekodifikácia občianskeho práva hmotného bez rekodifikácie civilného práva procesného?' in *Dny práva-2008: Days of Law* (Masarykova univerzita v Brne 2008).

Koziol H, 'Comparative Conclusions' in Koziol H (ed), *Basic Questions of Tort Law from a Comparative Perspective* (Jan Sramek Verlag 2015) [https://doi.org/10.26530/oapen_574832].

Lazar J, 'K stavu, problémom a perspektívam základnej občianskoprávnej úpravy' (1989) 72 *Prav Obzor* 388.

——, 'Aktuálna úvaha o postavení občianskeho práva v česko-slovenskom systéme práva' (1993) 132 *Právnik* 1048.

——, 'Základné aspekty nového občianskeho a obchodného práva' [1993] 15 *Acta Facultatis Iuridicae Universitatis Comenianae* 77.

——, 'Východiská a koncepčné otázky návrhu slovenského Občianskeho zákonníka' (1997) 49 (12) *Just Rev* 16.

——, 'K niektorým koncepčným otázkam rekodifikácie súkromného práva' (2001) 49 *Prav Praxe* 6.

——, *Otázky kodifikácie súkromného práva* (Iura edition 2006).

——, 'Základné aspekty kodifikácie slovenského Občianskeho zákonníka (úvodný referát)' in Lazar J (ed), *Návrh legislatívneho zámeru kodifikácie súkromného práva: Materiály z odbornej konferencie* (Ministerstvo spravodlivosti SR 2008).

Meder S, 'Die Krise des Nationalstaates und ihre Folgen für das Kodifikationsprinzip' (2006) 61 *JZ* 477 [https://doi.org/10.1628/002268806777248544].

Ministerstvo spravodlivosti Slovenskej republiky, 'Dôvodová správa' (*Ministerstvo spravodlivosti Slovenskej republiky*, 15 October 2018) <www.justice.gov.sk/Stranky/Ministerstvo/ Aktuality-obcianskeho-zakonnika.aspx> accessed 6 May 2020.

——, 'Vládny návrh zákona, ktorým sa mení a dopĺňa zákon č 40/1964 Zb Občiansky zákonník' (*Ministerstvo spravodlivosti Slovenskej republiky*, 15 October 2018) <www.justice. gov.sk/Stranky/Ministerstvo/Aktuality-obcianskeho-zakonnika.aspx> accessed 6 May 2020.

Ovečková O, 'Podstata a účel inštitútu premlčania de lege lata a de lege ferenda' (2019) 102 *Prav Obzor* 67.

Plank K, 'Koncepcia rekodifikácie občianskeho práva hmotného v Slovenskej republike' (1996) 48 (4) *Just Rev* 1.

Sedlačko F and Števček M, 'K podstate a účelu premlčania v súkromnom práve' (2019) 102 *Prav Obzor* 346.

Števček M and others, *Občiansky zákonník I: § 1–450: Komentár* (CH Beck 2015).

Wieacker F, *A History of Private Law in Europe* (Weir T tr, Clarendon Press 1995).

Windscheid B, 'Die geschichtliche Schule in der Rechtswissenschaft' in Oertmann P (ed), *Bernhard Windscheid: Gesammelte Reden und Abhandlungen* (Duncker & Humblot 1904).

Zimmerman R, 'Codification: History and Present Significance of an Idea' (1995) 3 *ERPL* 95.

——, 'Europäisches Privatrecht – Irrungen, Wirrungen' in *Begegnungen im Recht: Ringvor-lesung der Bucerius Law School zu Ehren von Karsten Schmidt anlässlich seines 70. Geburtstages* (Mohr Siebeck 2011).

——, 'Codification: The Civilian Experience Reconsidered on the Eve of a Common European Sales Law' (2012) 8 *ERCL* 367 [https://doi.org/10.1515/ercl-2012-1000].

——, 'Prescription' in Jansen N and Zimmerman R (eds), *Commentaries on European Contract Laws* (OUP 2018).

Zoulík F, 'Problematika rekodifikace soukromého práva v České republice' (1995) 43 *Prav Praxe* 126.

# 3 Recodifying tort law in Central Europe in the beginning of twenty-first century (Poland, Czech Republic, and Hungary)

*Ewa Bagińska and Paulina Wyszyńska-Ślufińska*

## 1 Introduction

Recodification processes in Central Europe in the beginning of the twenty-first century indicate a strong need to update the law of obligations, including not only contract law but also tort law. Historical, social, and economic factors, as well as the need to create a legal system compatible with the EU law and with the Strasbourg standards of human rights' protection, have had the greatest impact on the shape of new national codifications and recodifications.[1] The chapter discusses the recodification of tort law in selected Central European countries, but it should be noted that the process of updating civil law can be observed almost in the whole Europe.[2] The main aim of the chapter is to indicate the most significant changes introduced to different domestic legal systems and their legal effect on the injured parties.

## 2 The waves of codification and recodification

### 2.1 The first wave of codification

There is a distinction between the first wave of codification and a process of recodification which we can observe at present. The change of political and economic system led the post-social countries like Latvia, Albania, Lithuania, and Estonia to the implementation of entirely new legal regulations which would be adequate and appropriate to the new reality.[3] As regards Lithuania and Estonia in particular, it must be noted that the codifications were heavily based on a comparative work method.

1 Ewa Bagińska, 'Rekodyfikacja prawa odpowiedzialności cywilnej w Czechach i na Węgrzech – rewolucja czy ewolucja' in Ewa Bagińska, Władysław W Mogilski, and Monika Wałachowska (eds), *O dobre prawo dla ubezpieczeń: Księga jubileuszowa Profesora Eugeniusza Kowalewskiego* (TNOiK 2019) 329.
2 See Reiner Schulze and Fryderyk Zoll (eds), *The Law of Obligations in Europe: A New Wave of Codifications* (SELP 2013).
3 Ewoud Hondius, 'Recodification of Private Law in Central and Eastern Europe and in the Netherlands' [2014] (1) *ELTE LJ* 51, 51ff.

The Lithuanian Civil Code (*Lietuvos Respublikos civilinis kodeksas*,[4] CK) of 2000 came into force in 2001. It replaced the Civil Code of 1964, which could no longer be in use mainly due to its socialist spirit, where no private ownership and free market were allowed.[5] The new code is based mostly on the Dutch BW of 1992 and the Civil Code of Quebec of 1994.[6] Tort law, on the other hand, seems to derive from the Dutch BW and the French law.[7] The Principles of European Tort Law (PETL) and Draft Common Frame of Reference (DCFR) were adopted after the new code came into force, so they could not be used in the process of drafting the new CK.[8] Nevertheless, it is observed that the Supreme Court of Lithuania occasionally refers to the PETL as a source of inspiration and arguments in the motives of its judgments.[9]

The need to prepare a completely new act also appeared in Estonia, which as a former member of the Soviet Union could no longer depend on Soviet Civil Code.[10] The main method in creating the new Civil Code was also a comparative one,[11] and the Law of Obligations Act (*Võlaõigusseadus*,[12] VÕS) was adopted as a part of the new code, and entered into force on 1 July 2002. A mixture of sources was used to create the new act; some rules came from the Germanic legal culture (Germany, Netherlands, Switzerland, and Austria), some from the French one (France, Louisiana, Quebec, and Italy), and some from Scandinavian legal systems. The legislature decided to gain from the foreign legal experience instead of creating an original Estonian law. The materials used to create the new code also included the established court practice, the Vienna Convention on Contracts for International Sale of Goods (CISG), Principles of European Contract Law (PECL), UNIDROIT Principles of International Commercial Contracts (UPICC), and the EU law.[13]

---

4  Act VIII-1864 of 18 July 2000, *Žin* 2000, 74–2262, as later amended.

5  Simona Drukteiniene and Solveiga Paleviciene, 'Lithuania' in Britt Weyts (eds), *IEL Tort Law* (Kluwer Law International 2017) 19.

6  The impact of the civil codes of Italy, Switzerland, Germany, France, Latvia, and Japan, the Swiss OR, the Swedish regulations, as well as of the Russian Federation law, can be also observed. See ibid; Simona Selelionyté-Drukteiniené, Vaidas Jurkevičius, and Thomas Kadner Graziano, 'The Impact of the Comparative Method on Lithuanian Private Law' (2013) 21 *ERPL* 959, 972.

7  Drukteiniene and Paleviciene (n 5).

8  Selelionyté-Drukteiniené, Jurkevičius, and Kadner Graziano (n 6) 976.

9  Drukteiniene and Paleviciene (n 5) 33; Julija Kiršiené, Solveiga Palevičiené, and Simona Drukteiniené in Bénédict Winiger, Ernst Karner, and Ken Oliphant (eds), *Digest of European Tort Law: Vol 3: Essential Cases on Misconduct* (De Gruyter 2018) 72.

10  Paul Varul, 'The Creation of New Estonian Private Law' (2008) 16 *ERPL* 95, 98.

11  ibid 100.

12  *RT* I 2001, 81, 487, as later amended.

13  Varul (n 10) 105ff.

## 2.2 Recodification of tort law in selected jurisdictions

In the second category of countries, including *inter alia* Poland, Czech Republic, Hungary, and Romania, it was sufficient to amend the existing codes, largely based on European models, which made it easier to go through the first phase of transformation. The Romanian Civil Code of 1864 (based on the Napoleonic Code) and the post-war civil codes in Hungary (the Civil Code of 1959), Poland (the Civil Code of 1964), and Czech Republic (the Civil Code of Czecho-Slovakia of 1964) remained in force. Nevertheless, a complete reform of civil law was introduced and resulted in the creation of new civil codes in Romania (2009), Czech Republic (2012), and Hungary (2013).[14] The new Romanian Civil Code is a great example of a hybrid legal tradition, while the Czech and Hungarian civil codes seek a balance between the German and French tradition of civil liability law.[15] As all of these three countries introduced entirely new civil codes, we are going to examine them in more detail below.

## 2.3 Czech Republic: the Civil Code of 2012 – an evolution or a revolution?

The new Civil Code of the Czech Republic (*Občanský zákoník*,[16] NOZ) was enacted in 2012 and came into force on 1 January 2014. The new code has replaced the old Civil Code of 1964.[17] In comparison to the previous code, which consisted of 880 provisions, the new one seems to be much more detailed, as it consists of 3081 provisions. As concerns the regulatory novelties introduced to the NOZ of 2012, it must be said with certainty that the new Civil Code should be considered as a revolution instead of an evolution.[18]

One of the main aims of the Czech legislature was to create a code which would serve as a single act for all grounds of civil liability, *inter alia* in a case of product liability, unfair competition, and the employee liability. This target was only partially achieved, e.g. through the transfer of provisions governing the liability of organs of a legal entity into the new code.[19] Some issues governing civil liability, such as public authorities' liability rules and the liability of employees, still remain outside the scope of civil code.[20]

Focusing on the general structure first, one must emphasize the replacement of a monist system by a dualistic system of contractual and non-contractual liability regime. Thus, contrary to the previous monist system, the main prerequisite

---

14  Bagińska, 'Rekodyfikacja prawa' (n 1) 333.

15  ibid 330.

16  Act 89/2012, Civil Code (*Zákon 89/2012 Sb, Občanský zákoník*), as later amended.

17  Act 40/1964, Civil Code (*Zákon 40/1964 Sb, Občanský zákoník*), as later amended.

18  See Jiří Hrádek, 'The Czech Republic' in Ken Oliphant and Barbara C Steininger (eds), *European Tort Law 2012* (De Gruyter 2013) 119.

19  Bagińska, 'Rekodyfikacja prawa' (n 1) 333.

20  See Act 82/1998 (*Zákon 82/1998 Sb*) and the Labour Code of 2006 (*Zákon 262/2006 Sb, zákoník práce*).

for tort and contractual liability now differs. In the case of torts, the principle of fault still applies as a general clause, while contractual liability shall be deemed strict.[21] If a breach of contract occurs, the debtor may be exempted from the liability if she demonstrates that the non-performance of the obligation was due to an extraordinary, unforeseeable, and insurmountable obstacle, independent of her will.[22]

Second, the Czech legislature decided to codify the *neminem laedere* rule. According to § 2900 NOZ, every person is obliged 'to act as to prevent unreasonable harm to freedom, harm to life, bodily harm or harm to the property of another' if it is required by the circumstances of the case.

As was already mentioned, the general clause of tort liability is based on fault. Tort liability is provided for in §§ 2904, 2909, and 2910 NOZ.[23] § 2904 provides the grounds of the liability for an accident (*casus*). This responsibility lies with the person who caused the danger of the event, in particular by breach of a contractual obligation or damaging the protective device aimed to prevent the accident. It can be said that it is a specific *casus mixtus* or that it is a form of liability for breach of a legal obligation.[24] § 2909 establishes liability for an intentional breach of good morals, while § 2910 introduces liability for a culpable violation of a legal obligation leading to interference with absolute subjective rights, and for the culpable breach of laws protecting the interest of another. Thus, it can be observed that the new provisions are under a strong influence of the German BGB.[25]

Czech law clearly distinguishes between the condition of wrongfulness (construed as the violation of duties imposed by the law) and fault (considered as a state of mind of a party). Wrongfulness was expressed in §§ 415 and 420 of the Civil Code of 1964, while now it is reflected in the *neminem laedere* rule (§ 2900 NOZ), in § 2909 regarding an intentional breach of good morals, and § 2910 regarding a breach of legal obligation.[26] Fault is considered to be a failure to exercise the duty of care required of a reasonable person of average ability in private relations. The breach of professional diligence or special knowledge or skills possessed by the tortfeasor is considered to be her fault.[27] Taking into consideration the current shape of § 2912 the objectification of fault should be observed.[28] In addition, a duty to inform was codified and stipulated in § 2950

---

21  See Luboš Tichý, 'Czech Republic' in Miguel Martin-Casals (ed), *The Borderlines of Tort Law: Interactions with Contract Law* (Intersentia 2019) 51. See also NOZ, § 2913.

22  See NOZ, § 2913.

23  Luboš Tichý in Bénédict Winiger, Ernst Karner, and Ken Oliphant (eds), *Digest of European Tort Law: Vol 3: Essential Cases on Misconduct* (De Gruyter 2018) 78.

24  Jiří Hrádek and Andrew J Bell, 'The New Czech Civil Code and Compensation for Damage: Introductory Remarks' (2016) 7 *JETL* 300, 302.

25  See BGB, § 823(1) (breach of protected interest), § 823(2) (breach of legislative protective norm and intentional harm), and § 826 (intentional immoral infliction of loss).

26  Tichý in Winiger, Karner, and Oliphant (n 23) 78.

27  See NOZ, § 2912.

28  Tichý, 'Czech Republic' (n 21) 53; Tichý in Winiger, Karner, and Oliphant (n 23) 80.

NOZ. The term 'information tort' is relevant; it includes liability for incorrect or incomplete information or advice, if the information or advice was provided by a professional providing such information or advice (which constitutes her fault). Providing information or advice outside the scope of the professional activity may give rise to liability of the provider for damage only in the case of intentional fault.

The new code provides for the responsibility of supervisors with the presumption of fault in supervision; however, persons with mental illness and no legal capacity may be burdened with the duty to compensate where they were able to predict the consequences of their behaviour.[29]

As regards the causal link, the innovative solution adopted in PETL for concurrent causation is adopted by the Czech legislature. Accordingly, if there are several likely causes of single damage and it is not possible to establish with certainty which one was a cause, the tortfeasors' liability is joint and several. In justified cases, the court may determine the liability of the tortfeasor according to a degree corresponding to the likelihood that the damage resulted from her conduct. The latter rule, therefore, introduces proportional liability. This trend had already appeared in the case law of England, the Netherlands, Israel, as well as in the Austrian reform project.[30]

### 2.4 Hungary: a step forward or a status quo?

The new Hungarian Civil Code (*Polgári törvénykönyv*,[31] Ptk) was enacted on 7 February 2012 and entered into force on 15 March 2014. It replaced the Civil Code of 1959. As in the case of Czech NOZ, the tendency to broaden the scope of civil code provisions shall be observed. The new Hungarian Ptk consists of eight books including 6000 articles. By contrast, the previous Civil Code of 1959 contained only 685 articles. As a side note, it can be mentioned that the first project of a new code was prepared by the Codification Commission in 2002. Later, the Ministry of Justice took over the legislative work and prepared a new Civil Code in 2009. This Civil Code was characterized by a poor quality of regulations and a lack of important regulations (such as a public authority liability or wrongful life and wrongful birth claims), which led to loud criticism. In 2010 the Constitutional Tribunal declared the unconstitutionality of the provision introducing the Civil Code of 2009. The preparatory works were entrusted to the Codification Commission again, what resulted in the enactment of the new Ptk in 2012.[32]

---

29  See NOZ, § 2922(1).
30  Ewa Bagińska, *Odpowiedzialność deliktowa w razie niepewności związku przyczynowego: Studium prawnoporównawcze* (TNOiK 2013) 327ff.
31  Act V of 2013 on the Civil Code (*2013 évi V törvény a Polgári Törvénykönyvről*), MK 2013/31 (II 26), as later amended.
32  See: Attila Menyhárd, 'Hungary' in Helmut Koziol and Barbara C Steininger (eds), *European Tort Law 2002* (Springer 2003) 252; Attila Menyhárd, 'Hungary' in Helmut Koziol and Barbara C

The creation of an entirely new code was aimed to fulfil the following objectives: (i) the need of a consolidation of the jurisprudence practice developing in the light of the 1959 Code; (ii) introducing the amendments only when necessary and only if required due to the changing economic conditions; (iii) incorporation of family law and company law, as well as most of the civil law norms included in specific acts into the Civil Code (except the Labour Code and intellectual property law); and (iv) unification of regulation of professional and common trading.[33]

It must be emphasized that the Hungarian legislature, like the Czech one, decided to replace the monist system of liability with the dualistic system of contractual and torts regimes. Quite surprisingly, however, the Hungarian legislature decided to introduce a *non-cumul* rule for the claims grounded in both regimes. As a result, the parallel claims are excluded.[34] The solution was aimed at preventing the parties from circumventing the provisions on contractual liability and was not expressed in the previous code.[35] According to § 6:145 Ptk, which lays down the preference for the contractual regime, even if damage establishes both contractual and extra-contractual liability, the victim may claim damages only on the basis of contractual liability provisions. This solution has met with justified criticism in the academic legal writing, especially as concerns cases when the performance of a contract arises from a hazardous activity (e.g. the services provided by the amusements park operator) and causes personal injury.[36] The liability for extra-hazardous activities specified in § 6:535 Ptk is strict, but the application of *non-cumul* rule will exclude tort liability even when the improper performance of contract constitutes a delict. The victim will be entitled to claim damages only in the contractual regime. The *non-cumul* rule works in favour of the tortfeasors, as it is easier to exempt from liability in the contractual regime (by proof of an obstacle independent of the debtor) than in the tortious regime.[37]

---

Steininger (eds), *European Tort Law 2008* (Springer 2009) 345; Attila Menyhárd, 'Hungary' in Ernst Karner and Barbara C Steininger (eds), *European Tort Law 2013* (De Gruyter 2014) 305ff.

33  László Burián, 'Podstawowe zasady odpowiedzialności deliktowej i kontraktowej w nowym węgierskim kodeksie cywilnym' [2013] (9) *Prz Prawa Handl* 35, 35–41.

34  The rule was established by the courts in France in the '30s, but this process was related to the development of strict tort liability. The solution was aimed at preventing the parties from circumventing the provisions on contractual liability. See Jean-Sébastien Borghetti, 'France' in Miquel Martin-Casals (ed), *The Borderlines of Tort Law: Interactions with Contract Law* (Intersentia 2019) 156ff.

35  Ádám Fuglinszky, 'Some Structural Questions on the Relationship between Contractual and Extra-contractual Liability in the New Hungarian Civil Code' in Attila Menyhárd and Emőd Veress (eds), *New Civil Codes in Hungary and Romania* (Springer 2017) 112.

36  See Ádám Fuglinszky, 'Risks and Side Effects: Five Questions on the "New" Hungarian Tort Law' [2014] (2) *ELTE LJ* 221.

37  To compare the strict liability for hazardous liability see § 6:535(1) Ptk, under which 'the operator is relieved of this liability only if they are able to prove that the damage occurred due to an unavoidable event that falls beyond the scope of their highly dangerous activities'. All translations come from Attila Menyhárd, 'Hungary' in Ernst Karner, Ken Oliphant, and Barbara C Steininger (eds) *European Tort Law: Basic Texts* (2nd edn, Jan Sramek Verlag 2018) 165ff.

Regarding the causal link, it should be noted that the prerequisite of the foreseeability of damage is required both in contractual and tort liability.[38] According to § 6:521 Ptk, 'a causal link shall not be established in connection with losses which were not foreseen and were not such that they ought to have been foreseen by the tortfeasor'.[39] This is a material modification of the theory of causation accepted so far in the tort regime, which could be qualified as the theory of adequate causality.[40] The concept of burden of proof regarding tort liability is specific as it is a matter for the tortfeasor to provide the negative proof. The foreseeability (or a duty to foresee) should be ascertained with reference to the moment when the damage is caused.[41]

The rule of § 6:518 Ptk, contained in Book VI of the Ptk, constitutes a general clause: 'Causing damage unlawfully shall be prohibited by law.' The clause is supplemented by the next provision (§ 6:519), which formulates a general rule of liability for unlawfully caused damage. The tortfeasor is relieved from the liability if she proves her act was not wrongful. The provision of § 6:520 provides the presumption of unlawfulness, indicating that there is no unlawfulness of damage if: 1) the damage was caused with the victim's consent, 2) the conduct was permitted by the law and the conduct did not interfere with legally protected interests of another person or the law otherwise provides the compensation to the victim, 3) in a case of self-defence, or 4) in a case of necessity, in so far as it was proportionate. Otherwise, the damage will be considered unlawful (the presumption of wrongfulness).[42]

Although the Ptk does not regulate a general claim for the compensation of moral damages (non-pecuniary harm), § 2:52 introduces a *solatium doloris* (in Hungarian: *sérelemdíj*) – a new kind of pecuniary sanction for a violation of personal rights (but not a compensation), which may be granted only if personal rights were infringed.[43] It can be said that *solatium doloris* plays a role similar to compensation for non-pecuniary loss, yet more importantly, this pecuniary sanction was not envisaged in the provisions pertaining to liability, but in the Ptk chapter on natural persons. The Hungarian doctrine underlines that this sanction is not about compensation for the harm consisting in negative feelings or frustration, but about satisfaction in connection with unlawful infringement of personal rights. Mental pain and suffering will be the basis for increasing the amount of *solatium doloris*. The Hungarian legislature has established an irrebuttable presumption (*praesumptio iuris et de iure*) that pain and

---

38  Burián (n 33) 38.
39  Menyhárd, 'Hungary' in Karner, Oliphant, and Steininger (n 37) 165.
40  See Attila Menyhárd in Bénédict Winiger and others (eds), *Digest of European Tort Law: Vol I: Essential Cases on Natural Causation* (Springer 2007) 84.
41  Burián (n 33) 39.
42  ibid 38.
43  Menyhárd, 'Hungary' in Karner and Steininger, *European Tort Law 2013* (n 32) 306–8; cf Burián (n 33) 39.

suffering is the result of an infringement of personal rights. The new regulation could theoretically be seen as improving the protection of victims if not for the fact that it does not solve the problem of minimal claims and of commercializing non-commercial values.[44]

The Ptk maintains the court's right to mitigate the loss (§ 6:522), but – as a new solution – it replaces the preference for *restitutio in integrum* with the rule of pecuniary compensation.[45] Another interesting legal solution is the regulation of claims arising from *culpa in contrahendo*. In the Ptk, this kind of liability is based on the contractual regime. Previously, it was considered within tort liability like in many other European jurisdictions.[46]

Unfortunately, the Ptk does not contain the regulation of wrongful life or wrongful birth claims. Neither does it introduce changes regarding public authority liability. Instead of gaining from foreign experience or by using a comparative method, the new code seems to be a conservative act, reflecting the already existing and confirmed jurisprudence.

## 2.5 Romania – an example of a mixed jurisdiction

The new Romanian Civil Code (*Codul civil al României*,[47] NCC) was enacted in 2009 and came into force on 1 October 2011. It has replaced the old Civil Code of 1864, which had resembled the *Code Napoléon*.[48] It should be emphasized that the NCC was influenced by the globalization and Europeanization of private law with an aim to introduce adequate solutions to the problems of modern tort law.[49] The NCC should be deemed as a result of multinational comparative law influences as it is mostly based on Quebec's law (CCQ of 1991), but the impact of Swiss, Italian, and French law can be also observed. In creating the NCC, the European Union law could not be omitted due to the need to create a new code which would comply with the EU law.[50]

---

44  Menyhárd, 'Hungary' in Karner and Steininger, *European Tort Law 2013* (n 32) 307.
45  See § 6:527(1) Ptk, according to which: 'The tortfeasor shall provide compensation in money, or in kind, if that is more reasonable under the given circumstances.'
46  See Miguel Martin-Casals, 'Comparative Report' in Miguel Martin-Casals (ed), *The Borderlines of Tort Law: Interactions with Contract Law* (Intersentia 2019) 842.
47  Law 287 of 17 July 2009 on the Civil Code (*Lege 287 din 17 iulie 2009 privind Codul civil*), MO I 511, 2009, as later amended. There is a lot of controversy regarding the way of creating the new code, especially with the lack of parliamentary discussion. See Christian Alunaru and Lucian Bojin, 'Romania' in Helmut Koziol and Barbara C Steininger (eds) *European Tort Law 2009* (De Gruyter 2010) 525.
48  Christian Alunaru and Lucian Bojin, 'The Tort Law Provisions of the New Romanian Civil Code' (2011) 2 *JETL* 103.
49  Mónika Józon in Bénédict Winiger, Ernst Karner, and Ken Oliphant (eds), *Digest of European Tort Law: Vol 3: Essential Cases on Misconduct* (De Gruyter 2018) 91.
50  Alunaru and Bojin, 'Romania' in Koziol and Steininger (n 47) 528. Romania is a member of the EU since 2007.

The new code withdrew from a dualistic system of private law by the trans-position of the commercial and civil law into one act. Thus, the NCC repealed not only the previous Civil Code of 1864 but also the Romanian Commercial Code.[51] The NCC consists of seven books and 2664 articles. For the first time, a whole chapter of Romanian law was dedicated to the field of civil liabili-ty.[52] The NCC introduced a dualistic system of liability: (a) delictual liability, expressed in Art 1349, and (b) contractual liability, expressed in Art 1350. It is worth noting that forty-six articles (Arts 1349, and 1351 to 1395) are devoted to torts (for comparison, there were only six articles relating to torts in the previous code).[53] The issue of the concurrence of claims was solved in Art 1350(3), according to which a party may not replace the application of the rules of contractual liability by reference to other rules which would be more favourable unless otherwise stipulated by law.

As the case law on new tort law is still modest there is a question whether Art 1349 of the NCC, being a general provision of tort law, requires fault or just wrongfulness of conduct.[54] As a codification of a *neminem laedere* rule, Art 1349 imposes a duty on every person to comply with rules of conduct imposed by law and custom and not to harm the rights and legitimate interest of others (wrongfulness). Under the current wording, the rule has been supplemented by the violation of the personal legitimate interest. However, according to Art 1357 on liability for one's own acts, the tortfeasor is held responsible even for a slight fault. Moreover, the next provision provides special criteria for the assess-ment of fault. When estimating the fault, according to Art 1358, not only the circumstances surrounding the occurrence of the damage must be taken into account, but also, if applicable, the fact whether the damage was caused by a professional during the performance of his activity. Thus, we can see another example of the objectification of the fault.[55] These arguments may prevail in favour of considering fault as a prerequisite for liability, although there is no clear distinction between fault and wrongfulness in Romania and it is a role of courts to indicate the boundaries.[56]

51  Emőd Veress, 'The New Romanian Civil Code: Difficulties in the Transition towards a Monist Private Law' in Attila Menyhárd and Emőd Veress (eds), *New Civil Codes in Hungary and Romania* (Springer 2017) 28.
52  The Chapter IV of NCC which consists of six sections: (i) general provisions, (ii) circumstances precluding liability, (iii) liability for one's acts, (iv) liability for another person's acts, (v) liability for damage caused by animals and things, and (vi) reparation of damage. Christian Alunaru and Lucian Bojin, 'Romania' in Ernst Karner, Ken Oliphant, and Barbara C Steininger (eds) *European Tort Law: Basic Texts* (2nd edn, Jan Sramek Verlag 2018) 289–99.
53  Alunaru and Bojin, 'Romania' in Koziol and Steininger (n 47) 530.
54  Józon in Winiger, Karner and Oliphant (n 49) 92. See also the ÎCCJ decision of 24 June 2014, Sec II-a Civ, 2358, where the ÎCCJ stated that 'fault' is no longer a condition of liability, as it was not mentioned in the new Art 1349 (ibid).
55  ibid 93.
56  ibid.

For the first time in the history of Romanian civil law, the cases of strict liability for the liability caused by collision between vehicles (Art 1376(2) NCC) and the liability for damage caused by objects dropped or thrown off a building (Art 1379) were codified.[57] Other examples of strict liability are the liability for damage caused by animals (Art 1375) and things (Art 1376(1) NCC).

Regarding the issue of reparation of damage, the rule of full compensation (*damnum emerges* and *lucrum cessans*) recognized previously by the doctrine and case law was finally codified (Art 1385 NCC).[58] A true innovation, however, is the rule on the redress of a loss of chance. According to Art 1385(4), if the wrongful act caused a loss of chance to obtain an advantage, the party may obtain a reparation proportional to the likelihood of obtaining the advantage, considering the circumstances and the specific situation of the victim. For the first time, it was also expressly stated that non-pecuniary damages also shall be compensated in a case of the violation of physical integrity or health, as well as for diminished opportunities for family or social life (Art 1391). There are also special rules governing the violation of physical integrity and health (Art 1387) and damages for the death (Art 1390).[59]

Although the codification of tort rules by the NCC seems to be conducted in a detailed way, there are still some torts regulated outside the scope of the code e.g. liability of judges for judicial errors (Art 96 of Law 303/2004) and the liability of public authorities (Arts 16 and 19 of Law 554/2004, Arts 642 to 688 of Law 95/2006).[60]

## 3  Poland – a need for a new codification?

Polish private law is a 'hybrid civil legal system', i.e. one in which uniform solutions superseding the first classical European civil codes such as the French CCiv of 1804, the Austrian ABGB of 1811, and German BGB of 1896 were developed.[61] After World War I, instead of a synthesis of the existing great codes, the Polish Codification Commission chose to follow contemporary legislative trends, the then modern Swiss OR of 1911, as well as the unification processes that were taking place on supranational levels, including the French-Italian Draft Code of Obligations and Contracts of 1927. Eventually, the codification embraced the law of obligations (the Code of Obligations of 1933, *Kodeks zobowiązań*), commercial law (the Code of Commercial Companies of 1934), private international law, the law on bills of exchange and cheques, the law on unfair competition, and copyright law. In the areas not unified in the

---

57  Alunaru and Bojin, 'The Tort Law Provisions' (n 48) 104.
58  ibid 105.
59  ibid.
60  Józon in Winiger, Karner, and Oliphant (n 49) 95.
61  Wojciech Dajczak, 'The Polish Way to a Unified Law of Contract: Local Curiosity or Contribution to the European Debate Today?' in Christian von Bar and Arkadiusz Wudarski (eds), *Deutschland und Polen in der europäischen Rechtsgemeinschaft* (SELP 2012) 13ff.

interwar period, the four foreign codifications remained in force until the end of 1946, when they were finally repealed. The Civil Code (*Kodeks cywilny*,[62] KC) was enacted in 1964 and came into force in 1965. As far as the sources of obligations are concerned, while the Code of Obligations was mainly based on the Swiss OR, the KC followed more closely the structure of BGB, although it generally continued the substance of the Code of Obligations. The shape of fundamental legal institutions contained in the Code of Obligations was not only acceptable at a European level at the time but was also sufficiently modern to be brought back to Polish private law after 1990 by way of several amendments to the KC (1990, 1996, 2003, 2004, 2007, and 2008).[63]

As regards tort law rules, they were designed primarily in the third book of the KC on the law of obligations. In the Polish system, there is a dualistic model of liability.[64] Tort law is based on the 'general clause model'. The general clause of Art 415 KC[65] establishes tortious liability based upon proven fault. It is supplemented by a number of separate provisions located in the KC and in other pieces of legislation that regulate tortious liability in specified situations. While some of them are also based on fault, others are examples of strict liability or liability based on equity. Nevertheless, one should add that after World War II and before the KC was enacted, Polish law lacked rules on state liability. A slight relaxation in the political climate that took place in 1956 enabled the parliament to enact the Act of 15 November 1956 on the liability of the state for damages caused by state agents, which was subsequently rewritten into the KC of 1964. Articles 417 to 421 KC were considered to form a special regime of state liability and they were reformed only in 2004 with a view to adapt to the new constitutional standard of public authority liability for illegal conduct (Art 77 of the Polish Constitution). The reform of prescription of tort claims followed in 2007, and the reinstatement of bereavement damages in 2008 (which was regulated in Art 166 of the Code of Obligations) closed the reforms in the area of tort law.[66]

The preparatory works on the new code, which were undertaken in the late '90s by the Civil Law Codification Commission (*Komisja Kodyfikacyjna Prawa*

---

62  Act of 23 April 1964 – Civil Code (*Ustawa z dnia 23 kwietnia 1964 r – Kodeks cywilny, DzU* 1964, 16, 93), as later amended.

63  See Ewa Bagińska, 'The Meanders of Polish Tort Law (1933–2014)' in Johan Potgieter, Johann Knobel, and Rita-Marie Jansen (eds), *Essays in Honour of / Huldigingsbundel vir Johann Neethling* (LexisNexis 2015) 63ff.

64  The *non-cumul* rule does not apply. The concurrence of claims is regulated by Art 443 KC. The delictual regime works in favour of the injured party (due to, *inter alia*, the possibility to claim compensation for non-pecuniary loss, longer limitation period, and the burden of proof).

65  Article 415 KC, similarly to Art 134 of the Code of Obligations of 1933, followed Art 1382 of the French CCiv.

66  See Ewa Bagińska, 'Developments in Personal Injury Law in Poland: Shaping the Compensatory Function of Tort Law' (2015) 8 *J Civ L Stud* 309 <https://digitalcommons.law.lsu.edu/jcls/vol8/iss1/17> accessed 23 May 2020.

*Cywilnego*, KKPC), chaired by Zbigniew Radwański,[67] are presently continued in the academic community as part of the Academic Draft Civil Code (ADCC) project.[68] The activities focus on the specific part of contract law, thereby taking into account the hitherto achievements of KKPC (the draft of the General Part of the Civil Code published in 2008,[69] and the revision of the provisions of the general part of the contract law). In addition, in 2010 KKPC drafted common rules for both liability regimes and a new title on non-contractual (tort) liability. In another unfinished draft from 2015 the content of the individual provisions as well as their structure was significantly changed.

The general question of whether Poland needs a new civil code is highly disputed in doctrine. In one view the largest disadvantage of the present code lies in its inflexible pandectistic structure, which makes it difficult to adjust the Polish private law to European directives. The true need for recodification is, however, linked to the challenges of the modern world, which *inter alia* include problems arising from the new technologies, the prevalence of the need of access to services rather than to ownership of things, and the essential changes to the structure of a family.[70]

Considering the premise for the future reform of tort law, one should start with stating that the current scope of tort law regulation should be considered as overly broad when compared against the background of modern European codes. First of all, the present KC includes the most important cases of strict liability, such as liability for dangerous products and liability for traffic accidents. Outside of the KC, remain the operator liability in nuclear law, liability in aviation law, liability for genetically modified organisms (GMOs), and liability for the safety of mass events. There is no need to prove that the less specific rules outside the civil code (in contrast to the Germanic tradition), the fewer problems with the relationship between the code and *leges specialis*, and the fewer deviations from general principles implementing specific values (e.g. full compensation, increased protection of personal rights). Thus, the question arises whether it is worth extending the codified torts further, e.g. whether the liability of the organizer of a mass event should be included in the KC, or even to introduce a general liability based on the principle of risk. This approach is supported by the argument that too brief, or laconic, provisions which provide for liability for damage resulting from a specific activity and referring in details to the KC, usually raise many interpretative doubts, hence they had better be included in the code itself. On the other hand, against their inclusion, one may

---

67 A great Polish civil law scholar (1924–2012), a professor of law at the Adam Mickiewicz University in Poznań, and a long-time president of the KKPC.
68 Since the KKPC was resolved by the government at the end of 2015. No codification commission presently exists.
69 See also Zbigniew Radwański, *Zielona księga: Optymalna wizja Kodeksu cywilnego w Rzeczpospolitej Polskiej* (Ministerstwo Sprawiedliwości 2006).
70 See Fryderyk Zoll, 'A Civil Code Outside of Reality: The Polish Codification of the Year 1964, Its Origin, Development and Future' in Wen-Yeu Wang (ed), *Codification in International Perspective: Selected Papers from the 2nd IACL Thematic Conference* (Springer 2014) 134.

raise the argument of excessive growth of the code. The argument about the stability of the code's rules also remains relevant. The KC should serve as a basic act for all of the grounds of civil liability. Thus, the legislature should consider whether the provisions regarding commercial companies' liability should be transferred into the KC from the Commercial Company Code of 2000. The question refers also to delictual liability for the infringement of copyrights and employee liability. Having these types of liability in one single act would contribute to the unification of the scope and the prerequisites of the liability.

Within the limited framework of the chapter, it is impossible to present the whole subject matter of the tort reform.[71] It would be appropriate to propose a codification of the *neminem laedere* principle. This is one of the basic principles of liability for damages that the code should express. In Polish doctrine, this issue is currently disputed. Some authors claim that behaviour that violates the general duty of care that every person in society should observe in order not to cause harm to another person is wrongful (fault in the objective sense), while others claim that failure to observe the precautionary principles belongs to the category of fault. In the light of PETL, there is no general obligation to protect others from harm, but such an obligation may arise in situations provided for by law, or if an actor creates or controls a dangerous situation, or if there is a special relationship between the parties, or if a significant amount of harm, on the one hand, and the ease of avoiding it, on the other hand, indicates that such an obligation arises (Art 4:103 PETL). The burden of proof of fault can be reversed because of the degree of danger involved in the operation. The magnitude of the danger is determined by the extent of the potential damage and the likelihood of the damage being caused.

Furthermore, there is no doubt that fault as the basis for overall *ex delicto* liability has lost its dominant role in court practice. Strict liability has become on a par with the fault-based liability. This notwithstanding it is still controversial today to even allow the application of strict liability by analogy. Although the relationship between the principle of fault and risk is an extremely complex issue to codify, it is necessary to undertake this task as the scope of the subject matter of human activity subject to strict liability for damage is gradually broadening,[72] which is related to the distributive function of civil liability.

Certainly, the provisions on the liability of legal persons, liability for subordinates, as well as liability for minors and persons with no knowledge require reform. The model of liability of legal persons is another difficult issue. The current principle of liability of legal persons for damage caused by the full of their organs, reflecting the position of Germanic systems, is ill-suited to the realities of the modern world. In this respect, we share a critical view of the current model. Many other tort provisions need to be adjusted in order to

---

71  See Ewa Bagińska, 'Prawo deliktów w przyszłym kodeksie cywilnym (propozycje założeń)' (2019) 73 (10) *Panst Prawo* 124, 133ff.

72  See Bernhard A Koch and Helmut Koziol, 'Comparative Conclusions' in Bernhard A Koch and Helmut Koziol (eds), *Unification of Tort Law: Strict Liability* (Kluwer Law International 2002) 402.

maintain continuity. It is also worth considering regulating new torts, in particular, liability for wrongful conception and wrongful birth, and determining the (in)admissibility of wrongful life claims. Due to the developments of medical diagnostics, the preceding claims will be easier to establish in the future and will probably increase in numbers. Finally, consideration should be given to the introduction of the so-called information tort (like in the Czech system).

An entirely new issue is the problem of the grounds for claiming financial compensation for harm resulting from the violation of human rights and freedoms. A pecuniary claim has a fundamental function in terms of the effectiveness of the protection of rights and freedoms. Its importance can be seen especially when the legislature decides to leave this issue to the general principles of civil liability without introducing specific compensation mechanisms for selected cases of violations, or a general, separate basis for a pecuniary claim for a violation of freedoms and human rights. Such a state of affairs can be found in most European legislation,[73] including in Poland, where special protection measures constitute an exceptional solution. Meanwhile, claims based on a violation of human rights are increasingly frequent and often aim at questioning the established interpretation of rules on the protection of personal rights. A particular problem is caused by procedural rights which serve to ensure the effectiveness of the protection of human rights by the state. This raises the fundamental question of whether effective protection of human rights requires the introduction of a new, separate basis for a compensation claim in domestic law (e.g. in the civil code), or there is a need to create a new, separate liability regime – outside of tort law.[74]

## 4 Some concluding remarks

In conclusion, the need to modernize tort law and adapt it to modern forums for economic and social activity can be considered justified. However, it should be remembered that legal stability and continuity of jurisprudence are undoubtedly overriding values in this area. A deep doctrinal debate should not only answer the question of whether to modernize them, but also how to do it. The concept of the reform of tort law should, above all, be consistent. From an axiological point of view, civil liability reflects a flexible system of elements carrying certain values. A combination of several elements makes it possible to accept liability each time the overall balance of values forming the basis for liability for damages is not violated.

It is undeniable that recodifying tort law in Central Europe in the beginning of the twenty-first century constitutes an important answer to social and economic expectations formed in the society after the change in the economic and political regime. The changes introduced in the examined civil codes indicate

---

73 cf Czech NOZ, §§ 2956 and 2957.
74 Ewa Bagińska, 'Damages for Violations of Human Rights: A Comparative Analysis' in Ewa Bagińska (ed), *Damages for Violations of Human Rights: A Comparative Study of Domestic Legal Systems* (Springer 2015) 450.

a certain need for different prerequisites of delictual and contractual liability. Thus, in the case of the Czech Republic and Hungary, both countries withdrew from the monist system of contractual and delictual liability, thereby joining the rest of the legal systems (except for Austria). A common feature in the discussed recodifications is also the codification of the *neminem laedere* rule and modifications of strict liability rules. In general, fault remains the general condition for tort law, but the standard of its objectification prevails. The influence of PETL and DCFR can be observed in the fact that the general condition for compensation is fault, but strict liability for damage was set out also in greater detail. Despite some common themes, unique and novel solutions were also introduced to domestic systems e.g. *solatium doloris* in Hungary.

In Poland, there is still a debate on the directions of the development of a Polish tort law system. One of the main questions is whether some types of liability should be governed by the civil code instead of separate different acts, as well as whether to introduce a general clause of strict liability and, as regards the scope of damages, whether to regulate the claim for damages for violation of human rights.

## Bibliography

Alunaru C and Bojin L, 'Romania' in Koziol H and Steininger BC (eds), *European Tort Law 2009* (De Gruyter 2010).

—— and Bojin L, 'The Tort Law Provisions of the New Romanian Civil Code' (2011) 2 *JETL* 103 [https://doi.org/10.1515/jetl.2011.103].

—— and Bojin L, 'Romania' in Karner E, Oliphant K, and Steininger BC (eds), *European Tort Law: Basic Texts* (2nd edn, Jan Sramek Verlag 2018).

Bagińska E, *Odpowiedzialność deliktowa w razie niepewności związku przyczynowego: Studium prawnoporównawcze* (TNOiK 2013).

——, 'Damages for Violations of Human Rights: A Comparative Analysis' in Bagińska E (ed), *Damages for Violations of Human Rights: A Comparative Study of Domestic Legal Systems* (Springer 2015) [https://doi.org/10.1007/978-3-319-18950-5_20].

——, 'Developments in Personal Injury Law in Poland: Shaping the Compensatory Function of Tort Law' (2015) 8 *J Civ L Stud* 309 <https://digitalcommons.law.lsu.edu/jcls/vol8/iss1/17> accessed 23 May 2020.

——, 'The Meanders of Polish Tort Law (1933–2014)' in Potgieter J, Knobel J, and Jansen RM (eds), *Essays in Honour of/Huldigingsbundel vir Johann Neethling* (LexisNexis 2015).

——, 'Prawo deliktów w przyszłym kodeksie cywilnym (propozycje założeń)' (2019) 73 (10) *Panst Prawo* 124.

——, 'Rekodyfikacja prawa odpowiedzialności cywilnej w Czechach i na Węgrzech – rewolucja czy ewolucja' in Bagińska E, Mogilski WW, and Wałachowska M (eds), *O dobre prawo dla ubezpieczeń: Księga jubileuszowa Profesora Eugeniusza Kowalewskiego* (TNOiK 2019).

Borghetti JS, 'France' in Martin-Casals M (ed), *The Borderlines of Tort Law: Interactions with Contract Law* (Intersentia 2019) [https://doi.org/10.1017/9781780689135.007].

Burián L, 'Podstawowe zasady odpowiedzialności deliktowej i kontraktowej w nowym węgierskim kodeksie cywilnym' [2013] (9) *Prz Prawa Handl* 35.

Dajczak W, 'The Polish Way to a Unified Law of Contract: Local Curiosity or Contribution to the European Debate Today?' in Bar C von and Wudarski A (eds), *Deutschland und Polen in der europäischen Rechtsgemeinschaft* (SELP 2012) [https://doi.org/10.1515/9783866539464.13].

Drukteiniene S and Paleviciene S, 'Lithuania' in Weyts B (eds), *IEL Tort Law* (Kluwer Law International 2017).

Fuglinszky A, 'Risks and Side Effects: Five Questions on the "New" Hungarian Tort Law' [2014] (2) *ELTE LJ* 221.

——, 'Some Structural Questions on the Relationship between Contractual and Extracontractual Liability in the New Hungarian Civil Code' in Menyhárd A and Veress E (eds), *New Civil Codes in Hungary and Romania* (Springer 2017) [https://doi.org/10.1007/978-3-319-63327-5_9].

Hondius E, 'Recodification of Private Law in Central and Eastern Europe and in the Netherlands' [2014] (1) *ELTE LJ* 51.

Hrádek J, 'The Czech Republic' in Oliphant K and Steininger BC (eds), *European Tort Law 2012* (De Gruyter 2013) [https://doi.org/10.1515/etly.2013.3.1.119].

—— and Andrew J Bell, 'The New Czech Civil Code and Compensation for Damage: Introductory Remarks' (2016) 7 *JETL* 300 [https://doi.org/10.1515/jetl-2016-0014].

Koch BA and Koziol H, 'Comparative Conclusions' in Koch BA and Koziol H (eds), *Unification of Tort Law: Strict Liability* (Kluwer Law International 2002).

Martin-Casals M, 'Comparative Report' in Martin-Casals M (ed), *The Borderlines of Tort Law: Interactions with Contract Law* (Intersentia 2019) [https://doi.org/10.1017/9781780689135.020].

Menyhárd A, 'Hungary' in Koziol H and Steininger BC (eds), *European Tort Law 2002* (Springer 2003).

——, 'Hungary' in Koziol H and Steininger BC (eds), *European Tort Law 2008* (Springer 2009) [https://doi.org/10.1007/978-3-211-92798-4_17].

——, 'Hungary' in Karner E and Steininger BC (eds), *European Tort Law 2013* (De Gruyter 2014) [https://doi.org/10.1515/tortlaw-2014-0115].

——, 'Hungary' in Karner E, Oliphant K, and Steininger BC (eds), *European Tort Law: Basic Texts* (2nd edn, Jan Sramek Verlag 2018).

Radwański Z, *Zielona księga: Optymalna wizja Kodeksu cywilnego w Rzeczpospolitej Polskiej* (Ministerstwo Sprawiedliwości 2006).

Schulze R and Zoll F (eds), *The Law of Obligations in Europe: A New Wave of Codifications* (SELP 2013) [https://doi.org/10.1515/9783866539839].

Selelionyté-Drukteiniené S, Jurkevičius V, and Kadner Graziano T, 'The Impact of the Comparative Method on Lithuanian Private Law' (2013) 21 *ERPL* 959.

Tichý L, 'Czech Republic' in Martin-Casals M (ed), *The Borderlines of Tort Law: Interactions with Contract Law* (Intersentia 2019) [https://doi.org/10.1017/9781780689135.005].

Varul P, 'The Creation of New Estonian Private Law' (2008) 16 *ERPL* 95.

Veress E, 'The New Romanian Civil Code: Difficulties in the Transition towards a Monist Private Law' in Menyhárd A and Veress E (eds), *New Civil Codes in Hungary and Romania* (Springer 2017) [http://doi.org/10.1007/978-3-319-63327-5_3].

Winiger B and others (eds), *Digest of European Tort Law: Vol I: Essential Cases on Natural Causation* (Springer 2007) [https://doi.org/10.1007/978-3-211-36958-6].

——, Karner E, and Oliphant K (eds), *Digest of European Tort Law: Vol 3: Essential Cases on Misconduct* (De Gruyter 2018) [https://doi.org/10.1515/9783110535679].

Zoll F, 'A Civil Code Outside of Reality: The Polish Codification of the Year 1964, Its Origin, Development and Future' in Wang WY (ed), *Codification in International Perspective: Selected Papers from the 2nd IACL Thematic Conference* (Springer 2014) [https://doi.org/10.1007/978-3-319-03455-3_8].

# 4 Limitations of freedom of contract in the new codifications of the law of obligations in Central and Southeast Europe

An inspiration for the new Polish Civil Code?

*Dorota Miler*

## 1 Introduction[1]

The Polish Civil Code of 1964 (*Kodeks cywilny*,[2] KC) has been in force for over fifty-five years. It has been subject to many alterations that aimed at adjusting it to economic, social, and political transformations that took place since 1990, to the law of European Union, as well as to ongoing market developments.[3] Nevertheless, it has been proposed to replace it with a new codification. This idea is, however, highly controversial.[4] A group of Polish scholars is preparing an academic draft of a new Civil Code (ADCC).[5] The first draft was being prepared by the Polish Civil Law Codification Commission (advisory body of

1 I would like to thank Professor Ádám Fuglinszky for his help in collecting literature and information regarding the limitation of the freedom of contract under the Hungarian law. Many thanks should also be offered to the participants of the Zagreb Law of Obligations Conference for their comments on my presentation of an early draft of this chapter. Special thanks should be given to Matej Trkanjec for his help in obtaining literature and information on Croatian law of obligations. The author is grateful for financial support of the Young Researchers Travel Scholarship Program of the University of Augsburg.
2 Act of 23 April 1964 – Civil Code (*Ustawa z dnia 23 kwietnia 1964 r – Kodeks cywilny*), DzU 2019, 1145 (consolidated text).
3 Other post-communist countries have been faced with similar challenges, see e.g. Nekrosius Mizaras, 'Das neue Zivil- und Zivilprozessrecht in Litauen' [2002] *ZeuP* 466, 466–67.
4 Ewa Łętowska and Aneta Wiewiórowska-Domagalska, 'The Common Frame of Reference: The Perspective of a new Member State' (2007) 3 *ERCL* 277, 287. In favour of replacing the current code, e.g. Marian Kępiński in Mieczysław Sawczuk (ed), *Czterdzieści Lat Kodeksu Cywilnego: Materiały z Ogólnopolskiego Zjazdu Cywilistów w Rzeszowie (8–10 Października 2004 r.)* (Zakamycze 2006) 55, 62. Against replacing the current code, e.g.: Jerzy Poczobut, 'Geschichtlicher Hintergrund, heutiger Stand und Perspektiven des polnischen Privatrechts' in Rudolf Welser (ed), *Privatrechtsentwicklung in Zentral- und Osteuropa* (MANZ Verlag Wien 2008) 138; Andrzej Mączyński, 'Die Entwicklung und die Reformpläne des polnischen Privatrechts' in Rudolf Welser (ed), *Privatrechtsentwicklung in Zentral- und Osteuropa* (MANZ Verlag Wien 2008) 122–23 (but accepts novelizations of the current code). See also Zbigniew Radwański, 'Kodifikationsprobleme des Zivilrechts in Polen' in Peter Blaho and Jan Švidroň (eds), *Kodifikácia, europeizácia a harmonizácia súkromného práva* (Bratislava Iura Ed 2005) 174–75.
5 Information about the ADCC is available at: 'Akademicki Projekt Kodeksu Cywilnego' <www.projektkc.uj.edu.pl/> accessed 22 January 2020.

the Minister of Justice)[6] until 17 December 2015, when the members of the commission were relieved of their duties. Only the draft of the General Part of the Civil Code has been made public.

One of the fundamental principles of Polish private law is the freedom of contract. It provides parties of a contractual relationship with the freedom to decide whether to enter into a contract and to determine the contract's content.[7] Freedom of contract is, however, never unlimited. Therefore, one of the questions that the drafters of the new Polish Civil Code must answer is how to limit the freedom of contract in the drafted codification – where the provision should be located in the new Civil Code, what limits should apply, and how they should be interpreted. Hereinafter, only limitations that constrain the parties' freedom to determine the content (contractual stipulations) of their actions are being considered. No other constraints of the freedom of contract, including laws regulating customer protection and standard terms supplied by one of the parties, are taken into account. Also, the consequences of violating the limitations are not discussed hereinafter.

Since 1990, Central and Southeast European countries faced the challenge of recodifying their private law. They had to adjust their private law to new economic, social, and political conditions; to 'create more favourable legal conditions for development of enterprises, to strengthen protection of personal rights and freedoms as well as to build an effective legal protection system and, adapt their law to international law, especially EU law'.[8]

New civil codes came into force in Lithuania and Estonia in 2001 and 2002. At approximately the same time new acts regulating law of obligations were adopted in Croatia (2005) and Slovenia (2001). The newest codifications, adopted in Czech Republic and Hungary, have been in power since 2014. All these countries, and Poland, share the recent history and the legal obstacles encountered over the last thirty years. Which raises the question, should the solutions implemented in the legal acts adopted in these countries serve as inspiration for Polish scholars drafting the new Civil Code?

The author evaluates the proposed regulation of the limitations of concluding any legal transaction[9] proposed in the academic draft of a new Polish Civil Code by examining: the current regulation of the limitations of freedom of contract in Polish law and the necessity to modify it (section 2); and the limitations of freedom of contract in the newest codifications of the law of obligations in Central and Southeast Europe and their adaptability to the Polish

---

6 Ordinance of the Council of Ministers of 22 April 2002 on the establishment, organization, and operation of the Civil Law Codification Commission (*Rozporządzenie Rady Ministrów z dnia 22 kwietnia 2002 r w sprawie utworzenia, organizacji i trybu działania Komisji Kodyfikacyjnej Prawa Cywilnego*), DzU 2002, 55, 476.

7 Reinhard Zimmermann, 'The Civil Law in European Codes' in Hector L MacQueen, Antoni Vaquer, and Santiago Espiau Espiau (eds.), *Regional Private Laws and Codification in Europe* (CUP 2003) 57.

8 Mizaras (n 3) 466–67.

9 The term 'legal transaction' is used interchangeably with the term 'juridical act'.

legal system (section 3). In the analysis, the author relies mostly on secondary sources.

## 2 Limitations of freedom of contract under Polish law

The Article providing freedom of contract (Art 353¹ KC), in force since 1 October 1990,[10] is regulated as one of the general provisions of the law of obligations (Book Three of KC). Article 353¹ KC allows concluding any contract unless its aim or content contradicts: the nature of the (contractual) relationship, a statute, or the principles of community life. This legal provision applies only to contracts.[11]

Freedom of contract is also limited by the restrictions applying to all legal transactions. A relevant provision is regulated in the General Part of the Code (Book One of KC). Article 58 KC prohibits legal transactions that are contrary to a statute, whose purpose is to circumvent a statute (Art 58 § 1 KC) or that are contrary to the principles of community life (Art 58 § 2 KC). The limitations apply, at the very least, to the content and aim of the transaction.

Therefore, freedom of contract is limited by the nature of the relationship, statutes, and the principles of community life. The purpose of a contract – as a type of a legal transaction – cannot be to circumvent a statute.

KC does not provide statutory definitions of any of the limitations. They are defined in the legal literature and case law.

### 2.1 Nature of the (contractual) relationship

The majority of Polish scholars accept that the nature of a legal relationship is a general clause[12] that refers to legal factors, such as the content of the norms of the law of obligations and does not include any references to the non-legal factors.[13] The exact meaning of this clause is, however, understood in different ways.

Most Polish scholars[14] are of the opinion that the nature of a contractual legal relationship can be understood as an order or as a directive to respect 'certain basic features of a contractual legal relationship, that is, those of its elements, the

---

10  Added by Art 1(48) of the Act of 28 June 1990 amending the Civil Code (*Ustawa z dnia 28 lipca 1990 r o zmianie ustawy – Kodeks cywilny*), DzU 1990, 55, 321.

11  Marek Safjan in Krzysztof Pietrzykowski (ed) *Kodeks cywilny: Komentarz do art. 1–449¹⁰*, vol 1 (9th edn, CH Beck 2018) Art 353¹ para 4.

12  So e.g. Janusz Guść, 'O właściwości (naturze) stosunku prawnego' (1997) 51 (4) *Panst Prawo* 16, 16–17; Roman Trzaskowski, 'Właściwość (natura) zobowiązaniowego stosunku prawnego jako ograniczenie zasady swobody kształtowania treści umów' (2000) 10 *Kwart Prawa Prywat* 337, 347; Ewa Łętowska, *Prawo umów konsumenckich* (2nd edn, CH Beck 2002) 368.

13  See Piotr Machnikowski, *Swoboda umów według art. 353¹ KC: Konstrukcja prawna* (CH Beck 2005) 326. Contrary e.g. Guść (n 12) 16–17, 24–25; Łętowska, *Prawo* (n 12) 369–70.

14  E.g. Guść (n 12) 16–17, 20; Trzaskowski, 'Właściwość (natura)' (n 12) 348–49; Piotr Machnikowski in Ewa Łętowska (ed), *Prawo zobowiązań – część ogólna: System Prawa Prywatnego*, vol 5 (2nd edn, CH

absence of which may lead to undermining the sense (essence) of establishing a legal bond'[15] (broader meaning). It can be established 'directly from the very character of the contractual legal relationships as such, or from the character attributed to a particular category of these relations'.[16] For instance, according to this meaning, a legal transaction providing one party with the right to freely change the content of the contract would be contrary to the properties (nature) of a contractual legal relationship as being incompatible with the principle of equality of parties of a legal transaction.[17]

According to a narrower understanding, the nature of a contractual legal relationship is 'an order to respect these elements of a particular contractual legal relationship the omission or modification of which would lead to distorting the assumed model of the legal bond associated with a given type of relationship'.[18] The model can be distinguished on the basis of the minimal, necessary elements of a given contractual legal relationship regulated by the lawmaker that guarantee the economic purpose or 'internal axiological equilibrium' of that relationship.[19]

## 2.2 Statute

Polish literature accepts a broad understanding of a legal transaction contrary to a statute. Namely, a legal transaction (including a contract) can be found contrary to a statute (or to be more precise: to an act of statutory law) if (i) it lacks the minimal content required for this transaction's effectiveness by an act of statutory law;[20] (ii) it lacks (other than specific provisions of the content) elements required by law, in particular it lacks other statutory requirements ordered by a norm being a source of (conferring) competence;[21] (iii) it is concluded by a party that exceeded or abused his competences;[22] (iv) it causes legal results that are prohibited by legal norms.[23] The legal results intended by the

---

Beck 2013) ch VI § 29 para 133; Piotr Machnikowski in Edward Gniewek and Piotr Machnikowski (eds), *Kodeks Cywilny: Komentarz* (7th edn, CH Beck 2016) Art 353¹ para 18.

15 Marek Safjan, 'Zasada swobody umów (Uwagi wstępne na tle wykładni art. 353¹ k.c.)' (1993) 47 (4) *Panst Prawo* 12, 15–16; Safjan in Pietrzykowski (n 11) Art 353¹ para 15.

16 Safjan, 'Zasada swobody umów' (n 15) 15–16; Safjan in Pietrzykowski (n 11) Art 353¹ para 15.

17 SN resolution of 22 May 1991, III CZP 15/91, OSNC 1992, 1, 1; SN resolution of 19 May 1992, III CZP 50/92, OSP 1993, 3, 119. For more examples see Trzaskowski, 'Właściwość (natura)' (n 12) 349–67; Adam Olejniczak in Andrzej Kidyba (ed), *Kodeks Cywilny: Komentarz: Zobowiązania. Część ogólna*, vol 3 (2nd edn, Wolters Kluwer 2014) Art 353¹ para 11; Safjan in Pietrzykowski (n 11) Art 353¹ para 15.

18 Safjan, 'Zasada swobody umów' (n 15) 16; Safjan in Pietrzykowski (n 11) Art 353¹ para 16.

19 Safjan in Pietrzykowski (n 11) Art 353¹ para 16.

20 Maciej Gutowski, *Nieważność czynności prawnej* (CH Beck 2006) 229–33; Machnikowski in Gniewek and Machnikowski (n 14) Art 58 para 10.

21 Gutowski, *Nieważność* (n 20) 233–41.

22 Machnikowski in Gniewek and Machnikowski (n 14) Art 58 para 10.

23 Roman Trzaskowski in Jacek Gudowski (ed), *Kodeks Cywilny: Komentar: Część ogólna* (LexisNexis 2014) Art 58 para 29; Machnikowski in Gniewek and Machnikowski (n 14) Art 58 para 10.

parties are contrary to a general and abstract norm regulated in an act of statutory law if they are prohibited by a legal norm by being either excluded or not allowed (prohibited) from taking place or the 'full and simultaneous abidance of the contractual and legal norms by their addressee is impossible'.[24]

Any constitutional, statutory, or other provision that was issued on the basis of specific statutory authorization is considered to be 'a statute' under Art 58 KC[25] regardless of whether it belongs to civil, criminal, or administrative law.[26] Also, European Union law provisions,[27] ratified international agreements, and 'local law issued by the operation of organs . . . in the territory of the organ issuing such enactments' (Art 87(1) and (2) of Polish Constitution) fall within the category of 'a statute'.[28]

A legal transaction must contradict the norm provided in a statute.[29] In particular, a legal transaction is contrary to an act of a statutory law if it contradicts *iuris cogentis* (compulsory legal provisions) or *ius semidispositivum* (semi-imperative legal provisions).[30] Moreover, the Polish Supreme Court (*Sąd Najwyższy*, SN) found that 'the general legal rules that lie at the core of the legal system and the legal norms that can be interpreted from the act of statutory law' should be considered when deciding whether a legal transaction contradicts an act of statutory law.[31] Even though it remains controversial, extensive interpretation of a transaction *contra legem* also has been proposed in the legal literature.[32]

## 2.3 Principles of community life

The understanding of the principles of community life is controversial in Polish legal literature. Most of the scholars identify the principles as a general

---

24 Trzaskowski in Gudowski (n 23) Art 58 para 29.
25 Andrzej Wypiórkiewicz in Helena Ciepła (ed), *Kodeks Cywilny: Komentarz*, vol 1 (Wydawnictwo Zrzeszenia Prawników Polskich 2005) Art 58 para 1.
26 See e.g. Zbigniew Radwański, *Prawo cywilne – część ogólna: System Prawa Prywatnego*, vol 2 (CH Beck 2008) ch V § 23 para 26.
27 Radwański, *Prawo cywilne* (n 26) ch V § 23 para 13; Przemysław Sobolewski in Konrad Osajda (ed), *Kodeks cywilny: Komentarz*, vol 1 (CH Beck 2013) Art 58 paras 27–33.
28 Trzaskowski in Gudowski (n 23) Art 58 para 2.
29 Stefan Grzybowski, *System Prawa Cywilnego*, vol 1 (Ossolineum 1985) 515; Radwański, *Prawo cywilne* (n 26) ch V § 23 para 17. See also Grzegorz Tracz and Fryderyk Zoll, *Przewłaszczenie na zabezpieczenie* (Zakamycze 1996) 75; Sobolewski in Osajda, vol 1 (n 27) Art 58 paras 19–21.
30 Radwański, *Prawo cywilne* (n 26) ch V § 23 para 20; Machnikowski in Łętowska (n 14) ch VI § 29 para 77.
31 SN judgment of 29 March 2006, IV CK 411/05, LEX 179733. Contrary e.g. Maciej Gutowski, 'Sprzeczność z prawem Unii Europejskiej jako przesłanka nieważność czynności prawnej na podstawie Art 58 K.C.' (2006) 68 (1) *Ruch Praw Ekonom Socjol* 111, 122; Andrzej Janiak in Andrzej Kidyba (ed), *Kodeks Cywilny: Część ogólna*, vol 1 (2nd edn, Wolters Kluwer 2012) Art 58 para 12; Sobolewski in Osajda, vol 1 (n 27) Art 58 para 21.
32 See e.g. Grzybowski (n 29) 518; Stanisław Dmowski and Stanisław Rudnicki, *Komentarz do Kodeks cywilny: Księga pierwsza: Część ogólna* (LexisNexis 2011) 272–73, 280.

clause referring to moral norms.[33] Piotr Machnikowski specifies that these moral norms must be imperative and have a corresponding form: they must order certain morally accepted conduct or prohibit particular morally disapproved conduct.[34] These moral judgments are determined by 'values commonly accepted in the society'.[35]

Some scholars and judges give the principles (slightly) broader meaning. They are referred to as 'basic principles of ethical and honest behaviour, such as equity, morality or loyalty'[36] or as the 'idea of righteousness'[37] or even 'ethical norms'[38] or 'social norms' that are not necessarily identical with moral norms.[39]

Principles of community life refer only to a collection of rules of conduct of people towards each other.[40] They impose values that are universally recognized in Polish society and 'are both a heritage and a component of the European culture'.[41] Thus, it is assumed that despite the plurality of the values held by the members of Polish society, there is 'a certain objective order of values and moral norms'.[42]

In the legal literature and case law the principles are also interpreted not as a set of norms, but criteria for limiting, giving basis, and directing courts' discretion.[43]

It is commonly agreed that it is impossible to create a complete list of values and/or norms covered by the principles of community life.[44]

The catalogue of values to which the principles of community life refer to is not constant but evolves as a result of the evolution of the awareness of the members of the society.[45] This feature of the principles allows them to remain in Polish law, despite their origins.[46] Namely, they were transplanted to Polish private law from Soviet law and related originally 'to the Soviet moral doctrine and political goals of a state of "real socialism"'.[47] They were reinterpreted after

---

33  E.g. Adam Łopatka and Zygmunt Ziembiński, 'Próba systematyzacji zasad współżycia społecznego wg orzecznictwa S.N.' (1957) 12 (4–5) *Panst Prawo* 802, 803, 805.

34  Machnikowski in Gniewek and Machnikowski (n 14) Art 5 para 3.

35  Małgorzata Pyziak-Szafnicka in Małgorzata Pyziak-Szafnicka and Paweł Księżak (eds), *Kodeks Cywilny: Komentarz: Część ogólna* (Wolters Kluwer 2014) Art 5 para 30.

36  E.g. SN judgment of 5 June 2009, I UK 19/09.

37  E.g. SN resolution of 20 December 2012, III CZP 84/12, OSNC 2013, 7–8, 83.

38  E.g. Wypiórkiewicz in Ciepła (n 25) Art 5 para 3.

39  E.g. Stefan Grzybowski, 'Struktura i treść przepisów prawa cywilnego odsyłających do zasad współżycia społecznego' [1965] *Stud Cywilis* 3, 19.

40  Radwański, *Prawo cywilne* (n 26) ch V § 23 para 30.

41  ibid; Zbigniew Radwański and Maciej Zieliński in Marek Safjan (ed), *Prawo cywilne – część ogólna: System Prawa Prywatnego*, vol 1 (2nd edn, CH Beck 2012) ch VII § 29 para 51.

42  Trzaskowski in Gudowski (n 23) Art 58 para 8.

43  Ludwik Krąkowski, *Zasady współżycia społecznego w stosunkach pracy w PRL* (PWN 1970) 87.

44  So e.g. Radwański, *Prawo cywilne* (n 26) ch V § 23 para 31; Machnikowski in Łętowska (n 14) ch VI § 29 para 107; Dmowski and Rudnicki (n 32) Art 58 para 5.

45  Radwański, *Prawo cywilne* (n 26) ch V § 23 para 31.

46  ibid. Zbigniew Radwański is also of the opinion that this feature of the principles allows them to continue following the case law regarding the principles of community life given before 1989.

47  Radwański and Zieliński in Safjan (n 41) ch VII § 29 para 51.

1989; presently they have no political or ideological connotations to the political regime of the Polish People's Republic but relate to the values identified in the Polish Constitution of 1997.[48]

The use of the term 'principles of community life' is discontinued in the newest legislation. The recent acts do not contain any references to the principles, but, instead, they contain other terms, such as 'good morals' or 'considerations of equity'.[49]

### 2.4 Circumvention of the law

There are four definitions of circumvention of the law proposed in the Polish legal literature and used in the case law. Most frequently a legal transaction having as an objective circumventing an act of statutory law is understood as 'a transaction admittedly not covered by a legal prohibition, but one undertaken with the objective of achieving a legal result prohibited by law'.[50] According to an alternative definition that has been proposed in the recent literature, a legal transaction circumvents the law when its content and conclusion are not directly contrary to statutory law, but the parties of it 'consciously aim at producing a result which the circumvented norm sought to prevent'.[51]

Based on the case law of the SN, circumvention of the law can be established if (i) performing the contested legal transaction is not prohibited by statutory law and (ii) the transaction leads to the same result to which a transaction contrary to statutory law would have led, (iii) there is no rational justification confirming the need to perform the contested legal transaction, and (iv) at least one of the parties of the transaction had the intention to obtain a result which circumvents the law.[52]

### 2.5 The necessity to modify current limitations of the freedom of contract?

Current regulations of the limitations of the freedom of contract and of the freedom of concluding any legal transaction are criticized in the legal literature. Authors argue that having two legal provisions – one regulating the freedom of

48  ibid; Pyziak-Szafnicka in Pyziak-Szafnicka and Księżak (n 35) Art 5 para 26.
49  Observed by Radwański and Zieliński in Safjan (n 41) ch VII § 29 paras 53–54; Machnikowski in Gniewek and Machnikowski (n 14) Art 5 para 6; Janiak in Kidyba (n 31) Art 58 para 31; Krzysztof Pietrzykowski in Krzysztof Pietrzykowski (ed), *Kodeks cywilny: Komentarz do art. 1–44910*, vol 1 (8th edn, CH Beck 2015) Art 5 para 4. See also Tomasz Justyński, *Nadużycie prawa w polskim prawie cywilnym* (Zakamycze 2000) 113; Beata Janiszewska, 'Klauzula generalna dobrych obyczajów w znowelizowanych przepisach kodeksu cywilnego' [2003] (10) *Prz Prawa Handl* 12.
50  Zbigniew Radwański and Roman Trzaskowski in Adam Olejniczak (ed), *Prawo cywilne – część ogólna: System Prawa Prywatnego*, vol 2 (CH Beck 2019) 311. See also Aleksander Wolter, *Prawo cywilne: Zarys części ogólnej* (Wolters Kluwer 2001) 318.
51  Trzaskowski in Gudowski (n 23) 441.
52  Dorota Miler, 'Czynności mające na celu obejście ustawy na tle orzecznictwa sądów polskich' (2019) 81 (4) *Ruch Praw Ekonom Socjol* 109, 111ff.

contract and one regulating the freedom to conclude any legal transaction – is redundant. Also, not all currently binding limitations of freedom are necessary since some of them do not function independently of others.

### 2.5.1 *Two provisions regulating the freedom of contract and the freedom to conclude any legal transaction*

It was proposed in the legal literature that a separate provision restricting freedom of contract that modifies the provision constraining the freedom to conclude any legal transactions is unnecessary.[53] Removing the legal provision stating the freedom of contract is possible if the validity of a legal transaction (including a contract) will be dependent on the content and objective of the transaction. This is particularly since the existence of the separate provision stating the freedom of contract does not influence the interpretation of the other legal provisions regulating obligations.[54]

Moreover, regulating the freedom of contract and its limitations in a separate provision requires harmonizing its content with the legal provision providing limitations applicable to all legal transactions.[55]

Having two legal provisions might be seen as part of the Polish legal tradition since it has been this way for over thirty years. However, the act of introducing Art 353$^1$ KC is seen as having a symbolic and ideological dimension that nowadays has no meaning.[56]

### 2.5.2 *Redundant limitations*

#### 2.5.2.1 NATURE OF THE RELATIONSHIP

Most Polish scholars do not recognize the nature of the (contractual) relationship as a limitation of the freedom of contract that applies independently from the limitations prohibiting contracts contrary to an act of statutory law or the principles of community life. It has been postulated to interpret the term 'the nature of the (contractual) relationship' on the basis of the legal regulations and the principles of community life.[57] Further, it has been argued that the content of the nature is already covered by the content of the legal or moral norms[58]

---

53  Against removing Art 353$^1$ KC from the current civil code, e.g. Andrzej Koch in Sawczuk (n 4) 264, 266.

54  Piotr Machnikowski, 'Zasada swobody umów jako problem kodyfikacyjny' in Mieczysław Sawczuk (ed), *Czterdzieści Lat Kodeksu Cywilnego: Materiały z Ogólnopolskiego Zjazdu Cywilistów w Rzeszowie (8–10 Października 2004 r.)* (Zakamycze 2006) 229.

55  ibid 231.

56  ibid 232.

57  Radwański, *Prawo cywilne* (n 26) ch V § 23 para 29.

58  Machnikowski in Łętowska (n 14) ch VI § 29 para 133; Machnikowski in Gniewek and Machnikowski (n 14) Art 353$^1$ para 18.

and they include elements that were earlier applied as part of the other limitations.[59] Therefore, a legal transaction contrary to the nature of the (contractual) relationship is *per se* contrary to statutory law or the principles of community life.[60] Hence, this limitation is even described as 'empty, redundant, without its own normative content' and as one that should be removed.[61] Moreover, difficulties that are caused by the unclear meaning of this term provide courts with significantly wide discretion.[62]

Piotr Machnikowski points out that the usefulness of distinguishing the nature of a contractual legal relationship as a limitation of the freedom of contract 'depends mainly on the interpretation of the concept of statutory law and on the adopted theoretical assumptions, in particular concerning the rules of interpretation and inference in the process of applying the law'.[63] Namely, accepting a broad concept of statutory law or allowing extensive interpretation of law deems listing this limitation together with the other limitations unnecessary.

Only a minority of scholars hold the position that the nature of a contractual legal relationship is an independent and autonomous limitation of the freedom of contract.[64] This position is also expressed in some of the rulings of the SN.[65]

2.5.2.2 CIRCUMVENTION OF THE LAW

Scholars find distinguishing a legal transaction having as an objective circumventing an act of statutory law from a legal transaction contrary to an act of statutory law unnecessary.[66] First, the correct interpretation of a legal provision prevents the need for distinguishing a transaction evading the law. 'A legal norm reconstructed with the help of the rules of interpretation may include

59  Safjan, 'Zasada swobody umów' (n 15) 15.
60  Konrad Osajda in Konrad Osajda (ed), *Kodeks cywilny: Komentarz*, vol 2 (CH Beck 2013) Art 353[1] para 92.
61  ibid paras 80.2 and 96. Zbigniew Radwański goes a step further and proposes to eliminate the entire legal provision (art. 353[1] KC), see Radwański, *Prawo cywilne* (n 26) ch V § 23 para 29.
62  Machnikowski in Sawczuk (n 54) 225; Komisja Kodyfikacyjna Prawa Cywilnego działająca przy Ministrze Sprawiedliwości, 'Kodeks cywilny: Księga I: Część ogólna: Projekt z objaśnieniami' <www.projektkc.uj.edu.pl/index.php/projekty> accessed 22 January 2020 (ADCC with Commentary).
63  Machnikowski in Gniewek and Machnikowski (n 14) Art 353[1] para 18. See also Machnikowski in Łętowska (n 14) ch VI § 29 para 134.
64  Guść (n 12) 16–17; Kinga Bączyk, 'Zasada swobody umów w prawie polskim' in Ewa Kustry (ed), *Studia Iuridica Toruniensia: Przemiany Polskiego Prawa*, vol 2 (Wydawnictwo Naukowe Uniwersytetu Mikołaja Kopernika 2002) 55; Gutowski, *Nieważność* (n 20) 362–63, 368; Osajda in Osajda, vol 2 (n 60) Art 353[1] para 97.
65  E.g. SN judgment of 20 May 2004, II CK 354/03, OSN 2005, 5, 91.
66  E.g. Grzybowski (n 29) 515; Tracz and Zoll (n 29) 75; Radwański, *Prawo cywilne* (n 26) ch V § 23 para 19; Sobolewski in Osajda, vol 1 (n 27) Art 58 para 66. Against see e.g. Wojciech Wąsowicz, 'Obejście prawa jako przyczyna nieważności czynności prawnej' (1999) 9 *Kwart Prawa Prywat* 69; Marek Safjan in Pietrzykowski, vol 1 (n 49) Art 58 para 15.

prohibitions to accomplish states of affairs clearly unnamed in legal provisions.'[67] Also, because a legal transaction is contrary to an act of statutory law when it contradicts a norm interpreted from a legal provision, a legal transaction having as an objective circumventing an act of statutory law should be classified as *contra legem*.[68] Particularly, 'if a legal provision excludes the existence of legal relations with a specific content, then a legal norm decoded on the basis of this provision prohibits taking actions that lead to this result'.[69] Second, a legal transaction evading law can by definition be always classified as contradicting the law. Specifically, this is because not only the content but also the objective of a legal transaction is considered when the conformity of a legal transaction with an act of statutory law is examined; therefore, the definition of a legal transaction *contra legem* includes a legal transaction *in fraudem legis*.[70] Such understanding 'has the advantage of leading to ordering legal provisions under one legal norm'.[71] Third, not explicitly including circumvention of the law as a ground of invalidity of a legal transaction in other legal provisions (e.g. Art 353[1] KC) indicates that transactions *contra legem* should be so understood as to contain transactions *in fraudem legis*.

Some scholars support the opposite opinion.[72] Also, the SN distinguished in some of its rulings between the transactions *in fraudem legis* and *contra legem*.[73]

### 2.5.3 Anachronic terms

It has been debated since 1989 whether the term 'principles of community life' should be removed from all provisions of Polish law and replaced by other general clauses once and for all.[74] The authors suggesting removal of this general

---

67 Grzybowski (n 29) 516.

68 Sobolewski in Osajda, vol 1 (n 27) Art 58 para 66.

69 ibid.

70 Machnikowski in Gniewek and Machnikowski (n 14) Art 58 para 9.

71 Gutowski, *Nieważność* (n 20) 290.

72 Dmowski and Rudnicki (n 32) Art 58 para 1. See also e.g. Wąsowicz (n 66) 81; Piotr Karwat, *Obejście prawa podatkowego* (Wolters Kluwer 2002) 30; Tomasz Stawecki, 'Obejście prawa. Szkic na temat granic prawa i zasad jego wykładni' in Hubert Izdebski and Aleksander Stępkowski (eds), *Nadużycie prawa* (Liber 2003) 90; Safjan in Pietrzykowski, vol 1 (n 49) Art 58 para 15.

73 See e.g. SN judgment of 22 December 1970, II CR 517/70, LEX 6841; SN judgment of 27 June 2001, II CKN 602/00, OSNC 2002, 2, 28; SN judgment of 30 September 2016, I CSK 858/14, LEX 2152382.

74 Against the removal of the principles from the Polish private law, e.g. Adam Szpunar, 'Uwagi o nadużyciu prawa podmiotowego' in Romuald Sztyk (ed), *II Kongres Notariuszy Rzeczpospolitej Polskiej: referaty i opracowania* (Wydawnictwo Stowarzyszenia Notariuszy RP 1999) 340; Zbigniew Radwański and Maciej Zieliński, 'Uwagi de lege ferenda o klauzulach generalnych w prawie prywatny' (2001) 8 (2) *Prz Leg* 11, 19–20; Beata Janiszewska, 'O potrzebie zmiany klauzuli zasad współżycia społecznego (głos w dyskusji)' (2003) 56 (4) *Prz Ustaw Gosp* 7, 9–10; Ewa Rott-Pietrzykowska, 'Klauzule generalne rozsądku w kodeksie cywilnym' (2005) 14 *Kwart Prawa Prywat* 617, 657; Andrzej Śmieja in Sawczuk (n 4) 267; Pyziak-Szafnicka in Pyziak-Szafnicka and Księżak (n 35) Art 5 paras 26–28. In favour of, e.g. Tadeusz Zieliński, 'Klauzule generalne w nowym porządku konstytucyjnym' (1997) 51 (11–12) *Panst Prawo* 134, 144; Leszek Leszczyński, 'Funkcje

clause from legal texts find that it is necessary to cut off the legal system from the old, communistic system, and its axiology as well as to remove any form of general clauses that have political connotations; it would also help with fitting better within the Western legal tradition.[75] Some authors are also of the opinion that applying the principles leads to misuse of the court's discretion as it allows a judge to decide what is the content of the principles, particularly what principles are recognized in the society and must be followed.[76]

## 2.6  The proposed solutions

As mentioned earlier, it was proposed in Polish legal literature that including a provision explicitly stating the principle of freedom of contract has mostly symbolical and ideological dimension and is redundant nowadays.[77] So far, there is no provision regulating exclusively the freedom of contract planned in the draft of the Polish Civil Code. However, the draft includes a proposal of a provision expressly formulating freedom of determining the content of any legal transaction (Art 54 of the General Part of ADCC). The provision states: 'The parties to the contract may arrange their legal relationship at their discretion.' This legal provision differs from the current regulation of the freedom of contract in four ways: (i) it is regulated in the General Part of the drafted code rather than (as it is right now) in the part dedicated to the law on obligations; (ii) it extends the application of freedom of contract to any legal transaction (currently it applies only to contracts); (iii) it stipulates only the freedom to determine the content of a legal transaction and does not regulate any other aspect of the freedom of contract; and, finally (iv) it does not determine the limits of the freedom of contract.[78]

As in the current KC, the General Part of the academic draft includes a regulation limiting the freedom of concluding any legal transaction if its content, purpose, or performance contradict the law or decency (good morals). The legal transaction – and not a contract – remains the key term in Polish private law. Including this regulation in the General Part – applicable to all regulations that are to be included in the other parts of the draft and other statutes of private law character – prevents redundant repetitions of legal provisions and reinforces their uniform interpretation.[79]

---

klauzul odsyłających a model ich tworzenia w systemie prawa' (2000) 54 (7) *Panst Prawo* 3, 11–12; Mateusz Pilich, 'Zasady współżycia społecznego, dobre obyczaje czy dobra wiara? Dylematy nowelizacji klauzul generalnych prawa cywilnego w perspektywie europejskiej' [2006] (4) *Stud Prawn* 37, 54–56.

75  Marek Safjan, 'Klauzule generalne w prawie cywilnym (przyczynek do dyskusji)' (1990) 45 (11) *Panst Prawo* 48, 56–57; Justyński (n 49) 111–12; Tomasz Sokołowski in Sawczuk (n 4) 269.

76  Pilich (n 74) 54.

77  Machnikowski in Sawczuk (n 54) 232.

78  ADCC with Commentary (n 62).

79  Zbigniew Radwański, 'Aktualność posłużenia się częścią ogólną kodeksu cywilnego jako instrumentem regulacji prawa prywatnego' [2010] (4) *Transform Prawa Prywat* 13, 17.

Located in Chapter I (General provisions) of Section IV (Contradiction of a legal transaction with the law) of Title III (Declarations and legal transactions) of the Book One (General Part) of ADCC, Art 70 ADCC states:

§ 1 A legal transaction which content or purpose contradicts a statute or decency (*boni mores*) is invalid, unless the law provides otherwise or that due to the purpose of the violated norm, a different sanction is appropriate (effective and proportionate).

§ 2 A legal transaction the conclusion of which is contrary to a statute or decency, is invalid only if the statute so provides or when invalidity is the appropriate sanction because of the purpose of the violated norm.[80]

It seems that the critique of current regulations of the freedom of concluding any legal transaction and of the freedom of contract has been considered. The freedom to conclude any legal transaction is limited only by a statute and decency. The general clause of the principles of community life has been replaced with another clause.[81]

According to the commentary of Art 70 ADCC provided in the explanatory memorandum published together with the draft of the general part, 'statute' should be understood in a broad sense: 'It encompasses both norms that are directly named in a statute and the norms that are their necessary consequence.' That makes any references to public order or circumvention of the law unnecessary. The decency should be understood as moral norms binding in Polish society.[82]

Explicit listing of the content and purpose of a legal transaction provides clarity. It is based on the interpretation of Art 58 KC and the content of Art 353¹ KC. The provision serves the aim of guaranteeing a coherent system of legal consequences of violating limitations of freedom of concluding any legal transaction.

'The content of a legal transaction is its provisions, i.e. the decisions expressed in the declaration of intent (declarations of will) regarding individual, normatively relevant issues.'[83] That could be, for instance, the obligation to act in contradiction to the law or in contradiction to imperative norms regulating parties' rights and obligations. Transactions concluded by persons lacking competency to conclude a transaction with particular content or under particular circumstances should be also classified as contrary to law.[84]

---

80 ADCC with Commentary (n 62).
81 Zbigniew Radwański, *Zielona Księga: Optymalna wizja Kodeksu cywilnego w Rzeczpospolitej Polskiej* (Ministerstwo Sprawiedliwości 2006) 58; Zbigniew Radwański, 'Zielona Księga. Optymalna wizja kodeksu cywilnego Rzeczpospolitej Polskiej' (2007) 69 (1) *Ruch Praw Ekonom Socjol* 5, 9.
82 ADCC with Commentary (n 62).
83 ibid.
84 ibid. But if only the way in which an obligation is performed by a debtor is contrary to law (even if an alternative legal way existed) it does not deem the entire transaction contrary to law due to its content.

'The purpose of a transaction is a state of affairs which is to be achieved by concluding the legal transaction.'[85] It is the purpose that is common to all parties of a transaction or only of one of them but known to the other parties. Only if the purpose of one party is directed against the interests of the other party, can it be treated as the purpose of the transaction even though it is unknown to this other party.[86]

A transaction contrary to a statute or decency is deemed invalid (null and void) unless a court finds a different sanction more appropriate under the circumstances.

The second paragraph of the proposed provision regulates the situation in which the act of concluding a legal transaction is contrary to a statute that prohibits concluding such a transaction. The sanction for such a transaction must be decided through the interpretation of the violated statute.

## 3  Limitations of freedom of contract in other Central and Southeast European countries and their applicability under Polish law

### 3.1  General

Civil codes from Lithuania, Estonia, Czech Republic, and Hungary, as well as the regulations on obligations from Slovenia and Croatia, are considered hereinafter.

Lithuanian Civil Code (*Lietuvos Respublikos civilinis kodeksas*,[87] CK) was adopted on 18 July 2000 and entered into force on 1 July 2001.

Law on obligations in Estonia is regulated in the Estonian Law of Obligations Act (*Võlaõigusseadus*,[88] VÕS). The Act constitutes a part of the Estonian Civil Code that is made out of acts introduced after 1992 that gradually replaced the Civil Code of Soviet Estonia of 1965.[89] The VÕS itself was adopted on 26 September 2001 and entered into force on 1 July 2002. On the same day, the reviewed version of the General Part of the Estonian Civil Code Act (*Tsiviilseadustiku üldosa seadus*,[90] TsÜS), which was adopted on 27 March 2002, entered into force. Since then, the Estonian Civil Code has been completed.

The Slovenian Obligations Code (*Obligacijski zakonik*,[91] OblZ) was adopted on 25 October 2001 and entered into force on 1 January 2002. The private law in Slovenia is regulated by acts that determine the law applicable in each area of civil law separately and are traditionally named 'codes'. There is no one single

---

85  ibid.
86  ibid.
87  Act VIII-1864 of 18 July 2000, *Žin* 2000, 74–2262, with later amendments.
88  *RT* I 2001, 81, 487, with later amendments.
89  Harri Mikk, 'Zur Reform des Zivilrechts in Estland' (2001) 42 *Jb OstR* 31, 31–52; Martin Käerdi, 'Estonia and the New Civil Law' in Hector L MacQueen, Antoni Vaquer, and Santiago Espiau Espiau (eds), *Regional Private Laws and Codification in Europe* (CUP 2003) 251.
90  *RT* I 2002, 35, 216, with later amendments.
91  *UL RS* 83/2001, with later amendments.

piece of legislation that systematically codifies the entire private law.[92] Also, in Croatia, there is no civil code systematically regulating all areas of private law. The law of obligations is regulated by the Croatian Obligations Act (*Zakon o obveznim odnosima*,[93] ZOO) that came in force on 1 January 2006.

In the Czech Republic, the law of obligations is regulated by the Czech Civil Code (*Občanský zákoník*,[94] NOZ) that came into force on 1 January 2014. In the same year, but on 15 March, the Hungarian Civil Code (*Polgári törvénykönyv*,[95] Ptk) entered into force. The Hungarian Ptk was enacted on 11 February 2013.

A draft of the entire Polish Civil Code has not been prepared yet. Only the draft of the General Part of the Code accepted by the Polish Civil Law Codification Commission in 2015 has been made public. The draft of the book governing law of obligations has not been completed and made available yet.[96] However, even the members of the committee of the ADCC do not find a need to urgently replace the current civil code.[97] The group of academics that is preparing the ADCC is using the drafts prepared by the Civil Law Codification Commission that was resolved in December 2015. Continuity of the preparation work and no time pressure allow hoping that the prepared code will be a modern civil code of high quality.

### 3.2 Inspirations and historical background of the codifications

The drafters of all the discussed regulations considered civil codes adopted, *inter alia*, in Germany, Austria, and Netherlands, as well as the regulations proposed in documents aiming at harmonization of European private law.

Among the examined laws, only the legislation adopted in Lithuania and Estonia was based mainly on the solutions transplanted from abroad. The German BGB had significant impact on the preparation of the Lithuanian codification.[98] The drafters of the code used as sources also the Civil Code of Quebec, as well as the Dutch, Russian, French, Swiss, and Italian civil codes.[99] Also, the UNIDROIT Principles of International Commercial Contracts (UPICC) had a

---

92  Verica Trstenjak, 'Zivilrecht in Slowenien: Entwicklung und Stand der Dinge heute' [2000] *ZeuP* 77, 88; Verica Trstenjak, 'Das neue slowenische Obligationenrecht' [2002] *WGO* 90, 90.

93  *NN* 35/2005, with later amendments.

94  Act 89/2012, Civil Code (*Zákon 89/2012 Sb, Občanský zákoník*), with later amendments.

95  Act V of 2013 on the Civil Code (*2013 évi V törvény a Polgári Törvénykönyvről*), *MK* 2013/31 (II 26), with later amendments.

96  The remark is based on the information received from Jerzy Pisuliński (the former head of the Polish Civil Law Codification Commission and a member of the steering committee of the ADCC).

97  E.g. Jerzy Pisuliński in Sawczuk (n 4) 60–61.

98  Dimitri Steinke, *Die Zivilrechtsordnungen des Baltikums unter dem Einfluss ausländischer, insbesondere deutscher Rechtsquellen* (V&R Unipress, Universitätsverlag Osnabrück 2009) 220.

99  Ulrich Schulze, 'Das litauische Zivilrecht – Entwicklung, IPR und Allgemeiner Teil' [2001] *WGO* 331, 332; but see Martin Käerdi, 'Die Neukodifikation des Privatrechts der baltischen Staaten in vergleichender Sicht' in Helmut Heiss (ed), *Zivilrechtsreform im Baltikum* (Mohr Siebeck 2006) 22–23.

strong influence on the shape of the Lithuanian CK.[100] The remarks made in the Commentary to the UPICC were even adopted directly in the text of the code.[101]

The proposals of revision of German law of obligations and the new Dutch BW were considered during the preparation of the Estonian VÕS.[102] Further, Quebec's, Louisiana's, Swiss, and other regulations on obligations law have been suggested as additional sources of inspiration for the reform of Estonian private law.[103] Also, Estonian VÕS was strongly influenced by PECL, UPICC, and CISG.[104]

Such a significant impact of foreign law on the drafted acts can be explained if these countries' history is considered. As noticed in the legal literature, at the time these countries regained their independence, their legal system was fully regulated by Soviet Union legislation that was not responding to the needs of these newly established countries. Many norms were incompatible with new principles and a number of areas were not regulated completely or at all.[105] Therefore, in both countries a rapid change of laws – including the immediate introduction of a new civil law – was necessary.[106] As these two countries had limited human resources, were under time pressure, and did not have any legislation that was in force before the Soviet occupation that they could revive,[107] they could not prepare original drafts that would be grounded

100  Valentinas Mikelenas, 'Unification and Harmonisation of Law at the Turn of the Millennium: The Lithuanian Experience' (2000) 5 *Unif L Rev* 243, 251. See also Käerdi, 'Die Neukodifikation' (n 99) 22–23; Tadas Zukas, 'Reception of the Unidroit Principles of International Commercial Contracts and the Principles of European Contract Law in Lithuania' in Eleanor Cashin-Ritaine and Eva Lein (eds), *The UNIDROIT Principles 2004: Their Impact on Contractual Practice, Jurisprudence and Codification: Reports of the ISDC Colloquium (8/9 June 2006)* (Schulthess 2007) 232ff.

101  Tadas Zukas describes therefore the text of the Code as having also informative and educational functions and being like a textbook. Tadas Zukas, *Einfluss der 'Unidroit Principles of International Commercial Contracts' und der 'Principles of European Contract Law' auf die Transformation des Vertragsrechts in Litauen* (Stämpfli Verlag AG 2011) 58, 62–63.

102  Villu Kõve, 'Applicable Law in the Light of Modern Law of Obligations and Bases for the Preparation of the Law of Obligations Act' [2001] *Juridica Intl* 30, 36; Mikk (n 89) 39–40; Käerdi, 'Estonia and the New Civil Law' (n 89) 258–59; Irene Kull, 'Reform of Contract Law in Estonia: Influences of Harmonisation of European Private Law' [2008] *Juridica Intl* 122, 127–28.

103  Paul Varul, 'Legal Policy Decisions and Choices in the Creation of New Private Law in Estonia' [2000] *Juridica Intl* 104, 114; Paul Varul, 'Creation of New Private Law in Estonia' (2000) 31 *Rechtstheorie* 349, 363; Kõve (n 102) 36; Paul Varul, 'Estonian Private Law and the European Union' in Jānis Lazdiņš (ed), *Tiesību transformācijas problēmas sakarā ar integrāciju Eiropas Savienībā: starptautiskās konferences materiāli: Problems of Transformation of Law in Connection with European Integration* (Rīga Latvijas Univ, Juridiskā fak 2002) 200; Paul Varul, 'The Creation of New Estonian Private Law' (2008) 16 *ERPL* 95, 105.

104  Mikk (n 89) 39–40; Käerdi, 'Die Neukodifikation' (n 99) 22. For details see Kull, 'Reform of Contract Law' (n 102) 122, 127–28.

105  Varul, 'Creation of New Private Law' (n 103) 349.

106  Luboš Tichý, 'Processes of Modernisation of Private Law Compared, and the CFR's Influence' [2008] *Juridica Intl* 35, 36; Paul Varul, 'The Impact of Harmonisation of Private Law on the Reform of Civil Law in the New Member States' in Roger Brownsword and others (eds), *The Foundations of European Private Law* (Hart Publishing 2011) 287.

107  Varul, 'The Creation of New Estonian Private Law' (n 103) 98.

(solely or, at least) mostly in their legal culture. Transplanting legal solutions, which have been tried already in the Western countries, allowed constructing effective national law and enabled these countries to take part in international collaboration.[108]

The standards present in legislation applied in Western jurisdictions were also adopted in Croatia and Slovenia. However, the reform of the law involved transplanting legal solutions to a much smaller degree than it was done in the discussed Baltic states. In the post-Yugoslavian countries, the law of obligations was strongly influenced by the Yugoslav Obligations Act of 1978 that was binding in these jurisdictions before the legislative acts were introduced. According to the opinion represented in the legal literature, the current Slovenian OblZ is a slightly updated and extended, but not really modernized version of the Yugoslav Obligations Act.[109] The Slovenian OblZ is strongly based on the solutions adopted in the Yugoslav Obligations Act of 1978 that was – in turn – inspired by the ABGB; the OblZ has also been impacted by the EU law, CISG, and the developments in the German case law.[110] Also in case of the Croatian ZOO, most of the legal provisions included in it have been transferred from the Yugoslav Obligations Act of 1978.[111] Applying this solution is not surprising, as the Yugoslavian law on obligations has been described as 'very modern' and 'very capable of functioning under the changed economic circumstances'.[112] But it is also recognized that the transplanted provisions were enriched by general standard provisions responding to the needs of the time – provisions that were lacking in the earlier legislation.[113]

The two newest codifications, the one from the Czech Republic and the one from Hungary, are for the most part based on their own unique legal heritage. The Czech NOZ is based primarily on the revised draft of the Czechoslovak's Civil Code of 1937 for preparation of which ABGB served as an example.[114]

108 Varul, 'Creation of New Private Law' (n 103) 358.
109 Claudia Rudolf, 'Slowenien: Neues Schuldgesetzbuch in Kraft' [2002] WGO 7, 8; Damjan Možina, 'Harmonisation of Private Law in Europe and the Development of Private Law in Slovenia' [2008] *Juridica Intl* 173, 174–75. Similarly, Verica Trstenjak, 'Das ABGB in Slowenien' in Constanze Fischer-Czermak and others (eds), *Festschrift 200 Jahre ABGB*, vol 1 (MANZ Verlag Wien 2011) 298–99. See also Ada Polajnar-Pavcik, 'Neukodifikationen des Privatrechts in Slowenien' in Peter Blaho and Jan Švidroň (eds), *Kodifikácia, europeizácia a harmonizácia súkromného práva* (Bratislava Iura Ed 2005) 204–5.
110 Trstenjak, 'Das neue slowenische Obligationenrecht' (n 92) 110.
111 Zvonimir Slakoper, 'Allgemeines Bürgerliches Gesetzbuch (ABGB) und kroatisches bürgerliches Recht' in Michael Geistlinger and others (eds), *200 Jahre ABGB – Ausstrahlungen: Die Bedeutung der Kodifikation für andere Staaten und andere Rechtskulturen* (MANZ Verlag Wien 2011) 109.
112 Tichý, 'Processes of Modernisation' (n 106).
113 Slakoper (n 111) 109.
114 Luboš Tichý, 'Stand und Entwicklung des Privatrechts und der Tschechischen Republik' in Rudolf Welser (ed), *Privatrechtsentwicklung in Zentral- und Osteuropa* (MANZ Verlag Wien 2008) 27; Josef Bejcek, 'Das ABGB und das tschechische Zivil- und Handelsrecht' in Michael Geistlinger and others (eds), *200 Jahre ABGB – Ausstrahlungen: Die Bedeutung der Kodifikation für andere Staaten und andere Rechtskulturen* (MANZ Verlag Wien 2011) 169, 180; Kristian Csach and Miriam Laclavikova,

But influences of the Swiss OR, *Code civil du Québec,* Italian *Codice Civile,* and American common law can be identified in the Czech NOZ as well.[115] PECL, DCFR, and UPICC played no important role in the preparation of the Czech codification.[116]

The shape of the current Hungarian Ptk has been influenced by the earlier Hungarian Civil Code of 1959 and the unregulated law binding before 1959.[117] For instance, the regulation of the law of obligations follows in many aspects the regulation of the Civil Code of 1959.[118] But drafters of the newest code referred in their work also to the French CCiv, Austrian ABGB, German BGB, and the Swiss ZGB.[119] Dutch BW was an important source of inspiration. Hungarian drafters took into account UPICC, PECL, and DCFR. But also, CISG played a significant role in the preparation of the newest code.[120]

Each of these two countries (the Czech Republic and Hungary) retained a relative autonomy after the World War II thanks to which codifications of their private law were influenced by the Soviet law only to a certain degree.[121] In both countries, the civil codes were amended and new laws were introduced to adjust the legal systems to the changes that took place after the politically-economic transformation. There was no immediate need to draft a new civil codification.[122] However, unlike Hungary that used its Civil Code of 1959 as the basis for the new Ptk, Czech referred to the provisions of the draft of a civil code from 1937 for the preparation of their newest NOZ. That might be explained by looking at the content of the Czech Civil Code of 1964, which has been described as 'the most distinct attempt to deviate from the concept of civil law found in Roman law'.[123]

---

'Das ABGB und das slowakische Zivilrecht' in Michael Geistlinger and others (eds), *200 Jahre ABGB – Ausstrahlungen: Die Bedeutung der Kodifikation für andere Staaten und andere Rechtskulturen* (MANZ Verlag Wien 2011) 167.

115  Tichý, 'Stand und Entwicklung' (n 114) 27. Peter Bohata lists also German BGB as a source of inspiration for the new code: Peter Bohata, 'Neugestaltung des tschechischen Zivilrechts – Teil 1 – Allgemeiner Teil des zukünftigen BGB' [2011] *WiRO* 353, 354. Josef Bejcek adds also Dutch and Russian codification as having an impact on the new Czech NOZ: Bejcek (n 114) 180. For more possible sources see David Elischer, 'The New Czech Civil Code: Principles, Perspectives and Objectives of Actual Czech Civil Law Recodification: On the Way to Monistic Conception of Obligation Law?' (2010) 19 *Dereito* 431, 437.

116  Tichý, 'Stand und Entwicklung' (n 114) 27.

117  Herbert Küpper, 'Ungarns neues BGB – Teil 1: Entstehung und Inhalt' [2014] *WiRO* 129, 131.

118  ibid 133.

119  Lajos Vékás, 'Über die Expertenvorlage eines neuen Zivilgesetzbuches für Ungarn' [2009] *ZeuP* 536, 539. Herbert Küpper lists also Italy and Quebec's civil codes as sources of inspiration for the drafters: Küpper (n 117) 131.

120  Vékás, 'Über die Expertenvorlage' (n 119) 540; Gábor Hamza, 'Geschichte der Kodifikation des Zivilrechts in Ungarn' (2008) 12 *Anuario da Facultade de Dereito da Universidade da Coruña* 533, 543.

121  Tichý, 'Processes of Modernisation' (n 106).

122  András Kisfaludi, 'The Influence of Harmonisation of Private Law on the Development of the Civil Law in Hungary' (2008) *Juridica Intl*, 131–32; Varul, 'The Impact of Harmonisation' (n 106) 286.

123  Tichý, 'Processes of Modernisation' (n 106).

In the legal literature, it has been stated that the ADCC relies on the text of the current Polish KC 'as much as possible' and aims at including 'all the private law regulations dispersed throughout the entire system into the civil code'.[124] The explanatory memorandum published together with the General Part of the ADCC does not explicitly identify legislations used as the drafters' source of inspiration. But when discussing proposals of specific legal provisions references to Austrian, Dutch, French, German, Lithuanian, Russian, Swiss, and also Ukrainian legal provisions as well as to solutions applying under English common law are made. Also, provisions suggested in the chosen documents harmonizing European private law (e.g. DCFR) are considered. Moreover, the participation of Dutch experts in the preparation of the ADCC is also explicitly acknowledged. Furthermore, as Jerzy Pisuliński, a member of the steering committee of ADCC, in his publication in which he discussed the proposed structure of the book governing the law of obligations, considers the structure of this part in German and Swiss civil codes, as well as in the Dutch and Quebec's civil codes, it can be assumed that also Quebec's civil code was taken into account during the preparation of the General Part of the ADCC.[125]

It seems the history of the codification of Polish private law bears the strongest resemblance to the history of codifying the Hungarian private law. In both countries, modern civil codes were introduced around the year 1960 – in 1959 (for Hungary) and 1964 (for Poland) – that, after being modernized, were able to regulate private relationships even after (i) the political, economic, and social transformations that took place post-1990; (ii) accession of these countries to the European Union; and (iii) under the newest market developments. Unlike the Czech Civil Code, the Polish and the Hungarian civil codes were praised for their high quality. Unquestionably, the future Polish Civil Code should be based on the Polish legal heritage rather than on transplants of new and, unfamiliar to, Polish law solutions. Nevertheless, as was done during preparatory work of all the discussed acts, regulations adopted in other countries, as well as regulations proposed in documents aiming at harmonization of European private law, should be considered. Applying this method would facilitate drafting a modern civil code that could effectively function in the Polish legal system.

## 3.3 Freedom of contract and its limitations

### 3.3.1 General

The principle of freedom of contract is binding in the private law of all the discussed states, but it isn't expressly articulated in each of them.

---

124 Łętowska and Wiewiórowska-Domagalska (n 4) 288.
125 Jerzy Pisuliński, 'Struktura części ogólnej prawa zobowiązań (Wprowadzenie do dyskusji)' [2017]
    (2) *Transform Prawa Prywat* 37, 42–43.

Since 1992 the fundamental general principle of freedom of contract belongs to the primary principles of the Lithuanian legal system.[126] This principle is regulated in Art 46 of the Lithuanian Constitution. It is also regulated in the Lithuanian CK. In Lithuania, as it is also in Estonia, references to the principle of freedom of contract are made more than once in the civil code. In Lithuanian CK the freedom of contract is listed as one of the principles of legal regulation of civil relationships in the second article of the CK (Art 1.2), the limits of the freedom are regulated in Arts 1.80 and 1.81, and additionally, Art 6.156 provides a detailed explanation of the principle.[127] It has been stated that Lithuanian CK copied the rule regulated in UPICC, but provided it with 'greater detail by defining its content and limits'.[128] One of the purposes of this inclusion was to facilitate change in the way of thinking about law. Namely, to expressly confirm that not all legal provisions are binding.[129] The same culture – to 'write down in law everything that is covered in the developed countries by the laws and the legal dogmatics outside written law, [to] avoid disputes over the application and substance of law' – is identifiable in Estonia.[130] Under the Estonian legislation, the scope of the freedom of contract is regulated in the General Part of the Civil Code (TsÜS) as well as in the VÕS. Regulating it in the TsÜS aimed at allowing answering the question whether a legal transaction is valid – for the most part – on the basis of this part of the code.[131] In the legal literature discussing the law on obligations of these two countries, the multiple references to this principle are justified by the novelty of this concept to these two jurisdictions. Under Lithuanian law, neither the Civil Code of 1964 nor the Soviet legal doctrine recognized the principle of the freedom of contract.[132] Therefore, the additional explanation included in Art 6.156 aimed at assisting proper interpretation of the principle in Lithuania. In particular, 'the very detailed regulation is expected to be instrumental in ensuring a more authentic interpretation and more efficient application of these articles in the future.'[133] Also, under the Soviet civil law previously binding in Estonia, the principle of freedom of contract was not available to the parties of civil relationships.[134] Including this principle in Estonian law has been

---

126  Zukas, *Einfluss* (n 101) 56.

127  The practical interpretation of this provision raises a number of questions, see ibid, 58–59.

128  Mikelenas, 'Unification and Harmonisation of Law' (n 100) 253. But see Zukas, *Einfluss* (n 101) 58, 62–63.

129  Zukas, *Einfluss* (n 101) 58, 63.

130  Irene Kull, 'European and Estonian Law of Obligations: Transposition of Law or Mutual Influence?' [2004] *Juridica Intl* 32, 33. See also Marju Luts, 'Textbook of Pandects or New Style of Legislation in Estonia?' [2001] *Juridica Intl* 152, 157–58.

131  Paul Varul, 'The New Estonian Civil Code' in Helmut Heiss (ed), *Zivilrechtsreform im Baltikum* (Mohr Siebeck 2006) 53.

132  Valentinas Mikelenas, 'The Influence of Instruments of Harmonisation of Private Law upon the Reform of Civil Law in Lithuania' [2008] *Juridica Intl* 143, 147.

133  Mikelenas, 'Unification and Harmonisation of Law' (n 100) 253.

134  Irene Kull, 'Effect of Harmonisation of European Civil Law on Development of Estonian Law of Obligations' [1998] *Juridica Intl* 98, 98–102.

seen as one of the results of 'the process of harmonisation of the European civil law' influencing the nature of Estonian private law.[135]

The principle of freedom of contract is itemized as one of the fundamental principles of the law of obligations also in the Hungarian Ptk. Its meaning is explicitly articulated in § 6:59 Ptk.

The laws adopted in Slovenia, Croatia, and the Czech Republic do not include a provision that merely proclaims the principle of freedom of contract. Instead, they provide parties with the freedom of contract by allowing them to regulate their obligations at their discretion within the established limits (in Slovenian OblZ this freedom is stated twice: in Art 2 and Art 3). It can only be assumed that as this principle was known and applied in these jurisdictions before the new laws were introduced, there was no need of defining it in any additional way.

ADCC includes a provision expressly stating the freedom to determine the content of a legal transaction by its parties (Art 54 ADCC). However, it does not provide a detailed definition thereof. This provision is a successor of Art 353[1] KC.[136]

### 3.3.2 Limitations

In none of the discussed jurisdictions is the freedom of contract unlimited.

#### 3.3.2.1 THE LOCALIZATION OF THE LEGAL PROVISIONS REGULATING THE LIMITATIONS

The location of the provision limiting the freedom of contract varies in the discussed states within the given legal act and private law.

In Lithuanian, Estonian, and Czech civil codes the limitations of the freedom of contract are regulated in the first book (part) of the code. And so, under Lithuanian law, the limitations of the freedom of concluding any (legal) transaction is regulated in Arts 1.80 and 1.81 located in Chapter IV (Voidability of transactions) of Part II (Transactions) of Book One (General Provisions) of the CK.[137] In Estonian TsÜS the restrictions imposed upon the freedom to conclude any legal transaction – §§ 86 and 87 – are located in Division 1 (Void Transaction) of Chapter 5 (Invalidity of Transaction) in Part 4 (Transactions). In the Czech NOZ, the limitations of freedom of concluding any juridical act provided in § 1(2) are regulated already in the first chapter (Private law) of the Title I (Scope of regulation and its basic principles) of Book One (General provisions). In Estonia, the limitations of the freedom of contract (§ 5) are also regulated in Chapter 1 (General Provisions) of Part I (General Part) of the VÕS.

---

135  ibid.
136  ADCC with Commentary (n 62).
137  Regulating concept and form of transactions (Chapter III of Part II) and voidability of transactions (Chapter IV of Part II) in the Book One (General Provisions) strongly resemble the German regulation of the General Part of BGB. See Steinke (n 98) 220.

In the Slovenian OblZ, Art 3 is located in Title I (Basic Principles) of Book 1 (General Part of the OblZ). Also, in Croatian ZOO, the relevant provision (Art 2) is regulated in Title I (Basic Principles) of Part I (General Principles) of the ZOO. As there are no civil codes systematizing the entire private law in Slovenia and Croatia, it is understandable that the legal provision providing limitations of freedom of contract is one of the basic principles stated at the beginning of the acts regulating law on obligations. As there is no act governing the general part of civil (private) law, the provisions regulating contract law apply to other juridical acts as well.[138] Namely, Art 14 of the Slovenian OblZ extends the application of the sense of the provisions regulating contracts to other legal transactions and Art 14(3) of the Croatian ZOO extends, as far as it is appropriate, the application of provisions regulating contracts to other legal transactions.[139]

Under Hungarian law, limitations of the freedom of contract are regulated in Ptk, §§ 6:95 and 6:96. The provisions are located in a section dedicated to defects in the intended legal effects located in Chapter XVIII (Nullity and Avoidance) of Title VI (Invalidity) in the second part (General provisions on contracts) of Book Six (Law of obligations) of Ptk. Two reasons for that solution can be named. Namely, the Ptk does not include a general part applying to all areas of law regulated by the Code.[140] Further, this manner of regulation follows the pattern binding under the (previous) Hungarian Civil Code of 1959.[141]

In ADCC the limitations of the freedom to conclude a legal transaction are regulated in Art 70 located in Chapter I (General provisions) of Section IV (Contradiction of a legal transaction with the law) of Title III (Declarations and legal transactions) of Book One (General Part).

The Polish proposal harmonizes with the solutions adopted in the newest civil codes adopted in Central and Southeast European countries. The general tendency is to include limitations of the freedom of contract already in the general part of civil code (Hungarian solution is an exception). However, the position of the provision proposed by Polish scholars is not as prestigious as it is in the Czech NOZ, the first section of which regulates this matter. However, due to historical reasons, all provisions of the Czech NOZ are subordinated to this principle.[142] Namely, during the communism era, private law was seen as a

---

138  Trstenjak, 'Das neue slowenische Obligationenrecht' (n 92) 94.

139  Saša Nikšić, 'Contract Law' in Tatjana Josipović (ed), *Introduction to the Law of Croatia* (Wolters Kluwer 2014) 136.

140  Lajos Vékás, 'Über das ungarische Zivilgesetzbuch im Spiegel der neueren europäischen Privatrechtsentwicklung' [2016] *ZeuP* 37, 43; Küpper (n 117) 131.

141  Nevertheless, unlike the Civil Code of 1959, the new Ptk regulates in the first part of the Book Six common provisions relating to obligations and only in the second part general provisions on contracts. See Küpper (n 117) 132–33.

142  Peter Bohata, 'Grundsatzentwurf des neuen tschechischen Zivilrechts' [2001] *WiRO* 295.

tool used by the state to harass the private lives of Czech citizens.[143] Therefore, now, the application of limitations of private autonomy and its interpretation are restricted. Also, with exception of the Czech NOZ, in all considered civil codes (but not in the acts regulating the law on obligations), the regulation of the limitations of freedom of contract is located in the part discussing effects of any defects of the content of a contract or a juridical act. ADCC adopts the same solution.

### 3.3.2.2 ACTS TO WHICH THE LIMITATIONS APPLY

Under most considered civil codes the freedom of contract is formulated as the freedom to conclude any legal transaction (any juridical act) that creates obligations. That is the case under Lithuanian law (Arts 1.80 and 1.81 CK),[144] Estonian law (§ 86 TsÜS), and Czech law (§ 1(2) NOZ).[145]

It was a conscious choice of the drafters of the Hungarian Ptk to follow the decision made during the preparation of the Hungarian Civil Code of 1959 and treat the contract (and not juridical act) as the basic category for the regulation of the law of obligations. The decision was supported with arguments that 'the notion of juridical act, its types, creation, amendment, fulfilment and termination is in the closest relationship with the rules of contract; the juridical act as such is nothing else than a common denominator of artificially abstracted elements of contract and the exceptional cases of unilateral declarations'.[146] Therefore, §§ 6:95 and 6:96 Ptk apply to 'any contract'. Consequently, the Ptk includes provisions extending the application of common provisions on obligations and general provisions on contracts to obligations arising from unilateral acts (§ 6:2(2) Ptk). The general provisions on contracts regarding the effect, nullity, and invalidity apply also to legal statements (§ 6:9 Ptk).[147]

Also, Slovenian OblZ and Croatian ZOO use the terms 'an obligation or contract'. However, that seems instinctive since these acts regulate only the law on obligations. Moreover, as there is no act regulating the general part of civil (private) law, the provisions regulating contract law apply to other juridical acts as well.[148] Namely, Art 14 of the Slovenian OblZ and Art 14(3) of the Croatian ZOO generally extend the application (of the sense) of provisions regulating contracts to other legal transactions.[149]

---

143  Peter Bohata, 'Neugestaltung des tschechischen Zivilrechts – Teil 2 – Sachen und Rechtsgeschäfte' [2012] *WiRO* 7, 11.

144  In the legal literature it is expressly stated that the regulation applies also to contracts, see Valentinas Mikelenas, 'The Main Features of the New Lithuanian Contract Law System Based on the Civil Code of 2000' [2005] *Juridica Intl* 42, 43.

145  Bohata, 'Neugestaltung – Teil 1' (n 115) 354; Bohata, 'Neugestaltung – Teil 2' (n 143) 10.

146  Official Explanation prepared by the Minister of Justice (Budapest, 1963) 26 after Peter Gardos, 'Recodification of the Hungarian Civil Law' (2007) 15 *ERPL* 707, 718.

147  A legal statement is defined in § 6:4(1) Ptk as 'a unilateral act intended to have legal effect'.

148  Trstenjak, 'Das neue slowenische Obligationenrecht' (n 92) 94.

149  Nikšić (n 139) 136.

Proposal of Art 70 ADCC sets limits of the freedom to conclude any juridical act. Article 58 of the current Polish KC uses the same terminology. Further, it is proposed to locate the provision in the General Part of the new Civil Code, so it is only reasonable to make it clearly applicable to any legal transaction.

3.3.2.3 LIMITATIONS IMPOSED ON THE FREEDOM TO DETERMINE
THE CONTENT OF A LEGAL TRANSACTION OR A CONTRACT

The limitations of the freedom of contract (or of concluding any legal transaction) vary in the legal systems of the discussed states.

In Lithuania, the limitations of concluding any legal transactions are set in Arts 1.80 and 1.81 CK. Article 1.80(1) states that 'any transaction that fails to meet the requirements of mandatory statutory provisions shall be null and void'. Also, according to Art 1.81(1), 'a transaction that is contrary to public order or norms of good morals shall be null and void.' As a result of violating the limitations, a legal transaction is null and void;[150] parties are entitled to restitution.[151] The relationship between these limitations is controversial. A view that violation of legal provisions always amounts to a violation of public order and good morals has been presented in Lithuanian legal literature. However, some argue that violation of mandatory legal provisions can also be found if public order has not been violated. First, public order regards only the most important mandatory legal provisions involving fundamental values. Second, Art 1.81 provides different consequences for violating public order and good morals than Art 1.80 for violating mandatory norms.[152]

In Estonia, according to § 86(1) TsÜS, 'a transaction which is contrary to good morals or public order is void.'[153] A further limitation is established in § 87 TsÜS: 'A transaction contrary to a prohibition arising from the law is void if the purpose of the prohibition is to render the transaction void upon violation of the prohibition, especially if it is provided by law that a certain legal consequence must not arise.'[154] Additionally, § 5 VÕS states:

> Upon agreement between the parties to an obligation or contract, the parties may derogate from the provisions of this Act unless this Act expressly provides or the nature of a provision indicates that derogation from this Act

---

150 Unless the nullity would affect only a single term of a contract – in that case the rest of the contract remains valid, 'except if it appears that the contracting parties would not have entered into the contract without the condition affected by nullity', see Laurynas Didžiulis, *Contract Law in Lithuania* (Wolters Kluwer 2019) para 296.
151 ibid para 299.
152 For details see ibid para 287.
153 This paragraph was adopted on 25 February 2009 and entered into force on 1 May 2009 (*RT* I 2009, 18, 108).
154 As noticed by Paul Varul, 'the general rules on legal acts as provided in the GPCCA are of the greatest relevance to the law of obligations'. Varul, 'The Creation of New Estonian Private Law' in Lazdiņš (n 103) 102.

is not permitted, or unless derogation is contrary to public order or good morals or violates the fundamental rights of a person.

The principle of freedom of contract is based on the foundation that 'anything not prohibited is allowed'.[155] As it can be extracted from relevant provisions, the parties' freedom of contract is limited by mandatory provisions, public order, good morals, and the fundamental rights of a person. Nevertheless, as noted by Irene Kull in context of Estonian law, 'any restrictions concerning the content must be justified socially and economically because interference into contractual relations means recognition of certain way of life, standards, convictions and models of conduct.'[156]

Slovenian and Croatian provisions are similar to each other. In Slovenia, Art 3 OblZ states that 'participants shall be free to regulate obligational relationships, but may not act in contravention of the Constitution, compulsory regulations or moral principles'. Therefore, freedom of contract is limited by the principles of the Constitution of the Republic of Slovenia, compulsory legal provisions, and moral principles. The consequences of violation of one of the limitations are regulated in Arts 86 and following the OblZ.

In Croatia, Art 2 ZOO provides that 'the parties are free to regulate their obligations, and these must be in compliance with the Constitution of the Republic of Croatia, mandatory laws and the morals of the society'. Freedom of contract is limited by the principles of the Constitution of the Republic of Croatia, mandatory legal provisions, and public morality. As a result of violating any of these limitations, a contract is null and void and as such produces no legal effects.[157]

The Czech NOZ, § 1(2) states that

> unless expressly prohibited by a statute, persons can stipulate rights and duties by way of exclusion from a statute; stipulations contrary to good morals, public order or the law concerning the status of persons, including the right to protection of personality rights, are prohibited.

Therefore, the freedom of concluding any juridical act is limited by mandatory (imperative) statutory provisions, good morals, public order, and the law concerning the status of persons, including the right to protection of personality rights. Not all these limitations have the same function. Only a violation of mandatory (and not dispositive) statutory provisions or a violation of good

---

155 Kull, 'Effect of Harmonisation' (n 134) 98–102.
156 Irene Kull, 'Principle of Freedom of Contract in European Civil Law and Reform of Law of Obligations in Estonia' in Jānis Lazdiņš (ed), *Tiesību transformācijas problēmas sakarā ar integrāciju Eiropas Savienībā: starptautiskās konferences materiāli: Problems of Transformation of Law in Connection with European Integration* (Rīga Latvijas Univ, Juridiskā fak 2002) 232–33. See also Varul, 'Legal Policy Decisions' (n 103) 112.
157 Nikšić (n 139) 148, 152.

morals – regardless of whether actual damage occurred[158] – always leads to the invalidity of a juridical act.[159] In other words, violation of good morals, even if it does not violate statutory provisions, is a ground for a juridical act's invalidity.[160] But a violation of public order leads to the invalidity only if there is a legal provision stipulating a rule constituting part of the public order.[161] Also the limitation of the 'law concerning the status of persons, including the right to protection of personality rights' does not constitute an autonomous limitation, but has to be understood together with the legal provisions providing these laws (e.g. § 19 NOZ) and limits the freedom only if a provision of a juridical act is also contrary to statutory laws or good morals.[162]

In Hungary, the limitations are regulated in two separate legal provisions. Ptk, § 6:95 provides that 'any contract which is incompatible with the law or that was concluded by circumventing the law shall be null and void unless the relevant legislation stipulates another legal consequence'. Ptk, § 6:96 adds that 'a contract shall be null and void if it is manifestly in contradiction to good morals'. Therefore, freedom of contract is limited by the law and good morals. A contract cannot be concluded by circumventing the law.

### 3.3.2.4 INTERPRETATION OF THE LIMITATIONS

*3.3.2.4.1 Mandatory legal provisions*    All legal provisions setting limits for contractual freedom prohibit concluding contracts that violate mandatory statutory provisions. The most significant difference resides in the interpretation of this limitation and its application.

The most restrictive interpretation of the limitation of the freedom of concluding any legal transaction seems to apply in the Czech Republic. According to Czech scholars, statutory provisions limiting freedom of concluding any legal transaction should be understood as any provisions regulated in statutory law, but not necessarily as any legal norms that can be deduced from such provisions.[163] Therefore, legislation must explicitly prohibit contractual regulations for them to limit the parties' freedom.[164] Mandatory legal provisions can be identified because they prohibit, order invalidity, or impart no legal consequences of a particular contractual regulation. Only these provisions limit the freedom of concluding a judicial act.[165] This solution was applied to provide clarity and prevent any limitations of the freedom of concluding any legal transaction through an unfounded interpretation of legal provisions that

---

158  Jan Petrov, *Občanský zákoník: komentář* (CH Beck 2017) Art 1 para 46.
159  ibid Art 1 paras 38ff and 45.
160  But see exceptions ibid Art 1 para 45.
161  ibid Art 1 para 49.
162  ibid Art 1 paras 57–58.
163  Bohata, 'Neugestaltung – Teil 1' (n 115) 355.
164  ibid 356.
165  ibid.

would be too far-reaching (as has happened in the past).[166] Namely, under the previous Civil Code, there was a tendency to adjudicate invalidity of a legal transaction if its content contradicted statutory law to any extent.[167] Special emphasis is put on the protection of 'the law concerning the status of persons, including the right to protection of personality rights' (§ 1(2) NOZ). Violating these rights might be considered as an argument for finding a contractual stipulation contradicting a legal provision invalid.[168]

Compulsory regulations are also understood very narrowly in Slovenia. In this state they include only provisions providing legal prohibitions or provisions determining mandatory ways of carrying out certain actions.[169] Even though the Constitution of the Republic of Slovenia is explicitly named as a limitation of the freedom, it is unlikely that a contract could be found void based only on contradicting it. The Constitution includes only a few general rules that are applicable to contract law. Further, 'the human rights regulated by the Constitution are directly applicable against the state (vertical relationships) and principally not in contracts between private persons (horizontal relationships).'[170] Also in Croatia, as Croatian practitioners point out, it is unlikely that a contract or obligation would be found invalid solely on the basis of it contradicting the Constitution. The Constitution of the Republic of Croatia does not contain any provisions that could directly apply to contracts or obligations.

In these three countries and Estonia, provisions limiting the freedom of concluding any legal transaction also reference to a specific legal act (Constitution) or set of laws ('the fundamental rights of a person' and 'law concerning the status of persons, including the right to protection of personality rights'). As previously mentioned, in none of these countries do they function as autonomous limitations of the freedom of contract. It seems they were added to stress the importance of these laws and provide a directive of interpretation of other legal provisions.

Interpretation of the mandatory statutory provision is also significantly restricted under Lithuanian law. In Lithuania 'mandatory statutory provisions' are to be understood as 'imperative norms of legal act'.[171] Statutory provisions can be regulated in any area of law (public or private). However, if a contract

---

166 ibid. David Elischer commented the direction of the regulations of the Czech NOZ by stating: 'Philosophically said, the draft of Czech Civil Code seeks to achieve the ideals of Europeanism and humanism. The major axis of whole draft is a human being and his interests which are predominantly individual in private law sphere. It is the end of preferring any kind of collectivism and higher protection of collective interests.' Elischer (n 115) 438.

167 Milan Hulmak in Heinz-Bernd Wabnitz and Pavel Holländer (eds), *Einführung in das tschechische Recht* (CH Beck 2009) para 45.

168 Bohata, 'Neugestaltung – Teil 2' (n 143) 12.

169 Damjan Možina and Ana Vlahek, *Contract Law in Slovenia* (Wolters Kluwer 2019) para 176.

170 ibid para 175.

171 Jaunius Gumbis, 'The Impact of the ABGB on the Lithuanian Civil Law' in Michael Geistlinger and others (eds), *200 Jahre ABGB – Ausstrahlungen: Die Bedeutung der Kodifikation für andere Staaten und andere Rechtskulturen* (MANZ Verlag Wien 2011) 197, 206.

is concluded by a person lacking the administrative authorization mandatory to start regulated activities, considering current case law, its validity depends on the area of law in which the contract was regulated.[172] The broad scope of this limitation is restricted in the case law by 'adding the requirement to establish violation of fundamental public interest, which requires universally outlawing disputed transactions'.[173]

Estonian law, on the other hand, seems to allow a wider interpretation, as it includes content (in particular, legal prohibitions) and nature (meaning) of the law. Under Estonian Civil Code, parties' agreement may deviate from law, unless it deviates from explicitly articulated content or meaning (nature) of a legal provision interpreted on the basis of that mandatory provision.[174] In other words, the law is contradicted when it 'provides or suggests that deviation is not allowed'.[175] In particular, the content of a contract cannot contradict any legal prohibitions. That also includes laws regulating the extent to which parties may regulate certain issues (e.g. interest on interest is prohibited). Case law can be referred to, to identify such restrictions.[176] Moreover, § 5 VÕS prohibits agreements that violate 'the fundamental rights of a person'. As far as these rights are regulated under the law, they constitute mandatory provisions. Therefore, even though in the legal literature it has been stated that including 'the fundamental rights of a person' (individual rights)[177] as one of the limitations makes the provision 'particularly interesting and innovative',[178] it does not seem to set a new limitation of freedom of contract. As noted previously, it can be seen, however, as a way of stressing the importance of the rights of individuals.

In Hungary, the 'law' limiting the freedom of contract is understood as mandatory rules explicitly provided in a statute. Contractual stipulations cannot therefore violate and must comply with statutory provisions.[179]

The regulation proposed in ADCC also includes statutory law as a limitation of the freedom of concluding any legal transaction. However, it seems that the draft proclaims the widest possible interpretation, as it is supposed to include any imperative norms regulating parties' rights and obligations. This proposal significantly differs from laws binding in other Central and Eastern European countries. It leaves courts the most extensive discretion and provides no emergency valves that could limit it. It can be treated as an argument suggesting

---

172  See Didžiulis (n 150) para 283.
173  LAT judgment of 4 May 2005, 3K-3-263/2005, and LAT judgment of 21 September 2005, 3K-3-416/2005, after Didžiulis (n 150) para 282.
174  Kõve (n 102) 35. See also Dutch BW, Art 3:40.
175  Varul, 'Creation of New Private Law' in Lazdiņš (n 103) 361–62.
176  Kull, 'Principle of Freedom of Contract' in Lazdiņš (n 156) 232–33.
177  Kull, 'Effect of Harmonisation' (n 134) 98–102.
178  Norbert Reich, 'Transformation of Contract Law and Civil Justice in the New EU Member Countries: The Example of the Baltic States, Hungary and Poland' in Fabrizio Cafaggi (ed), *The Institutional Framework of European Private Law* (OUP 2006) 283.
179  Attila Menyhárd, 'Contracts' in Attila Harmathy (ed), *Introduction to Hungarian Law* (2nd edn, Wolters Kluwer 2019) 155.

that the drafting committee believes freedom of contract is a well-respected principle in Poland and Polish courts will not interpret the freedom's limits too extensively.

*3.3.2.4.2 Morals*   In all the discussed jurisdictions, morals (or good morals or decency) seem to be understood in similar ways: as moral or ethical norms generally acknowledged and followed in society.

In Estonia, § 86(2) TsÜS provides examples of when a transaction is contrary to good morals. That takes place:

> *inter alia*, if a party knows or must know at the time of entry into the transaction that the other party enters into the transaction arising from his or her exceptional need, a relationship of dependency, inexperience or other similar circumstances, and if: 1) the transaction has been entered into under conditions which are extremely unfavourable for the other party or 2) the value of the mutual obligations arising for the parties is out of proportion contrary to good morals.[180]

An additional explanation is provided in the legal literature and the case law. Irene Kull defines good morals as 'canons of ethical and moral conduct' commonly recognized by the majority that are based on 'normal sensitivity towards politeness and decency' and that change with time. Currently, 'the protection of individuals' interests, not of the whole society's interests, has become the main objective of legal practice when it comes to voiding a contract on grounds of good morals'.[181] Considering good morals obliges courts to 'proceed from their sense of propriety, and from the sense of propriety applied upon resolving analogous cases in the past'.[182] So far, for instance, the Supreme Court of Estonia (*Riigikohus*, RK) found entering into a contract by a company that was aware of its upcoming bankruptcy[183] or signing a lease for ninety-nine years without the right to terminate it earlier[184] contrary to good morals.

Unlike the other considered acts, the Hungarian Ptk requires that a contract 'manifestly' contradicts good morals.[185] But the understanding of good morals themselves does not vary from the meaning provided in other jurisdictions. Good morals can be defined as 'values generally accepted in the society'.[186]

---

180   For information on the way the provision has been applied see Kull, 'European and Estonian Law of Obligations' (n 130) 36–37.

181   ibid 36–37.

182   Kull, 'Principle of Freedom of Contract' in Lazdiņš (n 156) 232–33.

183   RK decision of 15 October 2002, 3–2–1–102–02, *RT* III 2002, 27, 301 after Kull, 'European and Estonian Law of Obligations' (n 130) 36–37.

184   RK decision of 16 October 2002, 3–2–1–29–02, *RT* III 2002, 14, 164, and RK decision of 24 May 2001, 3–2–1–76–01, *RT* III 2001, 19, 204 after Kull, 'European and Estonian Law of Obligations' (n 130) 36–37.

185   The earlier Civil Code of 1959 included a similar condition in § 200(2).

186   Menyhárd in Harmathy (n 179) 155.

Violation of good morals can be found when contractual stipulations are incompatible with public policy:

> Contracts that are oppressive, restrict the personal freedom excessively, were concluded with the intent to cause harm to others, are detrimental to the public interest, or are incompatible with basic professional and commercial standards, family values or other basic social and economic values, are null and void. The primary source of such basic values is the Fundamental Law.[187]

In most jurisdictions, the meaning of good morals is identified based on case law.

The Supreme Court of Lithuania (*Lietuvos Aukščiausiasis Teismas*, LAT) considers the content of the norms of good morals to be multifaceted and to relate not only to actions but also to their consequences. Moreover, considering good morals in the context of a legal transaction involves taking into account the impact of a legal transaction 'on society, the State and private individuals'.[188] Norms of good morals can be identified as norms regulated in the Decalogue. Therefore, it has been suggested in the legal literature that transactions relating to 'the prostitution, trade in human body parts and tissues' violate these norms.[189] The LAT found a violation of good morals, for example, when a bailiff sold seized property for a very low price[190] or when a transaction aimed at maintaining the unequal division of assets between spouses.[191]

In the Czech Republic, the judiciary defined good morals as 'a summary of social, cultural and moral norms that, in a historical context, confirm some immutability, reflecting important historical trends, are common to critical parts of society and are of basic nature'.[192] In Czech legal literature, good morals are identified as fundamental moral values generally shared by society, the violation of which causes a strong sense of injustice.[193] Inconvenience or departure from ordinary practice does not constitute a violation of good morals.[194]

Under Slovenian law, in particular, agreements violating the principle of good faith or the principle of good commercial practices are considered to be contrary to moral principles. Nevertheless, the practice shows that it is rare that a contract is invalidated solely based on the violation of one of these principles.[195]

Also, under the proposed ADCC the freedom of concluding any legal transactions is restricted by decency. Decency should be understood as moral norms binding in Polish society. It seems that this understanding follows the current interpretation of the principles of community life. As is currently practised, the

---

187  ibid.
188  LAT judgment of 16 January 2006, 3K-3-30/2006 after Didžiulis (n 150) para 284.
189  Didžiulis (n 150) para 286.
190  LAT judgment of 30 December 2008, 3K-3-617/2008 after Didžiulis (n 150) para 286.
191  LAT judgment of 19 June 2008, 3K-3-293/2008 after Didžiulis (n 150) para 286.
192  Petrov (n 158) Art 1 para 47.
193  ibid Art 1 para 46.
194  ibid.
195  Možina and Vlahek (n 169) para 177.

final interpretation of this limitation will be left to the courts and academics. The main difference between the provisions included in the current Polish KC and in the drafted one might be that the drafted provision uses a different name for the general clause than the current legal provisions. Eliminating the principles of community life from the legislative text – as it is recommended in the legal literature – will certainly facilitate a better understanding of this limitation in Poland and abroad.

*3.3.2.4.3 Public order* The limitation of public order (*ordre publique*) is only explicitly articulated in the Lithuanian, Estonian, and Czech civil codes.[196]

As in the case of the term 'good morals', the LAT relates the term 'public policy' not only to actions but also to their consequences.[197] The term encompasses 'main principles, which are the basis for the State legal system and functioning of State and society'. It 'consists of imperative norms of constitutional, administrative and other branches of Lithuanian law'.[198] Examples of transactions violating public order include:

> contracts with criminal content, transactions which hide evidence of a crime, creates illicit privileges, trades in chairs within the civil service, focuses on the evasion of taxes, facilitates hostile activities against the Republic of Lithuania or its allies, making donations solely in order to get State accolades.[199]

Moreover, the LAT decided that a legal transaction circumventing a mandatory bailiff's order made during the enforcement procedure violated public policy.[200]

In the Czech Republic, public order includes basic public policy principles that must be strictly followed.[201] However, a stipulation that contradicts public policy is invalid, only if it contradicts a legal provision at the same time.[202]

Even though public order is not explicitly listed as a limitation of the freedom of contract under Croatian law, its protection is the main purpose of imposing the limitations of freedom of contract.[203]

Even though public order has been listed as a separate limitation of the freedom of concluding any legal transaction, it seems that its application – at least in Lithuania and the Czech Republic – depends on the interpretation of statutory law. As this limitation has no independent standing, naming it in Art 70 ADCC has been rejected. Moreover, in the current Polish KC this restriction

---

196 For comparison see also Art 3:40 of the Dutch BW and Art 1373 CCQ that both include the limitation of 'public order'.
197 LAT judgment of 16 January 2006, 3K-3–30/2006 after Didžiulis (n 150) para 284.
198 Didžiulis (n 150) para 285.
199 ibid.
200 ibid.
201 Petrov (n 158) Art 1 para 49.
202 Bohata, 'Neugestaltung – Teil 2' (n 143) para 29.
203 See e.g. Zvonimir Slakoper and Vilim Gorenc, *Obvezno pravo: Opći dio: Sklapanje, promjene i prestanak ugovora* (Novi informator 2009) 47.

has not been explicitly imposed. There is also no clear reason, explaining the adoption of this limitation in Lithuania, Estonia, or the Czech Republic, that could be used as an argument for introducing it in Poland.

*3.3.2.4.4 Circumvention of the law*   Only Hungarian Ptk prohibits contractual stipulations that circumvent the law. The same limitation was also adopted in § 200(2) of the Hungarian Civil Code of 1959 and had been already known in the uncodified Hungarian law. Therefore, it seems that including it as a limitation of freedom of contract constitutes part of the Hungarian legal heritage. However, as Hungarian scholars point out, this limitation has no practical significance. Only in exceedingly rare cases circumvention of the law serves as a ground for invalidating a legal transaction.

Slovenian and Croatian laws on obligations do not limit the freedom of contract by explicitly prohibiting circumvention of the law. Nevertheless, in both legal systems, the general limitations of the freedom of contract are supplemented by a provision regulating the influence of the parties' impermissible motives (intention) on the validity of their obligations.[204] Namely, under Art 40(2) of the Slovenian OblZ and Art 273(2) of the Croatian ZOO, an impermissible motive that had a significant effect on (Slovenian law) or materially influenced (Croatian law) one of the parties' decision to conclude the contract – the motive that the other contracting party knows or should have known about – causes the contract's invalidity (under Slovenian law) or its ineffectiveness (under Croatian law).[205] Even despite lack of knowledge of the other contracting party, an impermissible motive that had a significant effect on the decision to conclude a contract of the first party deems a gratuitous contract null and void (Art 40(3) of the Slovenian OblZ and Art 273(3) of the Croatian ZOO). If it is accepted that parties' awareness of and the objective to circumvent the law are necessary prerequisites for establishing circumvention of the law, then limiting contractual freedom by considering parties' motives makes prohibiting circumvention of the law redundant. Applying both limitations is likely to lead to the same outcome.

In Polish legal literature, it is argued that including the prohibition of circumvention of the law in Art 58 KC was caused by the incorrect classification of legal transactions circumventing the law as violating the principles of community life before 1965. The explicit articulation of this prohibition in Art 58 KC aimed at preventing this classification after 1965 and at providing clarity.[206] According to the currently prevalent opinion represented in the legal literature, transactions having as an objective circumvention of the law are contrary to the law. However, the court practice shows that there are cases in which a legal

---

204 A contract was ineffective due to parties' prohibited motives also under the Yugoslav Obligations Act of 1978. See Art 53 YZOO.
205 For more information on Croatian law see Vilim Gorenc (ed), *Komentar Zakona o obveznim odnosima* (Narodne novine 2014) Art 273 paras 1ff.
206 Radwański, *Prawo cywilne* (n 26) ch V § 23 para 19.

transaction cannot be found invalid based on any other ground than the circumvention of the law.[207] As Art 70 ADCC explicitly names a contrary to law purpose of a legal transaction as a ground for a transaction's potential invalidity, stipulating the prohibition of circumvention of the law as a limitation of the freedom of contract seems unnecessary. Nevertheless, the proposed provision eliminates the flexibility of the nature of the prohibition of the circumvention of the law by refraining from giving any weight to the consideration of the parties' intention and potential justification confirming the need to perform the contested legal transaction.

## 4 Conclusions

There is clearly no one uniform solution – regarding the regulation of the limitations of the freedom of contract adopted in all the newest civil codifications in Central and Southeast Europe – that could be transplanted to Polish law. The regulation of freedom of contract and its limitations varies depending on the sources of inspiration of each legal act, its legislative history, and the past experiences of a given state. However, the regulations adopted in these codifications reinforce the decision of Polish scholars to regulate the law of obligations as a part of a civil code and to locate regulation of the limitations of freedom of concluding any legal transaction in the General Part of the Civil Code.

At the same time, the applied regulations put in question the minimalistic approach of Polish scholars who proposed to limit the freedom of concluding any legal transaction only by (mandatory) legal provisions and decency. The broad interpretation of these two terms – that corresponds to the meaning given to them under current case law and in the legal literature – makes other limitations redundant. This approach has not been applied in any other Central and Southeast European country.

Despite the common history that Poland shares with other Central and Southeast European countries, it seems that the scholars drafting the academic draft of a new Polish Civil Code represent a different standpoint than the one adopted by drafters of the other codes. Polish scholars, while supporting the liberal paradigm of contract law, seem not to fear that courts will abuse their discretion in applying the limitations of freedom. For that reason, no additional limitations that would emphasize democratic values and the importance of the rights of an individual have been suggested in addition to the standard limitations set by statutory law and decency. Moreover, according to the explanatory memorandum published together with the draft of the General Part of ADCC, the limitations are to be understood and applied in a very general way. No 'safety valves' – like deciding that particular words must be used in a legal provision for it to limit the content of a legal transaction – that have been applied in civil codes of the other countries from the region are to apply.

---

207 Miler (n 52) 118ff.

It is a rather isolated position that strongly contrasts with the stand taken by the drafters of civil codes binding in other Central and Southeast European countries. It could be argued that the philosophy behind the civil codes of the Baltic states and the acts regulating law of obligations in Croatia and Slovenia is in a sense 'outdated', as these legal acts are over 15 or even 20 years old. However, this argument cannot be used to discard the precautions that were adopted in the Czech NOZ. It is surprising how many similarities – regarding the limitations of the freedom of concluding any legal transaction – the Czech NOZ shares with the Lithuanian and Estonian civil codes, even though they were prepared and adopted over ten years apart. In the Czech legal literature, it is openly stated that the still vivid memories of how the private law was applied during communism influenced the current shape of the provision regulating the freedom of concluding any legal transaction and its restrictions. The concern about a possible repetition of the misuse of law and distrust of courts seems to be imprinted on the society, including its academics. In that context, the Polish approach reflects the position represented in the older Western civil codes and, in that sense, can be seen as more modern or universal. But the solutions adopted in other countries from the region – historically, socially, economically, and politically similar to Poland – cannot be simply ignored. Therefore, it could be questioned whether the proposed solution responds to the current or potential challenges. In particular, whether the regulation of the protection of the freedom of concluding any legal transaction is such as to prevent any misuse of the courts' discretion in interpreting statutory provisions or rules of decency in case the independence of courts in Poland was to ever be endangered. Or whether the solutions applied in other states from the region should serve as an inspiration to describe the proposed limitations in a more detailed manner, for instance by adding 'safety valves' or directives of interpretation.

## Bibliography

Bączyk K, 'Zasada swobody umów w prawie polskim' in Kustry E (ed), *Studia Iuridica Toruniensia: Przemiany Polskiego Prawa*, vol 2 (Wydawnictwo Naukowe Uniwersytetu Mikołaja Kopernika 2002) [https://doi.org/10.12775/sit.2002.003].

Bejcek J, 'Das ABGB und das tschechische Zivil- und Handelsrecht' in Geistlinger M and others (eds), *200 Jahre ABGB – Ausstrahlungen: Die Bedeutung der Kodifikation für andere Staaten und andere Rechtskulturen* (MANZ Verlag Wien 2011).

Bohata P, 'Grundsatzentwurf des neuen tschechischen Zivilrechts' [2001] *WiRO* 295.

——, 'Neugestaltung des tschechischen Zivilrechts – Teil 1 – Allgemeiner Teil des zukünftigen BGB' [2011] *WiRO* 353.

——, 'Neugestaltung des tschechischen Zivilrechts – Teil 2 – Sachen und Rechtsgeschäfte' [2012] *WiRO* 7.

Ciepła H (ed), *Kodeks Cywilny: Komentarz*, vol 1 (Wydawnictwo Zrzeszenia Prawników Polskich 2005).

Csach K and Laclavikova M, 'Das ABGB und das slowakische Zivilrecht' in Geistlinger M and others (eds), *200 Jahre ABGB – Ausstrahlungen: Die Bedeutung der Kodifikation für andere Staaten und andere Rechtskulturen* (MANZ Verlag Wien 2011).

Didžiulis L, *Contract Law in Lithuania* (Wolters Kluwer 2019).

Dmowski S and Rudnicki S, *Komentarz do Kodeks cywilny: Księga pierwsza: Część ogólna* (LexisNexis 2011).

Elischer D, 'The New Czech Civil Code: Principles, Perspectives and Objectives of Actual Czech Civil Law Recodification: On the Way to Monistic Conception of Obligation Law?' (2010) 19 *Dereito* 431.

Gardos P, 'Recodification of the Hungarian Civil Law' (2007) 15 *ERPL* 707.

Gniewek E and Machnikowski P (eds), *Kodeks Cywilny: Komentarz* (7th edn, CH Beck 2016).

Gorenc V (ed), *Komentar Zakona o obveznim odnosima* (Narodne novine 2014).

Grzybowski S, 'Struktura i treść przepisów prawa cywilnego odsyłających do zasad współżycia społecznego' [1965] *Stud Cywilis* 3.

——, *System Prawa Cywilnego*, vol 1 (Ossolineum 1985).

Gudowski J (ed), *Kodeks Cywilny: Komentarz: Część ogólna* (LexisNexis 2014).

Gumbis J, 'The Impact of the ABGB on the Lithuanian Civil Law' in Geistlinger M and others (eds), *200 Jahre ABGB – Ausstrahlungen: Die Bedeutung der Kodifikation für andere Staaten und andere Rechtskulturen* (MANZ Verlag Wien 2011).

Guść J, 'O właściwości (naturze) stosunku prawnego' (1997) 51 (4) *Panst Prawo* 16.

Gutowski M, *Nieważność czynności prawnej* (CH Beck 2006).

——, 'Sprzeczność z prawem Unii Europejskiej jako przesłanka nieważność czynności prawnej na podstawie Art 58 K.C.' (2006) 68 (1) *Ruch Praw Ekonom Socjo* 111.

Hamza G, 'Geschichte der Kodifikation des Zivilrechts in Ungarn' (2008) 12 *Anuario da Facultade de Dereito da Universidade da Coruña* 533.

Janiszewska B, 'Klauzula generalna dobrych obyczajów w znowelizowanych przepisach kodeksu cywilnego' [2003] (10) *Prz Prawa Handl* 12.

——, 'O potrzebie zmiany klauzuli zasad współżycia społecznego (głos w dyskusji)' (2003) LVI (4) *Prz Ustaw Gosp* 7.

Justyński T, *Nadużycie prawa w polskim prawie cywilnym* (Zakamycze 2000).

Käerdi M, 'Estonia and the New Civil Law' in MacQueen HL, Vaquer A, and Espiau Espiau S (eds), *Regional Private Laws and Codification in Europe* (CUP 2003) [https://doi.org/10.1017/cbo9780511495007.012].

——, 'Die Neukodifikation des Privatrechts der baltischen Staaten in vergleichender Sicht' in Heiss H (ed), *Zivilrechtsreform im Baltikum* (Mohr Siebeck 2006).

Karwat P, *Obejście prawa podatkowego* (Wolters Kluwer 2002).

Kidyba A (ed), *Kodeks Cywilny: Część ogólna*, vol 1 (2nd edn, Wolters Kluwer 2012).

—— (ed), *Kodeks Cywilny: Komentarz: Zobowiązania. Część ogólna*, vol 3 (2nd edn, Wolters Kluwer 2014).

Kisfaludi A, 'The Influence of Harmonisation of Private Law on the Development of the Civil Law in Hungary' [2008] *Juridica Intl* 130.

Komisja Kodyfikacyjna Prawa Cywilnego działająca przy Ministrze Sprawiedliwości, 'Kodeks cywilny: Księga I: Część ogólna: Projekt z objaśnieniami' <www.projektkc.uj.edu.pl/index.php/projekty> accessed 22 January 2020.

Kõve V, 'Applicable Law in the Light of Modern Law of Obligations and Bases for the Preparation of the Law of Obligations Act' [2001] *Juridica Intl* 30.

Krąkowski L, *Zasady współżycia społecznego w stosunkach pracy w PRL* (PWN 1970).

Kull I, 'Effect of Harmonisation of European Civil Law on Development of Estonian Law of Obligations' [1998] *Juridica Intl* 98.

——, 'Principle of Freedom of Contract in European Civil Law and Reform of Law of Obligations in Estonia' in Lazdiņš J (ed), *Tiesību transformācijas problēmas sakarā ar integrāciju Eiropas Savienībā: starptautiskās konferences materiāli: Problems of transformation of law in connection with European integration* (Rīga Latvijas Univ, Juridiskā fak 2002).

——, 'European and Estonian Law of Obligations: Transposition of Law or Mutual Influence?' [2004] *Juridica Intl* 32.

——, 'Reform of Contract Law in Estonia: Influences of Harmonisation of European Private Law' [2008] *Juridica Intl* 122.

Küpper H, 'Ungarns neues BGB – Teil 1: Entstehung und Inhalt' [2014] *WiRO* 129.

Leszczyński L, 'Funkcje klauzul odsyłających a model ich tworzenia w systemie prawa' (2000) 54 (7) *Panst Prawo* 3.

Łętowska E, *Prawo umów konsumenckich* (2nd edn, CH Beck 2002).

—— and Wiewiórowska-Domagalska A, 'The Common Frame of Reference: The Perspective of a New Member State' (2007) 3 *ERCL* 277.

—— (ed), *Prawo zobowiązań – część ogólna: System Prawa Prywatnego*, vol 5 (2nd edn, CH Beck 2013).

Łopatka A and Ziembiński Z, 'Próba systematyzacji zasad współżycia społecznego wg orzecznictwa S.N.' (1957) 12 (4–5) *Panst Prawo* 802.

Luts M, 'Textbook of Pandects or New Style of Legislation in Estonia?' [2001] *Juridica Intl* 152.

Machnikowski P, *Swoboda umów według art. 3531 KC: Konstrukcja prawna* (CH Beck 2005).

——, 'Zasada swobody umów jako problem kodyfikacyjny' in Sawczuk M (ed), *Czterdzieści Lat Kodeksu Cywilnego: Materiały z Ogólnopolskiego Zjazdu Cywilistów w Rzeszowie (8–10 Października 2004 r.)* (Zakamycze 2006).

Mączyński A, 'Die Entwicklung und die Reformpläne des polnischen Privatrechts' in Welser R (ed), *Privatrechtsentwicklung in Zentral- und Osteuropa* (MANZ Verlag Wien 2008).

Menyhárd A, 'Contracts' in Harmathy A (ed), *Introduction to Hungarian Law* (2nd edn, Wolters Kluwer 2019).

Mikelenas V, 'Unification and Harmonisation of Law at the Turn of the Millennium: The Lithuanian Experience' (2000) 5 *Unif L Rev* 243 [https://doi.org/10.1093/ulr/5.2.243].

——, 'The Main Features of the New Lithuanian Contract Law System Based on the Civil Code of 2000' [2005] *Juridica Intl* 42.

——, 'The Influence of Instruments of Harmonisation of Private Law upon the Reform of Civil Law in Lithuania' [2008] *Juridica Intl* 143.

Mikk H, 'Zur Reform des Zivilrechts in Estland' (2001) 42 *Jb OstR* 31.

Miler D, 'Czynności mające na celu obejście ustawy na tle orzecznictwa sądów polskich' (2019) 81 (4) *Ruch Praw Ekonom Socjol* 109 [https://doi.org/10.14746/rpeis.2019.81.4.9].

Mizaras N, 'Das neue Zivil- und Zivilprozessrecht in Litauen' [2002] *ZeuP* 466.

Možina D, 'Harmonisation of Private Law in Europe and the Development of Private Law in Slovenia' [2008] *Juridica Intl* 173.

—— and Vlahek A, *Contract Law in Slovenia* (Wolters Kluwer 2019).

Nikšić S, 'Contract Law' in Josipović T (ed), *Introduction to the Law of Croatia* (Wolters Kluwer 2014).

Olejniczak A (ed), *Prawo cywilne – część ogólna: System Prawa Prywatnego*, vol 2 (CH Beck 2019).

Osajda K (ed), *Kodeks cywilny: Komentarz*, vol 1 (CH Beck 2013).

—— (ed), *Kodeks cywilny: Komentarz*, vol 2 (CH Beck 2013).

Petrov J, *Občanský zákoník: komentář* (CH Beck 2017).

Pietrzykowski K (ed), *Kodeks cywilny: Komentarz do art. 1–44910*, vol 1 (8th edn, CH Beck 2015).

—— (ed), *Kodeks cywilny: Komentarz do art. 1–44910*, vol 1 (9th edn, CH Beck 2018).

Pilich M, 'Zasady współżycia społecznego, dobre obyczaje czy dobra wiara? Dylematy nowelizacji klauzul generalnych prawa cywilnego w perspektywie europejskiej' [2006] (4) *Stud Prawn* 37.

Pisuliński J, 'Struktura części ogólnej prawa zobowiązań (Wprowadzenie do dyskusji)' [2017] (2) *Transform Prawa Prywat* 37.

Poczobut J, 'Geschichtlicher Hintergrund, heutiger Stand und Perspektiven des polnischen Privatrechts' in Welser R (ed), *Privatrechtsentwicklung in Zentral- und Osteuropa* (MANZ Verlag Wien 2008).

Polajnar-Pavcik A, 'Neukodifikationen des Privatrechts in Slowenien' in Blaho P and Jan Švidroň J (eds), *Kodifikácia, europeizácia a harmonizácia súkromného práva* (Bratislava Iura Ed 2005).

Pyziak-Szafnicka M and Księżak P (eds), *Kodeks Cywilny: Komentarz: Część ogólna* (Wolters Kluwer 2014).

Radwański Z, 'Kodifikationsprobleme des Zivilrechts in Polen' in Blaho P and Švidroň J (eds), *Kodifikácia, europeizácia a harmonizácia súkromného práva* (Bratislava Iura Ed 2005).

——, *Zielona Księga: Optymalna wizja Kodeksu cywilnego w Rzeczpospolitej Polskiej* (Ministerstwo Sprawiedliwości 2006).

——, 'Zielona Księga. Optymalna wizja kodeksu cywilnego Rzeczpospolitej Polskiej' (2007) 69 (1) *Ruch Praw Ekonom Socjol* 5.

——, *Prawo cywilne – część ogólna: System Prawa Prywatnego*, vol 2 (CH Beck 2008).

——, 'Aktualność posłużenia się częścią ogólną kodeksu cywilnego jako instrumentem regulacji prawa prywatnego' [2010] (4) *Transform Prawa Prywat* 13.

—— and Zieliński M, 'Uwagi de lege ferenda o klauzulach generalnych w prawie prywatny' (2001) 8 (2) *Prz Leg* 11.

Reich N, 'Transformation of Contract Law and Civil Justice in the New EU Member Countries: The Example of the Baltic States, Hungary and Poland' in Cafaggi F (ed), *The Institutional Framework of European Private Law* (OUP 2006) [https://doi.org/10.1093/acp rof:oso/9780199296040.003.0008].

Rott-Pietrzykowska E, 'Klauzule generalne rozsądku w kodeksie cywilnym' (2005) 14 *Kwart Prawa Prywat* 617.

Rudolf C, 'Slowenien: Neues Schuldgesetzbuch in Kraft' [2002] *WGO* 7.

Safjan M, 'Klauzule generalne w prawie cywilnym (przyczynek do dyskusji)' (1990) 45 (11) *Panst Prawo* 48.

——, 'Zasada swobody umów (Uwagi wstępne na tle wykładni art. 353¹ k.c.)' (1993) 47 (4) *Panst Prawo* 12.

—— (ed), *Prawo cywilne – część ogólna: System Prawa Prywatnego*, vol 1 (2nd edn, CH Beck 2012).

Sawczuk M (ed), *Czterdzieści Lat Kodeksu Cywilnego: Materiały z Ogólnopolskiego Zjazdu Cywilistów w Rzeszowie (8–10 Października 2004 r.)* (Zakamycze 2006).

Schulze U, 'Das litauische Zivilrecht – Entwicklung, IPR und Allgemeiner Teil' [2001] *WGO* 331.

Slakoper Z, 'Allgemeines Bürgerliches Gesetzbuch (ABGB) und kroatisches bürgerliches Recht' in Geistlinger M and others (eds), *200 Jahre ABGB – Ausstrahlungen: Die Bedeutung der Kodifikation für andere Staaten und andere Rechtskulturen* (MANZ Verlag Wien 2011).

—— and Gorenc V, *Obvezno pravo: Opći dio: Sklapanje, promjene i prestanak ugovora* (Novi informator 2009).

Stawecki T, 'Obejście prawa. Szkic na temat granic prawa i zasad jego wykładni' in Izdebski H and Stępkowski A (eds), *Nadużycie prawa* (Liber 2003).

Steinke D, *Die Zivilrechtsordnungen des Baltikums unter dem Einfluss ausländischer, insbesondere deutscher Rechtsquellen* (V&R Unipress, Universitätsverlag Osnabrück 2009).

Szpunar A, 'Uwagi o nadużyciu prawa podmiotowego' in Sztyk R (ed), *II Kongres Notariuszy Rzeczpospolitej Polskiej: referaty i opracowania* (Wydawnictwo Stowarzyszenia Notariuszy RP 1999).

Tichý L, 'Processes of Modernisation of Private Law Compared, and the CFR's Influence' [2008] *Juridica Intl* 35.

——, 'Stand und Entwicklung des Privatrechts und der Tschechischen Republik' in Welser R (ed), *Privatrechtsentwicklung in Zentral- und Osteuropa* (MANZ Verlag Wien 2008).

Tracz G and Zoll F, *Przewłaszczenie na zabezpieczenie* (Zakamycze 1996).

Trstenjak V, 'Zivilrecht in Slowenien: Entwicklung und Stand der Dinge heute' [2000] *ZeuP* 77.

——, 'Das neue slowenische Obligationenrecht' [2002] *WGO* 90.

——, 'Das ABGB in Slowenien' in Fischer-Czermak C and others (eds), *Festschrift 200 Jahre ABGB*, vol 1 (MANZ Verlag Wien 2011).

Trzaskowski R, 'Właściwość (natura) zobowiązaniowego stosunku prawnego jako ograniczenie zasady swobody kształtowania treści umów' (2000) 10 *Kwart Prawa Prywat* 337.

Varul P, 'Creation of New Private Law in Estonia' (2000) 31 *Rechtstheorie* 349.

——, 'Legal Policy Decisions and Choices in the Creation of New Private Law in Estonia' [2000] *Juridica Intl* 104.

——, 'Estonian Private Law and the European Union' in Lazdiņš J (ed), *Tiesību transformācijas problēmas sakarā ar integrāciju Eiropas Savienībā: starptautiskās konferences materiāli: Problems of transformation of law in connection with European integration* (Rīga Latvijas Univ, Juridiskā fak 2002).

——, 'The New Estonian Civil Code' in Heiss H (ed), *Zivilrechtsreform im Baltikum* (Mohr Siebeck 2006) 53.

——, 'The Creation of New Estonian Private Law' (2008) 16 *ERPL* 95.

——, 'The Impact of Harmonisation of Private Law on the Reform of Civil Law in the New Member States' in Brownsword R and others (eds), *The Foundations of European Private Law* (Hart Publishing 2011) [https://doi.org/10.5040/9781472560995.ch-015].

Vékás L, 'Über die Expertenvorlage eines neuen Zivilgesetzbuches für Ungarn' [2009] *ZeuP* 536.

——, 'Über das ungarische Zivilgesetzbuch im Spiegel der neueren europäischen Privatrechtsentwicklung' [2016] *ZeuP* 37.

Wabnitz HB and Holländer P (eds), *Einführung in das tschechische Recht* (CH Beck 2009).

Wąsowicz W, 'Obejście prawa jako przyczyna nieważności czynności prawnej' (1999) 9 *Kwart Prawa Prywat* 69.

Wolter A, *Prawo cywilne: Zarys części ogólnej* (Wolters Kluwer 2001).

Zieliński T, 'Klauzule generalne w nowym porządku konstytucyjnym' (1997) 51 (11–12) *Panst Prawo* 134.

Zimmermann R, 'The Civil Law in European Codes' in MacQueen HL, Vaquer A, and Espiau Espiau S (eds), *Regional Private Laws and Codification in Europe* (CUP 2003) [https://doi.org/10.1017/CBO9780511495007.002].

Zukas T, 'Reception of the Unidroit Principles of International Commercial Contracts and the Principles of European Contract Law in Lithuania' in Cashin-Ritaine E and Lein E (eds), *The UNIDROIT Principles 2004: Their Impact on Contractual Practice, Jurisprudence and Codification: Reports of the ISDC Colloquium (8/9 June 2006)* (Schulthess 2007).

——, *Einfluss der 'Unidroit Principles of International Commercial Contracts' und der 'Principles of European Contract Law' auf die Transformation des Vertragsrechts in Litauen* (Stämpfli Verlag AG 2011).

# 5  Liability for breach of contract in Hungarian law

*Attila Menyhárd*

## 1 Introduction

The new Hungarian Civil Code of 2013 (*Polgári törvénykönyv*,[1] Ptk) changed the liability system of the previous Civil Code of 1959[2] and shifted to a system where liability in tort and liability of breach of contract constituted two separate regimes. While liability in tort remained a fault-based liability, liability for breach of contract is a strict liability. With this solution, the legislature attempted to bring the system of liability for breach of contract close to the liability system provided in the CISG. A foreseeability limit has been introduced as the statutory limitation of the liability for breach of contract. In the case of intentional breach of contract, full compensation must be provided as damages for breach of contract. The policy behind this solution is that contracts impose obligations that the parties undertook voluntarily, as a result of a bargain. This nature of the contractual obligation justifies strict liability. On the other hand, the foreseeability limit is justified by the idea that only risks that could be priced are to be allocated to the parties. The effect of shifting the burden of proof concerning foreseeability at the time of conclusion of the contract is an incentive for disclosing unusual or unexpected risks to the other party in order to bring them under the scope of liability. Contracts for services such as agency, medical practice, and legal services and advising create a specific type of contract in the system of specific contracts. In the context of such contracts, it is the failure to comply with the required duty of care that establishes a breach of contract. Thus, compliance with the required standard of duty excludes breach of contract and shall not establish liability. This holds for liability for medical malpractice as well. The policy underlying the strict nature of liability for breach of contract does not prevail if the contract relates to a gift. Thus, the fault-based regime is to apply to gratuitous contracts.

Hungarian court practice already faces the problem resulting from this system, especially with borderline cases, interferences of liability regimes (e.g.

---

1  Act V of 2013 on the Civil Code (*2013 évi V törvény a Polgári Törvénykönyvről*), MK 2013/31 (II 26), as later amended.
2  Act IV of 1959 on the Civil Code (*1959 évi IV törvény a Polgári Törvénykönyvről*), MK 1959/82 (VIII 11), as later amended.

liability for the extra hazardous activity of motor vehicle operators vs contractual liability), conceptual vagueness (e.g. interpreting 'beyond his control' as an element of exoneration from strict liability), or differentiation between deliberate and negligent wrongdoing from the point of view of the foreseeability limit. Liability for breach of contract in Hungarian contract law will be analysed here in the context of these issues as well as in the context of excluding liability and the agreed remedies like penalty and liquidated damages.

## 2  The binding force of a contract

### 2.1  Understanding the binding force of a contract

The binding force of contract lies at the heart of contract law. The function, the role, and the limits of liability for breach of contract are tightly connected to understanding the binding force of contract in a legal system. Historically, there are two paradigms of this understanding. According to the continental perspective, the binding force of contract means that if a party to a contract failed to keep his promise, the aggrieved party has the right to claim the enforcement in kind. This approach was the result of shifting the principle of in kind performance, originally provided by the law of Justinian for *dare* obligations,[3] to a general level. The other paradigm was provided by the English common law which is quite different from the continental perspective and which is similar to that of the early Roman law. According to the common law, as it has been expressed by Oliver Wendell Holmes, 'the only universal consequence of a legally binding promise is that the law makes the promisor pay damages if the promised act does not come to pass.'[4] Specific performance has become available only as an equitable remedy. The early history of specific performance seems to be, with the words of Brian Simpson, 'peculiarly obscure', and goes back to the mid-fifteenth century, when specific performance was decreed in the case of contracts conveying lands.[5] The Chancery, however, has never developed any coherent doctrine or clear guidelines for ordering specific performance. It seems likely that the Chancellor granted specific performance simply because it was in accordance with a good conscience to do so and the Chancellor never attempted to decree specific performance of all contracts: the granting of this relief might vary with the circumstances of each case[6] and remained exceptional. This origin of specific performance in English law determined its nature: it remains a discretionary remedy granted only upon the plaintiff's request and if the court finds it just to do so, but the plaintiff is not

3  István Szászy, *A kötelmi jog általános tanai* (Grill Kiadó 1943) 17; Reinhard Zimmermann, *The Law of Obligations: Roman Foundations of the Civilian Tradition* (Clarendon Press 1996) 772.
4  Oliver Wendell Holmes, Jr, *The Common Law* (Little, Brown and Co 1881) 301.
5  AW Brian Simpson, *A History of the Common Law of Contract* (Clarendon Press 1975) 595.
6  Gareth Jones and William Goodhart, *Specific Performance* (2nd edn, Butterworths 1996) 6, 8.

entitled to claim specific performance as of a right.[7] The Hungarian contract law, in line with other continental legal systems, follows the principle of in kind performance.

## 2.2 Morality of remedies

One may argue that the principle of the binding force of contract implies a moral aspect according to which promises are to be kept simply because they are promises and the right of choice of the debtor to buy off his duty to keep his promise would push this moral value into the background. This would not take into account the interests of the promisee, who surely had the good reason to request the contractual promise as a counter-value for his own obligation. Unavailability of specific performance also could lead to a decrease of mutual trust in the society since the interests of the promisee in a great bulk of cases surely cannot be compensated with money entirely. This is simply because there are idiosyncratic values and there are transactions where the aim of the parties is not or not only to make a profit. In absence of the possibility of enforcing performance in kind, in these cases, the promisee could not rely on that he can claim and get what he has bargained for if the promisor failed to perform his obligations. As Charles Fried argues, a contractual promise can be put into a wider context of conventions in society. With his words:

> The moralist of duty sees promising as a device that free, moral individuals have fashioned on the premise of mutual trust, and which gathers its moral force from that premise. The moralist of duty thus posits a general obliga-tion to keep promises, of which the obligation of contract will be only a special case – that special case in which certain promises have attained legal as well as moral force. But since a contract is first of all a promise, the contract must be kept because a promise must be kept.[8]

In commercial transactions, in most of the cases, the interests of the promisee may be compensated with monetary remedies either by enabling him to gain a substitute performance on the market with a cover transaction or by award-ing him the net gains that he lost because of the non-performance. One could assume that specific performance is, in the light of the aim and function of remedies for breach of contract, the proper method of enforcing contracts since it provides the promisee with the performance he had bargained for. There are, however, some restrictions applied in legal systems on specific performance. These limits may come from that courts try to avoid the waste of resources and are reluctant to order specific performance if supervision of performance would be too difficult or costly. Another policy for implementing such limits

7  ibid 2.
8  Charles Fried, *Contract as Promise: A Theory of Contractual Obligation* (HUP 1981) 17.

may come from protecting individual liberty. This may be the case where the performance of the contract involves personal services.[9]

The § 6:34 Ptk provides that obligations are to be performed according to their content. Contracts shall be performed as stipulated, at the place and in the time set forth and in accordance with the quantity, quality, and range specified therein. The general rule of the Ptk for breach of contract is specific performance. This is expressly provided in § 6:154(1) Ptk regulating the consequences of the delay in performance as a special breach of contract: if the party to the contract fails to perform his obligation as it falls due, the aggrieved party shall have the right to claim performance of the contractual obligation. Monetary compensation (damages) shall replace enforced performance only if the performance in kind is impossible or if it would be against the interests of the creditor. The original idea behind this principle in the Civil Code of 1959 was that this had been held as being in accordance with the state intervention and planning and was needed because of the shortage of resources. After the economic reform in 1968, the principle has not been abandoned but a new sense and meaning have been given to it and this new meaning of the principle of real performance has been the general rule of specific performance (the performance in kind).[10] This principle has been upheld with the new Ptk with the same content and the same understanding. Provisions regarding the enforcement of court decisions (judicial execution) attempt to support the general principle of enforced performance in the Ptk but – in absence of criminal law consequences – their efficiency is ambiguous. If the obligation of the debtor is to do something which is not the payment of money but a special act or behaviour, the court may enforce it in the phase of enforcement of the judgment.[11]

The main aim of the rules covering remedies for breach of contract is putting the aggrieved party into the same position as he would have been if the promisor had performed her promise. There are two possible methods to achieve this goal: one of them is to require the party in breach to perform the promised performance; the other is to require him to pay damages. There are strong arguments against and for both of them, as on the level of economical and legal theory as well as in the practice where the nature of the contractual obligation, the availability of substitution, the adequacy of damages, and the respect of personal liberty of the debtor may strongly support one or other of them.

---

9  Hugh Collins, *The Law of Contract* (2nd edn, Butterworths 1993) 392.

10  Attila Harmathy, 'The Binding Force of Contract in Hungarian Law' in Attila Harmathy (ed), *Binding Force of Contract* (Institute for Legal and Administrative Sciences of the Hungarian Academy of Sciences 1991) 29.

11  The court may, with issuing a decree, determine the manner of execution, such as ordering the obligor to pay the money equivalent of the definite act, granting authorization to the judgment creditor to perform or to cause to be performed the definite act at the cost and risk of the obligor, and concurrently ordering the obligor to advance the estimated costs of such, impose a fine on the obligor, or enforcing the definite act with police assistance. Act LIII of 1994 on Enforcement of Judicial Decisions (*1994 évi LIII törvény a bírósági végrehajtásról*), MK 1994/51 (V 11), as later amended, § 174.

## 2.3 Efficient breach of contract

The problem of an efficient breach is very tightly connected to specific performance because the availability of specific performance may prevent the efficient breach. From a point of view of economic analysis, breach of a contract in some cases may be more efficient than performing it. The breach is more efficient than performance when the costs of performance exceed the benefits to all parties. According to the theory of efficient breach, a unilateral breach of contract shall not only be permitted but even encouraged where the party in breach found a more profitable opportunity to invest the resources that would otherwise be dedicated to the performance provided that she is able to compensate the aggrieved party. According to this theory, the precondition of allowance of a breach is that the breaching party has to be willing and able to compensate the promisee for his full expectancy loss and still be able to realize gains from the new opportunity. All of this infers that the breach is Pareto superior, that is to say, as the result of the breach nobody is worse off and some are better off.[12] The breach is still efficient if the breaching party is in the position to compensate the aggrieved party while still being better off (Kaldor-Hicks efficiency).

Even if there are also strong arguments against the doctrine of efficient breach,[13] in commercial transactions this is a reality rather than a theory, which seems to be quite logical and inevitably has some sense. One of the main suggested strong limitations of this doctrine can be that it rests on the assumption that all of the values, preferences, and interests of the parties can be expressed in

---

12 Michael J Trebilcock, *The Limits of Freedom of Contract* (HUP 1997) 142. A widely cited and discussed four-players-example for the illustration of the paradigmatic situation of efficient breach has been created by Peter Linzer as follows:

> Assume that Athos owns a woodworking factory capable of taking one or more major project. He contracts to supply Porthos with 100,000 chairs at $10 per chair, which will bring Athos a net profit of $2 per chair, or $200,000 on the contract. Before any works takes place, Aramis, who sells tables, approaches Athos. Although there are several chair factories in the area, only Athos's factory can make tables. If Athos will supply Aramis with 50,000 tables, Aramis will pay him $40 per table. Athos can produce the tables for $25, so he can make a net profit of $750,000 if he uses his factory for Aramis's tables. But to do so, he must breach his contract with Porthos. There are other chair factories, and Porthos will be able to get the chairs from one of them – for example, from D'Artagnan's. Let us assume that because of his distress situation Porthos will have to pay D'Artagnan 20% more than Athos's price for comparable chairs, and that Porthos will sustain $100,000 in incidental administrative costs and consequential costs such as damages for delay to his customers. Even with these costs, Porthos will lose only $300,000 because of Athos's breach, and Athos can reimburse him in full and still make $450,000 profit, over twice the profit from his contract with Porthos.
>
> Peter Linzer, 'On the Amorality of Contract Remedies: Efficiency, Equity, and the Second *Restatement*' (1981) 81 *Colum L Rev* 111, 114–15.

13 One objection to this theory is that it 'encourages uncivil, unilateral, uncooperative attitudes towards contractual relationship' and that 'it deprives the non-breaching party of the possibility of sharing in the gains from the new opportunity presented to the breaching party, which a negotiated release from an entitlement to specific performance would probably engender'. Trebilcock (n 12).

monetary compensation and leaves out of sight that there are idiosyncratic non-market values and preferences which cannot be compensated in money. From this follows that the theory of efficient breach may be useful in commercial transactions where mostly the loss of the aggrieved party can be compensated in money and where, in most of the cases, there is a substitute performance available on the market. That is why Peter Linzer suggests the application of a two-step test to decide whether in a certain case specific performance or only compensation in money through paying damages shall be ordered. According to this test, in each of the cases, the courts first shall compare the efficacy of monetary damages with that of specific performance paying attention espe-cially to idiosyncratic interests. In commercial transactions involving tangible goods this test normally results in favouring monetary damages contrasting to specific performance. In non-commercial transactions, the promisee often has idiosyncratic values that are to be protected by the law. The recognition of such values should result in preferring specific performance to monetary damages because that is the more efficient solution. In the latter case the court:

> should then balance the cost to the promisee of receiving money damages in the place of performance against costs of judicial supervision, unusual hardships caused the promisor by threatened or actual punishment, and costs to a society that holds itself above imprisonment for debt or for mat-ters of conscience . . . only when these burdens are insurmountable in the particular case, and justify the costs to the promisee, should the court deny him specific relief and remit him to money damages.[14]

A further criticism contesting the efficient breach doctrine is that the general rule of enforced performance can be as effective a solution as the efficient breach: it all depends upon the actual transaction costs. The parties themselves are able to agree after the conclusion of the contract that they terminate it and that the party in the situation being able to breach the contract efficiently pays compensation to the other as a counter-value of non-performance. We shall leave it to the parties to do so and it does not seem to be necessary to 'shift' this bargain to the courts or to the level of a legal rule. According to Ian Macneil, if we assume the possibility of this bargain between the parties, as it is generally possible and we do not calculate with transaction costs, neither the doctrine of specific performance nor that of the efficient breach leads to more efficient use of resources than the other. It means that 'whether an expectation damages rule or a specific performance rule is more efficient depends entirely upon the relative transaction costs of operating under the rules'.[15] Despite the weaknesses of the theory of efficient breach, the economic analysis generates, as Hugh Collins emphasizes it, at least two important insights. One of them is that the general wealth of the community will be increased if an efficient

---

14  Linzer (n 12) 131.
15  Ian R Macneil, 'Efficient Breach of the Contract: Circles in the Sky' (1982) 68 *Va L Rev* 947, 957.

breach of contract is permitted. From this, it 'can be inferred that according to the regulatory policy of efficiency the law should not seek to compel performance of contracts where a party decides to breach and pay compensation after a suitable cost/benefit calculation'.[16] The other would suggest that the purpose of a legal sanction should be ensuring that neither party is worse off as a result of the breach of contract so that the remedy should match that loss exactly.[17]

Pushing specific performance as a primary remedy into the background also encourages self-help in commercial transactions. It seems to be reasonable to exclude the right to require performance in kind if the aggrieved party can obtain substitution of performance from other sources. This corresponds to such general principles of contract law as the principle of cooperation and the requirement of good faith and fair dealing too. One also could argue that in a situation where substitution of the performance is available in the market the claim for enforced performance is an abuse of rights (§ 1:5 Ptk) or is against the maxim of *nemo suam turpitudinem allegans* (§ 1:4 Ptk).

### 2.4 Proper guidelines for regulation

If one sums up the consequences and attempts to find some pillars for optimal regulation, the following points shall be taken into account. The binding force of contract and requirement of keeping the promises is based on social consent, implies also moral values, and must be considered in a wider context of the society. Contract law is bound to the market paradigm, so efficiency is an important factor, which the regulation must provide. Specific performance shall be available[18] but there also must be some limitations to the enforced performance. Specific performance definitely shall be the remedy if the monetary compensation is inadequate. Specific performance seems to be the appropriate remedy in case of unique goods[19] or if the obligation of the breaching party is 'to give' something, while monetary compensation seems to be a better one if the breaching party has 'to do' something. This distinction corresponds to the distinction between contracts for conveyance and contracts for services.[20]

---

16  Hugh Collins, *Regulating Contracts* (OUP 1999) 119.
17  ibid.
18  There are strong arguments for specific performance even in the Anglo-American legal theory. See Alan Schwartz, 'The Case for Specific Performance' (1979) 89 *Yale LJ* 271, 305.
19  This is the main starting point of the Uniform Commercial Code (UCC). The § 2–716(1) UCC provides that specific performance may be decreed where the goods are unique or in other circumstances. The notion of uniqueness seems to be a flexible one and the Comment 2 to § 2–716 UCC suggests a broader meaning, when it states that 'the test must be made in terms of the total situation which characterizes the contract. Output and requirements contracts involving a particular or peculiarly available source or market present today the typical commercial specific performance situation.' It also seems that the courts are 'thus encouraged to take notice of current market sources and commercial realities in determining whether goods are unique'. James J White and Robert S Summers, *Uniform Commercial Code* (5th edn, West Group 2000) § 6–6a.
20  This is the main distinction of French contract law for deciding whether specific performance is to be ordered. This solution also can be explained by a formal economic model, although it seems to

This distinction may be reasonable also from the point of view of the enforcement of judicial decisions, and also reflects the problems of supervising performance. The discretion power of the court in deciding whether to order enforced performance seems to be inevitable since in most of the cases it is necessary to consider the circumstances of the case and to balance the parties' interests including the assessment of the adequacy of damages or reasonableness of costs, burdens, efforts, time, and cover transaction. If the obligation of the promisor is to give a declaration, that declaration can be given by the court in judgment instead of the defendant. In commercial transactions damages are mostly an adequate remedy while in non-commercial transactions specific performance seems to be more often the proper remedy. That is why it seems to be appropriate to apply different standards in commercial and in non-commercial contracts, but this would not seem to be a final answer because we need more precise and refined guidelines. Private law regulation and court practice regarding specific performance are in tight connection with the execution (enforcement) of judgments. The rules of the enforcement must be suitable to enforce the order if the court renders specific performance.

Rules and guidelines regarding specific performance are tightly connected to different forms of impossibility: if one takes impossibility as a flexible concept (as doctrines of economic impossibility or hardship present all legal systems do it so) one can come to cases where hardship in performance may be a relief from a specific performance.

## 3 Liability for breach of contract in the Hungarian Civil Code of 1959

The Civil Code of 1959 in Hungary introduced a system of liability in which liability for breach of contract and liability in tort created one unitary system. The rules addressing liability in tort were to apply for liability for a breach of contract as well. That meant that liability for breach of contract, just like liability in tort, was a fault-based liability without statutory limitation. The main reason behind this solution was that if liability in tort and liability for breach of contract do fall under the application of the same rules, the issue whether the wrongdoing occurred within or outside of a contractual relationship becomes of a secondary nature. This way the issues of categorization were unimportant. As a result, the courts were able to focus their efforts on the merits of the case and on assessing the wrongful behaviour. Difficult bordering problems had been avoided and the idea of prevention of unlawful conducts could also be promoted. As early as 1945, Géza Marton considered the theoretical separation of contractual and non-contractual liability as an inconsistent and illogical consequence of liability theory. He described the theoretical distinction between

---

be a too simple one which must be refined. William Bishop, 'The Choice of Remedy for Breach of Contract' (1985) 14 *JLS* 299, 300, 320.

contractual and non–contractual liability as a 'burden that came with the legacy of Roman law for the modern legal systems'.[21] He was extremely critical of the solution to the French CCiv clearly reflecting this separation. Although it could be argued that the required duty of care in the context of liability for breach of contract should be strict and not be based on negligence, it did not cause any problems in court practice. Basically, there are two structural peculiarities of Hungarian private law making such unitary approach consistently possible. One of them is the concept of fault, which is rather flexible, providing that the required standard of conduct shall be established according to the circumstances of the case.[22] The other is the system of reversed burden of proof in tort law, shifting the risk of information asymmetry to the tortfeasor. According to this system, it is not on the victim to prove the tortfeasor's fault, but it is the tortfeasor who has to prove compliance with the required standard of conduct. Thus, the tortfeasor can be exonerated from liability only by proving the absence of fault on his side or on the side of the actual wrongdoer he was liable for. The reversed burden of proof shifts the risk to the tortfeasor in tort as well as in contract, while the flexible concept of fault provides a wide playing field to the courts in shifting the required standard of conduct to the level the court thinks it fit, according to the facts and circumstances of the case.

This resulted in applying different standards in the course of assessing liability for breach of contract contrasted to tort with maintaining the consistency of the liability system at the same time. While the concept of fault remained negligence-based in tort law, as to liability for breach of contract, the courts established strict liability simply by stating that in contractual relationships the required standard of conduct is performance. That is, failure of performance is fault *per se*.

## 4 Liability for breach of contract in the Hungarian Civil Code of 2013

The Ptk of 2013 changed the described system and shifted to a structure where liability in tort and liability for breach of contract constitute two separate regimes. While liability in tort remained a fault-based liability, liability for breach of contract is strict liability, where the obligor is to be exempted from liability if he proves that the breach of contract was caused by a circumstance that was beyond his control and was not foreseeable at the time of concluding the contract, and he could not be expected to have avoided that circumstance or averted the damage. With this formula, the legislature attempted to bring the system of liability for breach of contract close to the liability system provided in the CISG. Practically, the obligor can be exonerated only by proving

---

21  Géza Marton, *A polgári jogi felelősség* (TRIORG 1993) 50.
22  This concept is the same in the Civil Code of 1959 (§ 4(4)), as well as in the new Ptk of 2013 (§ 1:4(1)), providing that the parties shall proceed with the care that is generally expected under the given circumstances.

that *force majeure* caused the breach. The Hungarian legislature also introduced a foreseeability limit as the statutory limitation of the liability for breach of contract. In the case of intentional breach of contract, full compensation must be provided as damages for breach of contract. In the case of negligence, the damage incurred in the subject of the service must be compensated completely. However, other damage to the assets of the obligee and the loss of profit that occurred as a consequence of the breach of contract shall be compensated to the extent the obligee proved that the damage, as a possible consequence of the breach of contract, was foreseeable at the time of concluding the contract.

The basic policy behind this solution is that contracts impose obligations that the parties undertook voluntarily, as a result of a bargain. This nature of the contractual obligation justifies strict liability. On the other hand, the foreseeability limit is justified by the idea that only risks that could be priced are to be allocated to the parties. The effect of shifting the burden of proof concerning foreseeability at the time of conclusion of the contract is an incentive to disclose unusual or unexpected risks to the other party in order to bring him under the scope of liability. The foreseeability limit, however, is to apply only if the breach of contract was negligent. If the breach of contract was the result of a deliberate act of the obligor, he is not protected by this rule of limitation of liability. This rule – together with further solutions – pushes intention to the background as an element of risk allocation. The problem with this is that 'intent' does not have a clear meaning or clear contours in private law. It may be understood widely, as a resolution of the party, or narrowly, covering only cases of wrongful intent. Policy, creating incentives, may play a role in shaping the content of this concept as well.[23] The intent in private law should have an abstract understanding because legal entities (e.g. companies) should have been assumed as having an intent too. Thus, there is a conceptual vacuum in this respect in private law, or, at least there is an absolute lack of common understanding and consent about conceptualizing intent.

### 4.1 Strict liability for breach of contract

The § 6:142 Ptk provides that the party causing damage to the other party by breach of contract shall be required to compensate for it. He shall be exempted from liability if he proves that the breach of contract was caused by a circumstance that was outside of his control and was not foreseeable at the time of concluding the contract, and he could not be expected to have avoided that circumstance or averted the damage. The key factor of exoneration from liability is the concept of 'beyond control'. If the cause of the breach of contract fell within the control of the party, he could hardly argue successfully that it was not foreseeable at the time of concluding the contract, and that he could

---

23 Ákos Szalai, 'A szerződésszegés szándékossága. Tudatosság és ösztönzők' in Fruzsina Gárdos-Orosz and Attila Menyhárd (eds), *Az Új Polgári Törvénykönyv első öt éve* (Társadalomtudományi Kutatóközpont Jogtudományi Intézet 2019) 195.

not be expected to have avoided that circumstance or averted the damage. The phrase 'beyond control' did not have preliminaries in Hungarian contract law, neither in theory nor in practice. It is a legal transplant taken from products of unification of private law, especially from the CISG, the PECL, the DCFR, and from the UPICC. The main goal of the legislature was to express that compliance with the required standard of conduct or duty of care shall not be a ground for exoneration. The rule establishes strict liability in the sense that the absence of fault shall not be enough ground for exoneration. In the context of a contractual relationship, this rule is not about responsibility or about establishing the consequences of a wrongful behaviour but is about pure risk allocation: the obligor undertook an obligation voluntarily for the agreed price. Thus, the cost of performance shall be borne by the obligor in order to shift the costs where the benefits are. The protection of the reliance on the promise of the obligor also requires such strict liability. The fact that the party breaching the contract was not able to influence the circumstance resulting in a breach of contract does not qualify the ground as falling 'beyond control'. Beyond control shall be understood in the context of Hungarian contract law as expressing *force majeure*. Circumstances that the obligor was not able to influence and could not be avoided even with the utmost duty of care, may still be qualified as falling under the scope of the party's control.

## 4.2  Contracts for services and agency

Contracts for services such as agency, medical practice, and legal services and advising create a specific type of contract in the system of Hungarian contract law. A contract for services is a very wide category, embracing all the contractual relationships where the obligation of the agent is not to provide a certain result but to proceed in the interests of the principal. It is the *differentia specifica* of this specific contract. Although in most cases the agent is imposed with the duty to proceed in order to reach a certain result in the interests of the principal or to represent him, failure to reach the intended result does not constitute a breach of contract *per se*. The agent breaches the contract if he failed to proceed according to the standard of conduct required by the law or by the contract. Although the parties may agree that presenting the result triggers the agent's right to claim the fee, in such cases the failure of the agent does not mean a breach of a duty. If the parties agree that presenting the intended result is a contractual duty of the agent, the contract shall not qualify as a contract for services but a contract for work on goods. A duty of loyalty is imposed on the agent, as he must follow the interests of the principal and not his own. Failure to comply with this duty is a breach of contract. Contracts for legal or medical services, auditors, managers, and officers of a company are typical agency relationships. The rules of contracts for services cover commercial intermediaries and trust as well.

Conveyances, leases, contracts for work on goods, building contracts, etc. are, on the other hand, contracts where the promisor is obliged to perform a certain result. If the result was not performed, it is a breach of contract *per se*. The rules of liability for breach of contract are designed for these types of contracts. In case of contracts for services or agency, the duty of the agent is to perform services according to the standard of required duty of care. Failure to comply with the required duty of care establishes a breach of contract. From this, it follows that compliance with the required standard of duty excludes breach of contract and shall not establish liability. With these types of contract, the obligor is be exonerated from liability if he proves compliance with the required standard of care. This holds for medical malpractice cases too.

### 4.3 'Non-cumul'

The attempt of the legislature to provide different regimes for liability in tort and liability for breach of contract could be undermined if the plaintiff had the opportunity to choose between the two systems. That is why the rules provided in the Ptk draw a Chinese wall between the two regimes. Under the heading of exclusion of parallel claims for damages, the Ptk provides that the obligee shall enforce his claim for damages against the obligor in accordance with the rules on liability for damage caused by a breach of contract, even if the claim for liability in tort could also be established (*non-cumul*). The legislative considerations this separation of liability for breach of contract and non–contractual liability is based on can only be implemented if the plaintiff does not have a choice as to the applicable rules of liability, even if the facts of the specific case could establish both. Although the rule is criticized in scholarship,[24] the *non-cumul* is not a legislative choice but a logical consequence of the separation of the two regimes and a necessary element of this system of liability. The result of this rule is that the plaintiff is prevented from shifting to a title of the claim for damages in tort if the claim can be formulated as a liability for breach of contract. The rule, however, does not prevent the plaintiff from choosing the defendant. Parties may employ other persons in order to exercise their duties and perform their obligations. The concept of a vicarious agent is to be interpreted very broadly. For example, the shop selling the spare parts built into the object of a contract for work on goods shall be deemed a vicarious agent of the contractor. In order to provide the recourse claim against the employed person as long as the obligation against the party is enforceable, the obligor may enforce his rights against the vicarious agent arising from the vicarious agent's breach of contract for as long as he is required to be liable towards the obligee. In chains of contracts, the *non-cumul* rule of liability for breach of contract does not exclude the claims of the obligee directly against the intermediary or agent on the basis of tort.

The *non-cumul* system has the obvious consequence that it is a preliminary issue for each claim for damages whether a contract has been concluded

---

24 Ádám Fuglinszky, 'Risks and Side Effects: Five Questions on the "New" Hungarian Tort Law' [2014] (2) *ELTE LJ* 199, 217.

between the parties, and whether this contract is valid and enforceable. In addition, the court must also check whether the wrongful conduct results in a breach of contract. This must be answered in the affirmative if the conduct constitutes a breach of a contractual obligation expressly stated in the contract or specified of an implied term. It is particularly difficult to assess under what conditions conduct that was realized in connection with the performance of the contract falls within the scope of performance or falls outside of it. At some points, this separation of contractual and non-contractual liability cannot be maintained consequently. Product liability is provided in Hungarian private law as a specific form of liability in tort. With applying the *non-cumul* rule also for product liability cases, the Hungarian legislature proved to be reluctant to draw the consequences of the interpretation of product liability rules provided by the ECJ. According to the ECJ, if the claim falls under the scope of product liability, the national court is prevented from applying parallel regimes of national law even if the alternative could be more beneficial for the victim.[25] The interpretation handed down by the ECJ established very clearly that product liability is a maximum harmonization in European law. That is, cases falling under the scope of product-liability legislation are to be decided according to the rules of product liability. The member state shall not apply any form of a parallel regime of liability, even if that would be more favourable for the victim. The *non-cumul* regime of liability provided in the Ptk hence does not seem to comply with European law in this respect.

### 4.4 Accommodation relationships, gratuitous contracts, and 'non-cumul'

The risk allocation policy underlying the strict nature of liability for breach of contract does not prevail if the contract relates to a benefit transferred without a counter-value. That is why there is a specific rule provided for accommodation relationships. The person undertaking the performance of a service free of charge shall be liable for the damage incurred in the subject of the service if the obligee proves that the obligor caused the damage by an intentional breach of contract, or failed to provide information on a substantial characteristic of the service which was unknown to the obligee. A person undertaking the performance of a service free of charge shall be required to compensate the aggrieved party for the damage caused by his service. He shall be exempted from liability if he proves that he was not at fault (§ 6:147 Ptk). The party shall be liable for the damage incurred in the subject of the service if the obligee proved that the obligor caused the damage by an intentional breach of contract, or that he failed to disclose a substantial characteristic of the service which was unknown to the obligee. The party undertaking the performance of a service free of

---

25 Case C-183/00 *Maria Victoria González Sánchez v Medicina Asturiana SA* [2002] ECR I-3901 ECLI:EU:C:2002:255; case C-52/00 *EC Commission v French Republic* [2002] ECR I-3827 ECLI:EU:C:2002:252; case C-154/00 *EC Commission v Hellenic Republic* [2002] ECR I-3879 ECLI:EU:C:2002:254.

charge shall be required to compensate for the damage caused by his service to the assets of the obligee. He shall be exempted from liability if he proves that he was not at fault by breaching the contract.

So far, Hungarian jurisprudence and practice have not developed a specific doctrine for accommodation relationships. One consequence of this is the uncertainty as to the liability for gratuitous services. In practice, the question arises in connection with accidents suffered as a passenger in a motor vehicle. If the gratuitous service for transporting the passenger (e.g. someone takes her colleague or family member by her own car) is regarded as a contract and the liability relationship is examined in the light of the liability for breach of contract, the application of the *non-cumul* rule typically has detrimental consequences for the victim. If it does not qualify a contract, the liability goes with the rules of liability in tort. If such gratuitous services are to qualify as contracts, one of the detrimental consequences is that liability is fault-based contrasted to the strict liability provided for the operator of extra-hazardous activity which is normally to apply for liability of owners of motor vehicles. A further consequence is that since liability for breach of contract is not covered by compulsory third-party insurance for motor vehicles, the injured party is not protected by the insurance cover. If such gratuitous services are not to qualify as contracts, strict liability for owners of motor vehicles is to apply and claims are covered with the compulsory motor vehicle insurance regime. The attempt of the legislature does not seem to change the risk allocation of tort law and insurance provided for such cases, which certainly would support this latter outcome. The assessment of these cases in professional discussions is highly controversial.

There is an opinion that such cases create contracts simply because the service was provided. The consequence is that these claims are covered by contractual liability even if the outcome can be dramatic for the victim because his position is much worse than applying a specific form of liability in tort and due to absence of insurance coverage.[26] There is, however, another competing view, which takes as a starting point that conclusion of a contract is a necessary prerequisite of applying the rules of liability for breach of contract.[27] Performing gratuitous services does not create a contractual relationship *per se*. In order to establish a contractual relationship, there is a need for exchange of contractual promises. Without promises, there is no contract. The contract stems from the mutual and concordant juridical act of the parties from which the obligation to perform the service and the right to claim the service arises (§ 6:58 Ptk). A juridical act is a declaration of intent aiming at producing a legal effect, either made orally, in writing, or by way of implied conduct (§ 6:4 (1) and (2) Ptk). In order to decide if there was a mutual intent for creating a legal effect behind the declarations, i.e. whether they are to qualify as juridical acts,

26 Ádám Fuglinszky, *Kártérítési jog* (HVGORAC 2015) 71.
27 Attila Menyhárd and Emőd Veress, 'Kontraktuális felelősség a magyar és a román polgári jogban' [2020] *MJ* 288, 291.

they are to be construed according to the rules of construction of declaration of the parties. According to § 6:8(1) Ptk, a juridical act shall be construed like it had to be interpreted by the addressee on the basis of the presumed intent of the party making the statement and of the circumstances of the case, in accordance with the generally accepted meaning of words. If the result of this test is that, under the given circumstances of the case, a contract was concluded between the parties, the liability for gratuitous service is to be assessed according to the fault-based liability provided for accommodation contracts. If the result of this test is that, under the given circumstances of the case, there was no contract concluded between the parties, the liability for gratuitous service is to be assessed according to rules covering non-contractual liability. Non-contractual liability is fault-based as a main rule, but, especially for the liability of operators of a motor vehicle, strict liability is provided.[28]

In Hungarian contract law theory, it is not established that mere facts may create a contract. The contract is the result of juridical acts that are to be construed. That is, performing and accepting a service cannot create a contract *per se*. It is to be assessed on a case-by-case basis, in accordance with the circumstances of the case and the rules for the construction of juridical acts (contracts), whether juridical acts of the parties created a legally enforceable mutual intent, that is, a contract. The fact that the service, performed under an accommodation relationship, may also be provided as a contractual service is not a sufficient basis for establishing the conclusion of the contract.

## 5 Penalty, liquidated damages, and limitation of liability

In the course of preparing the Ptk, the Hungarian legislature decided not to have commercial law as a separate regime[29] but designing contract law as to comply with the requirements of commercial relationships.[30] The most important aspect of contracting in the commercial area is the allocation of risks. One of the characteristic features of commercial relationships is that stepping into the market as a market player is always a choice: no one is forced to play the game and if someone decides to do so, he may be supposed to have accepted the rules of the game. If the main rule is that players take care themselves, it has to be assumed then that everyone is playing according to this rule, at the same time accepting that others keep themselves to this rule of autonomy too. The situation is quite the opposite to consumer transactions, where it is not a choice to become a consumer, but consumers are, due to the characteristic features of their bargaining position, consumers simply by their existence in modern society. Keeping commercial transactions in mind, the legislature has to assume

---

28   The § 6:535 Ptk provides that a person carrying out hazardous activities shall compensate for the resulting damage. He shall be exempted from liability if he proves that the damage was caused by an unavoidable event outside the scope of the hazardous activity.

29   Lajos Vékás, *Az Új Polgári Törvénykönyv elméleti előkérdései* (HVGORAC 2001) 38.

30   Lajos Vékás, *Parerga: Dolgozatok az Új Polgári Törvénykönyv tervezetéhez* (HVGORAC 2008) 271.

that contracting parties are at relatively equal bargaining strength. This is a strong argument for minimizing state intervention and giving as a wide playing field to the parties as it is possible. This approach might have two implications, as far as contractual risk allocation is concerned. One of them is that agreed remedies shall be enforceable, the other is that parties – as the main rule – shall be allowed to limit their liability for breach of contract and shall be free in allocating risks of improper performance within the boundaries of public policy.

Agreed remedies are always the part of the regime of remedies for breach of contract. They may specify a sum to be paid on an event defined in the contract or breach, may give the aggrieved party the right to terminate the contract or entitle the party to retain a sum of money. Parties may include agreed remedies in their contract for different reasons, like avoiding the expensive assessment of damages in the event of a breach; enabling each party to plan for the financial consequences of the breach; enabling the aggrieved party to recover for losses that might otherwise be irrecoverable under the ordinary rules of assessment of damages; enabling the aggrieved party to get recovery where damages would be difficult to assess; enabling the parties to allocate the risk of particular losses occurring; acting as an incentive to performance, where performance is more valuable to the paying party than damages.[31]

From the point of view of contract law regulation, the three most problematic aspects of agreed remedies and contractual risk allocation are the limitation of liability, enforceability of liquidated damages, and enforceability of penalty clauses.

### 5.1 Exclusion clauses

Clauses of excluding or limiting the liability for breach of contract are the most important tools of risk allocation in the hand of the contracting parties. There are, however, certain statutory limits for enforcing such clauses. The § 6:152 Ptk provides that contract clauses limiting or excluding liability for damage caused by a breach of contract intentionally, as well as for the breach of contract harming human life, physical integrity, and health shall be null and void. Regulatory and judiciary restriction of contractual limitation and exclusion of liability for breach of contract has been a general answer in modern legal systems to the abuse of bargaining power. Limitation clauses reaching beyond the acceptable degree in most of the cases appeared in standard contract terms. This might be the reason that the reaction of the legal systems was generally twofold. One of the answers of the courts and later the legislation was disclaiming exclusion clauses; the other was the control of standard contract terms. One of the main arguments in favour of regulatory or judicial restriction on the enforceability of exclusion clauses is that if the party to a contract was allowed

---

31  Louise Gullifer, 'Agreed Remedies' in Andrew Burrows and Edwin Peel (eds), *Commercial Remedies: Current Issues and Problems* (OUP 2003) 191.

to exclude her liability for all kind of breach, it would deprive the contract as a legal instrument of its substance because the contract actually would not create any rights and obligations. The thought of treating some clauses as a kind of the core of a contract and assessing them differently from the aspect of exemption clauses as the other terms and conditions has also appeared in the Hungarian court praxis. The Hungarian Supreme Court in a case decided that the seller is liable for that the thing sold fits for purpose and is suitable for proper use even if it has been sold on a reduced price on the ground of its lower quality.[32]

An adverse consequence of the statutory restriction of exclusion clauses is that the restriction may prevent contracting parties from defining the scope of their liability and adjusting it to the agreed price of their performance. Fixing the limits of liability may be seen as one form of defining the rights and duties of the parties; that is, defining the contractual performance. If the parties agree to the contractual price with having regard to the scope of the liability of the obligor, the intervention into the contractual relationship with widening the scope of liability compared to the agreed limits of liability upsets the balance of contractual rights and obligations stipulated by the parties. If parties conclude the contract with relatively equal bargaining position, as it is assumed in commercial transactions, and there is not any ground for invalidity because of duress, mistake, abuse of standard contract terms or contractual power, etc. it does not seem to be reasonable to limit the party autonomy and freedom of contract in such a far-reaching way, provided that it is not contrary to public policy (like the exclusion of liability for personal injury or for consequences of an intentional breach that may be qualified as such).

Perhaps risk allocation is the most important aspect of establishing contractual rights and obligations. As parties draw the boundaries of their obligations, they define their promised performance. From this point of view exclusion or limitation of liability in commercial transactions may be seen only as a form of the definition of contractual duties as in general it is very hard to distinguish exclusion clauses and definition clauses. Clauses defining the performance and clauses defining liability do the very same. To some extent, Hungarian courts seem to accept as a defence the defining character of a clause. Courts seem to construe the rules on limiting the enforceability of exclusion clauses restrictively, for as much as they differ between exclusion clauses and clauses defining what must be treated as a breach of contract; or clauses defining the rights and obligations of the parties and the main subject matter of the contract. According to the court practice, clauses defining defective performance shall not be deemed as exemption clauses. Only the performance that is defective according to the terms of the contract can be qualified as a breach of contract.[33]

32  Supreme Court of Hungary decision Legf Bír Gf I 30 274/1986, BH 1987, 19.
33  E.g. if the parties of a building contract stipulate in the contract that hair-cracks on the wall shall not be treated as a defect of the building, this is not an exclusion clause and cannot be declared void on the ground of absence of adequate compensation. According to a decision of the Hungarian

If one assumes that parties of equal bargaining power consented freely and consciously upon clauses drawing the boundary of their liabilities, it does not seem to be reasonable to distinguish between definition clauses and exemption clauses, because limiting freedom of contract makes the non-mandatory character of contract law relative. In commercial transactions, regulatory limitations on exclusion clauses restrict the freedom of the parties in agreeing lump-sum damages making the boundaries of the obligation undertaken as the result of the bargain clear. This is a question of pricing too: the price the party would ask for his performance is normally adjusted to the risk imposed on him by the law and by the contract. Statutory restrictions on exclusion clauses restrict the playing field of the parties for the bargain too: the law simply prevents the parties from agreeing freely on the risk to be undertaken for the agreed price.

### 5.2 Liquidated damages

In commercial contracting parties usually attempt to standardize the compensation the obligor has to pay in case of breach of contract. This way they can make their risks foreseeable and can pre-estimate the compensable loss the obligee may suffer in case of a breach. The penalty is not suitable for this purpose because it is one-sided: it relieves the obligee from the burden of proving the loss he suffered within the penalty, but in certain jurisdictions, just like the Hungarian one, it would not limit the obligations of the obligor. If penalty in a legal system fixes only the minimum to be paid in case of a breach but does not set the maximum (like Hungarian law does not do that) it is not suitable for standardizing damages and providing a proper allocation of risks. Liquidated damages clauses are certainly the most reasonable and optimal way of risk allocation in commercial relationships. They make the risks of the obligor as well as the recovery of the obligee predictable and help to avoid the costs of a later dispute emerging from the uncertainties of the necessity of proving the loss of the aggrieved party.

Liquidated damages clauses are widely applied in commercial transactions; they are, however, to be distinguished from penalty clauses. It is a penalty, if 'a payment of money stipulated as *in terrorem* of the offending party' while a liquidated damages clause is 'a genuine attempt by the parties to estimate in advance the loss which will result from the breach'.[34] Where the clause in a contract shall be construed as liquidated damages, the aggrieved party would recover the agreed sum irrespectively of the actual loss he suffered or whether he proved any loss at all. If the actual loss is greater than the stipulated liquidated damages, the claim of the aggrieved party is limited to the stipulated sum.[35] A stipulated sum to be paid as a consequence of the breach of the other party shall be

Supreme Court in this case defect (breach of contract) is only a crack, which is deeper than a hair-crack. Supreme Court of Hungary decision Eln Tan G törv 31 848/1989, BH 1990, 343.

34 Guenther H Treitel, *The Law of Contract* (10th edn, Sweet and Maxwell 1999) 929.
35 Jack Beatson (ed), *Anson's Law of Contract* (27th edn, OUP 1998) 591.

qualified as liquidated damages (not a penalty) if the parties intended to provide for damages rather than a penalty, if the injury caused by the breach was – at the time of concluding the contract – uncertain or difficult to quantify, and if the stipulated sum had been a reasonable pre-estimation of the probable loss.[36] There are cases where a very fine distinction is to be made between payment triggered by breach and payment which is conditional on an event other than breach.[37] One of the main – and perhaps the worst – side-effects of statutory or judicial restriction on the enforceability of exclusion clauses is that it may create an inherent restriction on liquidated damages too: if it turns out that under the liquidation damages clauses the party in breach should pay less than the damage suffered by the aggrieved party, the enforceability of the liquidated damages clause shall be assessed as an exclusion clause.

Liquidated damages clauses are to be enforceable despite their atypical character in Hungarian law. There is, however, a risk of being construed as penalty clauses or deemed as exclusion clauses falling under the limits of enforceability, i.e. they cannot be enforced in cases of breach of contract with intentional conduct or in order to limit liability for personal injury. In both cases, the result is that – as a remedy for breach of contract – the aggrieved party is not prevented from claiming compensation for the loss exceeding the liquidated damages despite the agreement. Penalty clauses, however, can be reduced on the basis of the discretion of the courts. Thus, if the clause in the contract is to qualify as a penalty clause, it is up to the discretionary power of the court to reduce it. If the clause were to standardize damages, such a qualification may undermine the balance of the contract.

## 5.3 Penalty

As Victor Goldberg points out, acceptability of penalty seems to be culturally dependent.[38] The inconsistency in making the distinction between penalty clauses and independent guarantees suggests that discrediting penalty clauses may not be convincing and reasonable but authors often stress the advantages of penalty clauses which may serve three important and advantageous functions. First, the punitive element may serve as insurance provided by the promisor in favour of the aggrieved party. Second, penalty clauses often convey information about the reliability of the promisor. Third, in most of the cases penalties can be restated as bonuses: rejecting enforcement of penalty clauses provides incentives to simply re-draft identical contracts with bonuses.[39] Regulation may bring penalty close to liquidated damages if it does not allow claiming damages

---

36  This latter criterion is generally determinative. See John D Calamari and Joseph M Perillo, *The Law of Contracts* (4th edn, West Group 1998) 590.

37  Gullifer (n 31) 203.

38  Victor P Goldberg, 'Further Thoughts on Penalty Clauses' in Victor P Goldberg (ed), *Readings in the Economics of Contract Law* (CUP 1989) 161.

39  Robert Cooter and Thomas Ulen, *Law & Economics* (5th edn, Pearson 2008) 260.

exceeding the default penalty. The disadvantage of this solution is that it compels the parties to imply less probable damages too as they stipulate the sum of penalty. This may be avoided by the minimum-damages concept of penalty where damages exceeding penalty are recoverable.[40] Looking for a proper solution of regulating penalty and/or liquidated damages clauses the starting point shall be that remedies imposed by the parties shall generally be enforced by the courts (whether they are typical or atypical or have a punitive character or not) because self-imposed remedies reflect the parties' efforts to maximize the value of the contract.[41] Only solutions which allow the parties as great freedom as possible – within the boundaries of public policy – in designing and stipulating their agreed remedy and which are flexible enough to cover different types of agreed remedies according to the will of the parties shall be optimal.

A penalty in Hungarian contract law is a secondary obligation. Under a penalty clause stipulated in the contract, the obligor shall pay a certain sum of money if he fails to perform the contract or his performance is not in conformity with the contract for reasons attributable to him (default penalty). The payment of a penalty does not relieve the party of his obligation to perform, because the obligor is also entitled to enforce payment for those damages exceeding the default penalty, as well as other rights resulting from a breach of contract. The obligee is entitled – in accordance with the relevant regulations – to demand compensation for damages caused by the breach of contract, even if he has not enforced the claim for default penalty. In commercial contracting practice, the parties usually try to standardize the compensation the obligor has to pay in the event of a breach of contract, in this way trying to make their obligations foreseeable and to pre-estimate all the damages the obligee may suffer in the case of a breach. A penalty is not suitable for this purpose because it is one-sided: it relieves the obligee from the burden of proving the loss she suffered as far as the penalty extends, but in certain jurisdictions, it would not limit the obligations of the obligor. If the penalty in a legal system fixes only the minimum to be paid in the event of a breach but does not set the maximum (like in Hungarian law) it is not suitable for standardizing damages and providing a proper allocation of risks. Liquidated damages clauses are certainly the most reasonable and optimal way of risk allocation in commercial relationships: they make the risks of the obligor, as well as the recovery of the obligee, predictable and help to avoid the costs of a later dispute emerging from the uncertainties of needing to prove the loss of the aggrieved party.

Penalty clauses have a double function: they provide lump-sum compensation to the aggrieved party and they also provide a deterrent sanction in the event of a breach of contract, even in absence of damage, in order to compel the party to perform even if breaching the contract would be preferable for

---

40  Detlev Fischer, *Vertragsstrafe und vertragliche Schadensersatzpauschalierung* (Alfred Metzner Verlag 1981) 161.
41  Thomas J Miceli, *The Economic Approach to Law* (Stanford University Press 2004) 158.

him. That is, the function of the penalty is to increase the costs of the breach of contract for the obligor and this way to prevent an efficient breach.

## 6  Conclusions

The main structural and determining feature of contract law is if the performance of contractual obligations is enforced in kind, and if yes, to what extent. Specific performance is the underlying principle of the Hungarian contract law. Liability for breach of contract is embedded in this context. The Civil Code of 1959 established a unitary regime where liability for breach of contract as well liability in tort were fault-based. The flexible concept of fault made it possible for the courts to adjust the required standard of conduct to the circumstances of the case. There were no significant difficulties experienced in this regime. The new Ptk of 2013 changed the system of liability with drawing a Chinese Wall between liability in tort and liability for breach of contract. While liability in tort remained fault-based liability, liability for breach of contract is construed, with the implementation of the CISG, as a strict liability with a foreseeability limit. The conceptual elements of this system, like the 'beyond control' or foreseeability, are widely discussed in scholarship. However, there are no experiences with this new system yet. The difficulties with applying the *non-cumul* rule, bordering cases, assessing contracts for services, and accommodation relationships suggest that this new system may not bring significant advantages. In transactions, exclusions clauses, stipulated penalty, and liquidated damages clauses play an important role. Although liquidated damages clauses are enforceable in Hungarian contract law, there is a risk that they are to qualify as a penalty clause or exclusion clause according to the circumstances of the case. Such qualification may undermine the structure and the balance of contractual rights and obligations. The main function of the penalty is to increase the transactional costs of breaching the contract. That is, penalty, as well as the principle of specific performance, are to prevent an efficient breach of contract.

## Bibliography

Beatson J (ed), *Anson's Law of Contract* (27th edn, OUP 1998).

Calamari JD and Perillo JM, *The Law of Contracts* (4th edn, West Group 1998).

Collins H, *The Law of Contract* (2nd edn, Butterworths 1993).

——, *Regulating Contracts* (OUP 1999).

Cooter R and Ulen T, *Law & Economics* (5th edn, Pearson 2008).

Fischer D, *Vertragsstrafe und vertragliche Schadensersatzpauschalierung* (Alfred Metzner Verlag 1981).

Fried C, *Contract as Promise: A Theory of Contractual Obligation* (HUP 1981).

Fuglinszky Á, 'Risks and Side Effects: Five Questions on the "New" Hungarian Tort Law' [2014] (2) *ELTE LJ* 199.

——, *Kártérítési jog* (HVGORAC 2015).

Goldberg VP, 'Further thoughts on Penalty Clauses' in Goldberg VP (ed), *Readings in the Economics of Contract Law* (CUP 1989) [https://doi.org/10.1017/CBO9780511528248.037].

Gullifer L, 'Agreed Remedies' in Burrows A and Peel E (eds), *Commercial Remedies: Current Issues and Problems* (OUP 2003).

Harmathy A, 'The Binding Force of Contract in Hungarian Law' in Harmathy A (ed), *Binding Force of Contract* (Institute for Legal and Administrative Sciences of the Hungarian Academy of Sciences 1991).

Holmes OW Jr, *The Common Law* (Little, Brown and Co 1881).

Jones G and Goodhart W, *Specific Performance* (2nd edn, Butterworths 1996).

Linzer P, 'On the Amorality of Contract Remedies: Efficiency, Equity, and the Second Restatement' (1981) 81 *Colum L Rev* 111 [https://doi.org/10.2307/1122187].

Macneil IR, 'Efficient Breach of the Contract: Circles in the Sky' (1982) 68 *Va L Rev* 947 [https://doi.org/10.2307/1072886].

Marton G, *A polgári jogi felelősség* (TRIORG 1993).

Menyhárd A and Veress E, 'Kontraktuális felelősség a magyar és a román polgári jogban' [2020] *MJ* 288.

Miceli TJ, *The Economic Approach to Law* (Stanford University Press 2004).

Schwartz A, 'The Case for Specific Performance' (1979) 89 *Yale LJ* 271 [https://doi.org/10.2307/795838].

Simpson AWB, *A History of the Common Law of Contract* (Clarendon Press 1975).

Szalai Á, 'A szerződésszegés szándékossága. Tudatosság és ösztönzők' in Gárdos-Orosz F and Menyhárd A (eds), *Az Új Polgári Törvénykönyv első öt éve* (Társadalomtudományi Kutatóközpont Jogtudományi Intézet 2019).

Szászy I, *A kötelmi jog általános tanai* (Grill Kiadó 1943).

Trebilcock MJ, *The Limits of Freedom of Contract* (HUP 1997).

Treitel GH, *The Law of Contract* (10th edn, Sweet and Maxwell 1999).

Vékás L, *Az Új Polgári Törvénykönyv elméleti előkérdései* (HVGORAC 2001).

——, *Parerga: Dolgozatok az Új Polgári Törvénykönyv tervezetéhez* (HVGORAC 2008).

White JJ and Summers RS, *Uniform Commercial Code* (5th edn, West Group 2000).

Zimmermann R, *The Law of Obligations: Roman Foundations of the Civilian Tradition* (Clarendon Press 1996).

Part II

# Specific institutes and recent developments in the law of obligations in Central and Southeast Europe

# 6 Ascertainment of a claim as a requirement for set-off

## Different approaches in comparative and the Czech law

*Jiří Handlar*

## 1 Introduction

Set-off is a way of extinction of claims that consists in discharging of fungible claims in the scope in which they meet each other.

Set-off facilitates the performance of obligations. If the parties are mutually bound to give one another the same fulfilment, the provision of fulfilments by both parties is not necessary as the same result can be achieved when one party's obligation is deducted from the other party's obligation, i.e. via their set-off. Set-off accelerates and simplifies the payment system and lowers the costs related to the mutual provision of the respective fulfilments. Therefore, the law of obligations strongly tends to support set-off and define its requirements in a way that would make set-off admissible in most cases.

Set-off can operate *ipso iure*, that is by means of the law itself, if the requirements for set-off have been met (automatic set-off); or on the basis of a declaration made by one of the parties (set-off by declaration); or by court decision (judicial set-off).[1]

The chapter is limited to set-off by a declaration of a party, which is a mode of set-off typical for most European jurisdictions as well as for international systems of law of obligations (UPICC, PECL, or DCFR).

## 2 Set-off by declaration and its legal effects

In this concept, the party can set-off its claim against the other party's claim if the requirements of set-off are met. Declaration of set-off must be addressed to the other party, and the discharging effect of set-off takes place at the moment when the declaration of set-off is received by the other party.

---

1 See for details Pascal Pichonnaz and Louise Gullifer, *Set-Off in Arbitration and Commercial Transactions* (OUP 2014) 21ff. Claims can be set-off by the agreement of contractual parties too (set-off by agreement). In these cases, the ascertainment of the claims is not the necessary requirement for the set-off. This chapter does not deal with this type of set-off.

In this chapter, the following terminology is used. *Main claim* is the claim of the party against which set-off is declared. The party is a main creditor. In the civil proceedings, the main creditor is a plaintiff. *Cross-claim* is the claim of the party declaring set-off. The party is a cross-claim creditor. In the civil proceedings, the cross-claim creditor is a defendant.

Set-off by declaration can operate retrospectively (*ex tunc*) as of the moment when the mutual claims could have been fulfilled for the first time (*retrospective effect*). In such a case the accrued interests, as well as late payment charges (consequences of delayed payment, namely the obligation to pay interests for delayed payment, contractual penalties, or damages due to the delay), will retrospectively extinguish together with the claims. It has to be stressed that the discharging effect of set-off differs from the discharging effect of performance.

Set-off has retrospective effects in most legal systems in Europe (including German, Austrian, Swiss, Dutch, and Czech law).[2]

Moreover, set-off by declaration can operate only in respect to the future (*ex nunc*), it means from the time the declaration of set-off is received by the other party (*prospective effect*). In this case, the set-off discharges only the claims of the parties; interests and consequences of the delay are not affected by that set-off. In this case, the discharging effect of set-off is the same as the discharging effect of performance.

Prospective effects of set-off are seen especially in the international systems of law of obligations (UPICC, PECL, and DCFR).[3]

## 3 Ascertainment of a claim

General requirements for set-off are mutuality of claims and fungibility of claims (the claims have to be of the same kind). Moreover, a cross-claim has to be matured and enforceable.

A requirement for set-off also can be an ascertainment (often called *liquidity*) of a claim. The requirement of ascertainment usually relates only to the claim of the party declaring set-off (cross-claim).

Ascertainment (liquidity) of a claim can be considered in different ways; in this chapter we will distinguish its following substantive and procedural meaning.

### 3.1 Substantive ascertainment

Substantive ascertainment (liquidity) means that a claim has to be ascertained as to its existence and as to its amount and is not disputable.

---

2 Christian von Bar and Eric Clive (eds), *Principles, Definitions and Model Rules of European Private Law: Draft Common Frame of Reference (DCFR)*, vol 2 (SELP 2009) 1132–33.
3 UPICC 2016, Art 8.5(3); PECL, Art 13:106; DCFR, Art III-6:107.

A claim ascertained as to its existence and as to its amount is especially a claim awarded by a judgment, established by a valid agreement of the parties, or acknowledged by a debtor. The claims that have been ascertained as to their existence but not yet as to their amount are not considered as ascertained (liquid) claims. Typical examples of those are claims for damages.

A claim is disputable if a debtor can contest its existence or its value. It is generally acknowledged that the mere denial of its existence or value is not sufficient. To contest the claim, the debtor has to have serious reasons.[4]

### 3.2 Procedural ascertainment

Procedural ascertainment (liquidity) means that a claim is ascertained if it can be easily and readily proved in the civil proceedings. The cross-claim invoked to be set-off in the civil proceedings is considered illiquid if the proceedings on such a claim significantly protract the proceedings on the main claim. The requirement of procedural ascertainment (liquidity) of the cross-claim protects the plaintiff who exercises a claim at the civil proceedings that can be quickly awarded to him and prevents the defendant from delaying the court proceedings by raising the objection of set-off.

## 4 Main approaches to the issue

The particular jurisdictions view the ascertainment of the cross-claim as the requirement for set-off from several basic perspectives: ascertainment as a substantive requirement (4.1.), procedural approach (4.2.), judicial discretion (4.3.), and no ascertainment of the cross-claim (4.5.).

### 4.1 Ascertainment as a substantive requirement

Ascertainment (liquidity) of a cross-claim is another substantive requirement for set-off. The cross-claim that is to be set-off has to be ascertained as to its existence and as to its amount. If there is not an ascertained cross-claim there is no valid declaration of set-off. In this case, the cross-claim creditor has to wait until the cross-claim becomes ascertained and then he can make a declaration of set-off again.

Even if the ascertainment of a cross-claim as a substantive requirement is more typical of set-off operated automatically (Italian law or Belgian law), we can find it also in the legal systems where set-off is made by declaration.

---

4 See Pascal Pichonnaz in Stefan Vogenauer (ed), *Commentary on the UNIDROIT Principles of International Commercial Contracts (PICC)* (2nd edn, OUP 2015) 1050.

### 4.1.1 UNIDROIT Principles

According to Art 8.1(1) UPICC 2016,

> where two parties owe each other money or other performances of the
> same kind, either of them ('the first party') may set off its obligation against
> that of its obligee ('the other party') if at the time of set-off, . . . the other
> party's obligation is ascertained as to its existence and amount and perfor-
> mance is due.

Under Art 8.1 (2) UPICC 2016, 'if the obligations of both parties arise from
the same contract, the first party may also set off its obligation against an obligation of the other party which is not ascertained as to its existence or to its
amount.'

According to the UPICC, the requirement of ascertainment is fully depen-
dant on the fact whether the main claim and the cross-claim arise from the same
contract. If so, then there is no requirement of ascertainment at all. But if the
claims do not arise from the same contract the cross-claim has to be ascertained.

The Official Comment explains that:

> an obligation is ascertained when the obligation itself cannot be con-
> tested, for example, when it is based on a valid and executed contract or
> a final judgment or award which is not subject to review. Conversely, an
> obligation to pay damages is not ascertained when the obligation may be
> contested by the other party. Even if the existence of the other party's obli-
> gation is not contested, it is not possible to exercise set-off if the obligation
> is not ascertained as to its amount.[5]

Consequences of this definition for set-off in practice are controversial. Pascal
Pichonnaz points out that the requirement of ascertainment 'restricts the ability
to set-off obligations arising from different contracts to a significant extent; it
is rather unusual for the obligation of the other party to be ascertained where
there is doubt'.[6] Moreover, in the systems where set-off operates by a declaration of a party, there are no justifiable doctrinal reasons for including the ascertainment of cross-claim in requirements of set-off (in contrast with the systems
where set-off operates automatically).[7]

Pichonnaz concludes that for practical purposes the requirement of ascertainment should be softened, 'however, it would be wiser to abandon the
requirement altogether'.[8]

5 International Institute for the Unification of Private Law (UNIDROIT), 'UNIDROIT Principles of
International Commercial Contracts 2016' (UNIDROIT 2016) 295 <www.unidroit.org/instruments/
commercial-contracts/unidroit-principles-2016> accessed 29 February 2020.
6 Pichonnaz in Vogenauer (n 4) 1051.
7 ibid.
8 ibid 1053.

*4.1.2 French law*

In the past, set-off in French law operated automatically when the requirements for set-off were met, i.e. without any activity of the parties. Ascertainment (liquidity) of both claims (not only of a cross-claim) was another substantive requirement for set-off. A claim was ascertained if it was indisputable (certain) as to its existence and as to its amount.

Because the requirement of ascertainment (liquidity) limited set-off to a significant extent, the automatic set-off was supplemented by judicial set-off (set-off operated by the court decision). The court was empowered to order set-off in two cases. First, if the claim was not ascertained, the judge was allowed to ascertain it provided that it could easily be done. In this case, set-off did not have a retrospective, but a prospective effect. Second, the judicial set-off was available if the claims were sufficiently connected even if they were not ascertained. It means that 'connectivity replaced liquidity'. The set-off operated retrospectively; the discharging effect took place at the moment when the first claim became due.[9]

The reform of the French law of obligations[10] has changed the mode of set-off. The automatic set-off was replaced by set-off made by declaration. According to Art 1347 of the French CCiv, set-off operates if it is invoked by a party, and it has the retroactive effect.

However, the requirements and effects of set-off have not been changed. Ascertainment (liquidity) of both claims is still a requirement for set-off.[11] The judicial set-off is also available; the court may order set-off even if the claims have not been ascertained (liquidated) yet, then the court decision has an only prospective effect. If the claims are connected the court has to order set-off regardless of whether or not the claims have been ascertained. In this case, the decision has retroactive effect.[12]

We can conclude that current French law is another example of the law system where set-off operates by a declaration of a party and where ascertainment of a claim is another substantive requirement for set-off. However, the requirement is softened by judicial set-off and excluded in the case of connected claims.

### 4.2 Procedural approach

This approach can be found in German law. According to German law, ascertainment (liquidity) of a cross-claim is not a substantive requirement for set-off

---

9  Gérard Légier, *Droit Civil: Les Obligations* (18th edn, Dalloz 2005) 197, Pichonnaz and Gullifer (n 1) 144, 150.

10 Ordinance 2016–131 of 10 February 2016 (*Ordonnance 2016–131 du 10 février 2016 portant réforme du droit des contrats, du régime général et de la preuve des obligations*), JORF, 0035 of 11 February 2016, 26 (came into force on 1 October 2016).

11 See CCiv, Art 1348.

12 See CCiv, Art 1348–1. Laurent Jourdan, 'La compensation: consécrations et interrogations' (2016) 14 (144) *JdS* 32.

at all. The cross-claim creditor can set-off the cross-claim even if it is unascertained (disputable). The set-off is valid and has a discharging effect on the claims concerned.

However, in the civil proceedings, it can be relevant if the defendant declares set-off of a cross-claim that cannot easily be proved (procedural ascertainment). In this case, the court should consider – according to the circumstances of the case – whether adjudication of the cross-claim could delay the proceedings or not.

If the defendant invokes a cross-claim that is not ready for decision unlike the main claim, the court can decide separately on the main claim by a provisional judgment (a decision with reservation).[13] The provisional judgment does not deal with the cross-claim; the decision on the cross-claim is reserved to a later stage of the proceedings.

The provisional judgment is fully enforceable and can be executed.[14] It means that the main creditor can enforce the decision at the court and obtain fulfilment from the main claim regardless of whether or not the set-off has already been validly exercised.

On the other side, the provisional judgment does not influence the set-off and its substantive effects. The court – subsequently deciding on the cross-claim – has to consider whether the declaration of set-off has been valid. If it concludes that the set-off has been valid and has discharged the claims (the cross-claim as well as the main claim) the court sets aside the provisional judgment and dismisses the action. If it concludes that the set-off has not been valid, it upholds the original judgment but overrules the reservation.[15]

If the provisional judgment has already been enforced the main creditor is fully responsible for damages.[16] The responsibility of the main claim creditor (plaintiff) is an objective responsibility (it does not require the proof of culpability) and includes all material damage as well as immaterial damage that the cross-claim creditor (defendant) incurred due to the enforcement of the main claim.[17]

### 4.3 Judicial discretion

In this approach, it is the judge who is to decide whether or not the set-off of the cross-claim is to be admitted. Depending on the circumstances of each

---

13 See German Code of Civil Procedure (*Zivilprozessordnung*, ZPO) in the version promulgated on 5 December 2005 (*BGBl* I 3202; 2606 I 431; 2007 I 1781), last amended by Article 2 of the Act of 12 December 2019 (*BGBl* I 2633), § 302(1).

14 See ZPO, § 302(2).

15 Adolf Baumbach and others (eds), *Zivilprozessordnung*, vol 1 (74th edn, CH Beck 2016) 1394.

16 See ZPO, § 302(3).

17 Christoph Thole in Hanns Prütting and Markus Gehrlein (eds), *Zivilprozessordnung: Kommentar* (10th edn, Luchterhand Verlag 2018) § 302 998–99.

particular case, the judge takes into consideration whether or not set-off of the cross-claim would unduly delay the civil proceedings concerning the main claim. This approach can be found in the DCFR and in Dutch law.

### 4.3.1 DCFR

According to Art III – 6:103(1) DCFR, 'a debtor may not set off a right which is unascertained as to its existence or value unless the set-off will not prejudice the interests of the creditor.' Under Art III – 6:103(2) DCFR, 'where the rights of both parties arise from the same legal relationship it is presumed that the creditor's interests will not be prejudiced.'[18]

The meaning of the Article is explained in the Official Comment. The solution of the issue adopted by the DCFR is considered as a compromise between the approach, where ascertainment is a substantive requirement for set-off and the approach, where the cross-claim does not have to be ascertained.[19]

According to the DCFR, ascertainment of a cross-claim is not a further substantive requirement of set-off. However, the requirement of ascertainment may be applied in the proceedings. In every single case, the judge should consider all the circumstances of the case and decide whether interests of the main creditor will not be prejudiced by the set-off. It is presumed that the creditor's interests will not be prejudiced if the claims arise from the same legal relationship.

The Official Comment states:

> if the cross-right cannot be readily ascertained, the judge is empowered to adjudicate upon the principal right without taking account of the set-off declared by the debtor, provided that the principal right is otherwise ready for adjudication. The judge is thus given a discretion and will have to take account of all the circumstances of the case, such as the probable duration of the proceedings concerning both, principal right and cross-right, or the effect of a delay on the creditor.[20]

If the judge comes to the conclusion that the main creditor will be prejudiced by the set-off, he decides only on the main claim. The cross-claim is not taken into account, and the main claim is regarded 'as being unaffected by the declaration of set-off. As a result, the declaration of set-off must be regarded as ineffective'.[21]

It means that the decision on the main claim is final, not only provisional. There is no other decision on the cross-claim; the cross-claim is no longer

---

18  The same regulation is contained in PECL, Art 13:102.
19  Bar and Clive (n 2) 1121.
20  ibid.
21  ibid; Ole Lando and others (eds), *Principles of European Contract Law: Part III* (Kluwer Law International 2003) 145.

taken into account in the present proceedings. It has to mean that the court decision has a substantive effect and makes the set-off ineffective.

Pascal Pichonnaz and Louise Gullifer point out that:

> these concerns can be followed when notice of set-off is made for the first time in proceedings. They may be less valid if they relate to a situation of notice of set-off given outside a courtroom. To be taken seriously, The Official Comment's remark that ascertainment is not a substantive requirement would mean that set-off should be accepted in all cases, despite an unascertained cross-claim.[22]

### 4.3.2 Dutch law

A similar approach can be found in Dutch law, although it is derived from quite different wording of the law.

According to the Dutch BW, the judge may grant judgment in favour of the plaintiff even though the defendant invokes compensation, where the validity of this defence cannot easily be ascertained, and the action would otherwise succeed.[23]

The provision empowers the judge to reject the defence of set-off if the cross-claim is not ready for adjudication. Hugo van Kooten explains that this is the case if the content of the cross-claim cannot be established immediately or if the cross-claim is contested by the plaintiff and if it can only be ascertained by complicated or time-consuming proof. The judge must take into account all the relevant circumstances of the case, such as the relationship between the claims and the probable duration of the inquiry into the validity of the claims.[24]

### 4.4 No ascertainment of the cross-claim

This approach can be found in Swiss law. Article 120(2) of the Swiss OR expressly provides that 'the debtor may assert his right of set-off even if the countervailing claim is contested'.

Ascertainment of a cross-claim is not a requirement of set-off at all. The cross-claim can be set-off regardless of whether or not it has been ascertained. Set-off of a claim that has not been ascertained is valid and has a discharging effect. In the event of a dispute between parties, the judge has to determine the exact amount for which set-off has discharged the main claim and the cross-claim. Similarly, the ascertainment (liquidity) of the cross-claim is not a requirement for set-off in the civil proceedings. It seems that there is no special regulation of the issue in Swiss procedural law.[25]

---

22  Pichonnaz and Gullifer (n 1) 194.
23  See BW, Art 6:136.
24  Hugo van Kooten in Danny Busch and others (eds), *The Principles of European Contract Law (Part III) and Dutch Law* (Kluwer Law International 2006) 151.
25  Wolfgang Peter in Heinrich Honsell, Nedim Peter Vogt, and Wolfgang Wiegand (eds), *Basler Kommentar: Obligationenrecht I: Art. 1–529 OR* (6th edn, Helbing Lichtenhahn Verlag 2015) 733–34; Pichonnaz and Gullifer (n 1) 163–64.

# 5  Advantages and disadvantages of the main approaches

## 5.1  *Ascertainment as a substantive requirement*

There are legal systems where ascertainment of a cross-claim is a substantive requirement for set-off. Without an ascertained cross-claim there is no valid declaration of set-off. The requirement of ascertainment aims primarily at the protection of the main creditor. Set-off is a way of private enforcement of the cross-claim that is exercised only based on the will of the cross-claim creditor and without the involvement of the main-claim creditor. If the cross-claim is illiquid or disputable, the illiquidity or disputability should not be transferred via the set-off to the main claim which is not illiquid or disputable.

The main deficiencies of that approach lie in the definition of the term 'an unascertained claim' in its substantive meaning. There are no doubts that if there were the 'completely strict' approach to the requirement of ascertainment and only incontestable cross-claims would be suitable for set-off it would improve legal certainty of the parties and it could simplify the process of set-off. But at the same time, it would represent such a significant limitation to the set-off that it would make it hard to be accepted.

There cannot be the 'strict' approach to the requirement, not every contest can make the cross-claim unascertained, but it is hard to define how serious the contest has to be. The definition mentioned earlier that a claim is ascertained when it cannot be contested is not thus sufficient because it does not give the satisfying answer to the question. Moreover, how Pichonnaz highlights,[26] even if the requirement of ascertainment is softened (and not every contested cross-claim is excluded from set-off) this approach stays too strict and restricts the ability to set-off to a significant extent.

Another trouble of the approach is the fact that the requirement can be abused by the main creditor. In cases where the contest of the cross-claim is crucial for the set-off, the main creditor can contest the cross-claim to make it disputable using artificial reasons or objections.

Another question is in as much the fact that the cross-claim is disputable should be relevant in the field of substantive law. Set-off of a cross-claim that has been contested does not prejudice the interests of the main creditor in the field of substantive law. If the cross-claim does not exist, the set-off is invalid and has no discharging effect (because the cross-claim that does not exist cannot be set-off at all). If the cross-claim exists (even if it has been disputed) and set-off discharges the main claim and the cross-claim, the interest of the main creditors usually will not be prejudiced because the main creditor has been obliged to perform the cross-claim and the set-off only discharges his obligation (admittedly disputable, but existing) in accordance with the nature and purpose of set-off. If the cross-claim is disputable there is no possibility how to solve the dispute in the field of substantive law (but an agreement of the

---

26  Pichonnaz in Vogenauer (n 4) 1050–51.

parties), only a judge can solve the dispute of the parties. Here the question of ascertainment of the cross-claim is not an issue of the substantive law anymore and it becomes the issue of the procedural law. Now the disputability of the cross-claim is of no importance as the only thing that matters is the fact whether it can be easily proved in the civil proceedings (which is, however, the question of procedural ascertainment, not substantive ascertainment).

We can conclude that in legal systems where set-off operates by declaration the requirement of ascertainment as a substantive requirement causes legal uncertainty and at the same time too much restricts the ability to set-off, and often it is not necessary to achieve the wished aim for which it was determined. These inconveniences can be partially solved if the requirement is softened by judicial set-off or by exceptions from the requirement (e.g. the requirement is not to be applied to claims arising from the same contract).

### 5.2 Procedural approach

In this approach, the ascertainment of the cross-claim is not a substantive requirement, therefore it does not cause the difficulties mentioned earlier.

The approach deals with the question of ascertainment in its procedural meaning and tries to find a balanced solution. On the first side, there is the interest to allow set-off to the greatest extent; on the other side there is the danger that the cross-claim creditor (as a defendant) can delay the civil proceedings by invoking an unfounded set-off.

The solution is simple and clever. Set-off of a cross-claim is allowed even if the cross-claim is disputable, but if invoking the set-off might delay the civil proceedings the court can decide separately on the main claim by a provisional judgment and leave the adjudication of the cross-claim to a later stage of the proceedings. If set-off is valid the court will set aside the provisional judgment.

The main advantage of the approach is that the ability of the parties to set-off is not limited to any extent. Nevertheless, the approach prevents the cross-claim creditor from declaring an unfounded set-off because the set-off cannot prevent the court from the adjudication of the main claim. At the same time, it prevents the main claim creditor from contesting the cross-claim without reasonable reasons because the contest is not able to prevent the cross-creditor from set-off.

In other words, this approach does not prevent the cross-claim creditor from declaring set-off even if the cross-claim is disputable; such a set-off does not delay the civil proceedings about the main claim yet.

But we can also find some disadvantages of the approach. The first one is that in some cases the approach could prejudice the cross-claim creditor. The provisional judgment might be enforced even if the main claim has been discharged by a valid set-off. In this case, the provisional judgment is subsequently set aside and the cross-claim creditor has a claim for damages caused by the execution, but it seems that it does not have to be always sufficient for the protection of the cross-claim creditor, especially if the main creditor has become insolvent in the meantime. In this case, it can be difficult for the cross-creditor to get back the money he had to pay to perform the main claim.

Another disadvantage of the approach is that it can be used only if German procedural rules apply. These rules are to be applied in the court proceedings, but in the arbitral proceedings special procedural rules that can regulate the issue of procedural ascertainment of the cross-claim in another way are often applied.[27]

## 5.3 Judicial discretion

In this approach an ascertainment of a cross-claim is not a substantive requirement of set-off; it is the judge who is to decide whether or not the set-off of the cross-claim is to be admitted depending on the circumstances of each particular case.

It means that the ascertainment of the cross-claim is relevant in its procedural (not substantive) meaning and that the approach is only a special kind of procedural approach.

Before the civil proceedings, there is no judicial discretion (there is nobody who would be able to decide whether the cross-claim can easily be proved and is suitable for adjudication) and the approach thus should not be applied. In other words, the approach is to be applied only to the set-off that is made for the first time in civil proceedings.

The main advantage of the approach is obvious. It prevents a defendant from invoking an unfounded set-off that can unduly delay the civil proceedings.

But we can also name some disadvantages of this approach. First, the approach can probably be applied only to a limited extent because it only relates to set-off that is declared in the civil proceedings. It limits the application of the approach to a significant extent.

Second, in the civil proceedings, it reduces the ability of the parties to set-off. The reduction is not considerable but exists (contrary to the other procedural approach mentioned above).

Third, the approach is more suitable for law systems where set-off has a prospective effect. In these systems, the discharging effect of set-off is the same as the discharging effect of performance. If a court in the civil proceedings does not admit the set-off of an unascertained cross-claim the cross-claim creditor can immediately perform his obligation instead of the set-off and achieve the same legal effect (the discharging of the main claim at the time of the performance). But in legal systems where set-off operates retrospectively, there is a completely different situation. In these systems, set-off does not have the same legal effect as performance. Set-off retrospectively discharges not only mutual claims but also the accrued interests and consequences of the delay, whereas by the mutual performance of obligations just and only the obligations of the

---

27 Pichonnaz and Gullifer (n 1) 165.

parties extinguish. If a court in the civil proceedings does not admit the set-off of an unascertained cross-claim there is no way for the cross-claim creditor to achieve the same legal effect as he would have achieved if the set-off had been admitted. In this case, it seems to be inequitable to deprive the cross-claim creditor of the possibility to set-off.

### 5.4 No ascertainment of the cross-claim

In law systems based on this approach, there is no requirement of ascertainment of a cross-claim at all. A cross-claim, even if it is unascertained (disputable), can be set-off regardless of whether the set-off has been declared in the civil proceeding or out of it.

The advantages of the approach are obvious; there are no issues with the requirement of ascertainment mentioned earlier. The ability of the parties to declare set-off is not limited to any extent. The approach prevents the main claim creditor from contesting of the cross-claim based on artificial reasons because the contest cannot prevent the cross-creditor from declaring set-off. In the civil proceedings, there is no separate adjudication on the claims that have been set-off; a judge decides on the claims by only one judgment.

The main disadvantage of the approach is obvious as well. The cross-creditor can delay the civil proceedings by invoking set-off of the unascertained (disputable) cross-claim. But it does not mean that the matter cannot be solved by procedural rules.

The procedural regulations define the way the respondent can contest the action and exercise objections. If the defendant wants to contest the main claim by raising the objection of set-off, he has to do so only under the conditions set by the procedural regulations. These regulations can lay down especially the period of time within which the defendant can contest the action by exercising his procedural defence or objections. Objections raised later can be taken into consideration only exceptionally, under the pre-set conditions. The procedural regulations can limit the right to exercise the objection of set-off (by allowing it only at the early stage of the proceedings) and as such significantly limit the eventual abuse of set-off for the purpose of protracting the court proceedings.[28]

## 6 Ascertainment of a cross-claim and Czech law

The position of Czech law on this matter is very unclear yet. According to the old Civil Code, which was in force until 2013, there was no requirement of ascertainment of a cross-claim at all. This regulation did not cause any trouble in the field of substantive law, but courts sometimes faced attempts to protract the civil proceedings by invoking set-off of obviously unfounded cross-claims.

28  See ibid 19.

It should be noted that there have not been any special regulations of that issue in Czech procedural law. According to Czech procedural law the parties usually can present facts and evidence only before the end of the first court hearing in their case (however, there are some exceptions laid down by the law). Therefore, the defendant can base his defence just and only on the facts that were presented at the court before the end of the first court hearing.[29]

However, it has been disputable whether or not that regulation applies also to the set-off, namely whether the defendant can use only the set-off made before the end of the first hearing as his procedural defence or whether it is allowed to invoke the set-off that was made later in the proceedings. According to the most recent decision of the Supreme Court of the Czech Republic (*Nejvyšší soud České republiky*, NSČR), a defendant can declare set-off and use it as a procedural defence after the first hearing even if he could have done it before the first hearing had ended.[30]

The new Czech Civil Code (*Občanský zákoník*,[31] NOZ), which came into force in 2014, contains a provision that may regulate the issue. According to § 1987(2) NOZ, 'an uncertain or indeterminate claim is not eligible for set-off.'

The explanatory memorandum to the NOZ does not explain the meaning of the provision. There is written only the following:

> In compliance with the standard regulations, it is newly suggested that it should be expressly laid down that neither the uncertain claims nor inde-terminate claims can be unilaterally set-off, as the aim of the set-off is to discharge the mutual claims of the participants and not to invoke the dis-crepancies and follow-up disputes.

However, the purpose has not been achieved. The regulation is still one of the most disputed in the NOZ. All authors agree that the 'uncertainty or indeter-minateness' is another substantive requirement for set-off and it is to be applied only to cross-claims. If the uncertain or indeterminate cross-claim is set-off, the declaration of set-off is voidable (it has legal effect unless the main creditor invokes its invalidity).

But the authors differ significantly in their opinion on what is the exact meaning of the requirement of 'uncertainty or indeterminateness' of the cross-claim and how the requirement influences the ability of parties to set-off. The fact whether the requirement means the non-ascertainment of the cross-claim,

---

29 See especially Czech Civil Procedure Code (*Zákon* 99/1963 *Sb, Občanský soudní řád*), as later amended, § 118b. The Czech procedural regulations on the way, when, and how new facts and evidence are to be presented at the court are much more complicated; however for the purpose of this chapter the preceding simplification will suffice.

30 NSČR decision of 28 August 2018, 32 Cdo 4182/2016. It has to be mentioned that the decision was not approved for publication in the official Collection of the Supreme Court decisions.

31 Act 89/2012, Civil Code (*Zákon* 89/2012 *Sb, Občanský zákoník*), as later amended.

as it is mentioned in this chapter, is not clear either. There are three differing opinions on this issue.

According to the first opinion, the requirement of 'uncertainty or indeterminateness' of the cross-claim does not mean its non-ascertainment. The uncertainty or indeterminateness of the cross-claim is usually understood as some specific attribute of the cross-claim. For example, a cross-claim is uncertain or indeterminate if it is a conditional claim, if it is a future claim, if it exists but its value cannot be established yet, or if it can be contested as to its enforceability. Only these special attributes of the cross-claim prevent set-off, otherwise, the cross-claim can be set-off without any other limitation.[32]

According to the second opinion, the requirement of 'uncertainty or indeterminateness' of the cross-claim means its non-ascertainment. To be suitable for set-off the cross-claim has to be ascertained as to its existence and as to its amount and may not be disputable. Following the DCFR it is suggested that the strict requirement of ascertainment should be softened and should not be applied if the set-off does not prejudice the main creditor's interests. It is especially the case of the claims that arise from the same contract or from contracts that are economically or legally connected.[33]

It has to be noted that the opinion has the same inconveniences as were described in part 5.1 of the chapter. Moreover, in Czech law, the judicial set-off that might soften the requirement of ascertainment is not available.

There is the third opinion presented in the recent decision of the NSČR.[34] The NSČR concluded that:

> if it can be expected that the raising of the objection of set-off in the court proceedings would unreasonably protract the proceedings on the main-claim (that has been exercised in an action) due to the difficulty of the examination of the existence and value of the to-be-set-off cross-claim, it can be stated that the claim cannot be set-off due to its uncertainty and indeterminateness.

If the uncertain or indeterminate cross-claim is used for set-off, the set-off is voidable.

The approach of the NSČR is very unusual and different from all the approaches described in this chapter. The NSČR defines the 'uncertainty or indeterminateness' of the cross-claim as non-ascertainment in procedural meaning (the cross-claim is not certain if it cannot easily be proved in the civil proceedings pending on the main claim), but simultaneously considers the requirement as the substantive one (if the cross-claim is not certain at the time when set-off is declared the set-off is voidable in the field of substantive law).

---

32 Jiří Handlar, 'Započtení' in Zbyněk Pražák, Josef Fiala, and Jiří Handlar (eds), *Závazky z právních jednání podle občanského zákoníku: Komentář k § 1721–2893 OZ* (Leges 2017) 612–13.

33 Josef Šilhán, 'Započtení pohledávky "nejisté nebo neurčité"' (2018) 26 (22) *Prav Rozhl* 763.

34 NSČR decision of 1 October 2018, 28 Cdo 5711/2017.

The approach differs from the approach described in part 4.1 (ascertainment as a substantive requirement), because the requirement of ascertainment of the cross-claim has completely procedural content. It also differs from the approach described in part 4.2 (procedural approach), because the lack of requirement has a substantive effect. Finally, it differs from the approach described in part 4.3 (judicial discretion), because the lack of the requirement has substantive effect without any activity of the court (the court only finds out whether or not the set-off has been valid; it has no power to declare valid set-off as ineffective).

It seems that the connection of the ascertainment as the substantive require-ment with its procedural content (that can be derived only from the course of the civil proceedings) does not make reasonable sense. Finally, it has to be noted that the decision was not approved for publication in the Official Col-lection of the NSČR decisions, but it was afterwards followed in one other deci-sion of the NSČR.[35] The position of Czech case law thus stays a little unclear.

We can conclude that even if numerous opinions concerning the signifi-cance and consequences of the § 1987(2) NOZ have been presented, it remains a questionable and contestable issue. Contrary to the intention declared in the explanatory memorandum, the NOZ has brought great legal uncertainty to the process of set-off. The legal regulation of the issue in the NOZ cannot be considered better than the regulation that was contained in the old Civil Code.

## 7 Conclusions

Ascertainment (liquidity) of a cross-claim as a requirement for set-off can be considered first in its substantive meaning (a cross-claim has to be ascertained as to its existence and as to its amount and may not be disputable). Ascertainment as a substantive requirement, however, causes legal uncertainty and too much restricts the ability of parties to set-off. These inconveniences can be partially solved if the requirement is softened by judicial set-off or by exemptions from the requirement.

Ascertainment (liquidity) of a cross claim can be considered second in its procedural meaning (a cross-claim can be easily proved in the civil proceed-ings). Ascertainment in this meaning can be particularly useful because it can prevent a cross-claim creditor (as a defendant) from invoking an unfounded set-off in order to delay the civil proceedings. This is the reason why some legal systems have introduced special procedural rules that limit or exclude set-off in the civil proceedings if the cross-claim is not ripe for adjudication.

We can distinguish two different kinds of procedural approaches. The first one is a purely procedural approach with no consequences in the field of sub-stantive law (German law). In this approach – if there is a set-off that can delay the civil proceedings – the court can decide separately on the main claim by a provisional judgment and leave the adjudication of the cross-claim to a later

---

35  NSČR decision of 22 January 2019, 20 Cdo 4713/2018.

stage of the proceedings. The second one is a procedural approach with impact on the substantive effect of set-off. In this approach, the judge decides whether or not the set-off of the cross-claim is to be admitted according to the circumstances of each particular case.

If we compare these procedural approaches, the first one seems to be better because it does not limit the ability to set-off to any extent, but still prevents the defendant from delaying the proceedings by invoking an unfounded set-off.

Finally, we can say that similar result can be achieved even if there is no special requirement of ascertainment of a cross-claim, namely by general regulation of procedural law that requires that all facts and evidence used by a defendant as a procedural defence have to be submitted at the early stage of the civil proceedings.

## Bibliography

Bar C von and Clive E (eds), *Principles, Definitions and Model Rules of European Private Law: Draft Common Frame of Reference (DCFR)*, vol 2 (SELP 2009).

Baumbach A and others (eds), *Zivilprozessordnung*, vol 1 (74th edn, CH Beck 2016).

Busch D and others (eds), *The Principles of European Contract Law (Part III) and Dutch Law* (Kluwer Law International 2006).

Honsell H, Vogt NP, and Wiegand W (eds), *Basler Kommentar: Obligationenrecht I: Art. 1–529 OR* (6th edn, Helbing Lichtenhahn Verlag 2015).

International Institute for the Unification of Private Law (UNIDROIT), 'UNIDROIT Principles of International Commercial Contracts 2016' (UNIDROIT 2016) <www.unidroit.org/instruments/commercial-contracts/unidroit-principles-2016> accessed 29 February 2020.

Jourdan L, 'La compensation: consécrations et interrogations' (2016) 14 (144) *JdS* 32.

Lando O and others (eds), *Principles of European Contract Law: Part III* (Kluwer Law International 2003).

Légier G, *Droit Civil: Les Obligations* (18th edn, Dalloz 2005).

Pichonnaz P and Gullifer L, *Set-Off in Arbitration and Commercial Transactions* (OUP 2014).

Pražák Z, Fiala J, and Handlar J (eds), *Závazky z právních jednání podle občanského zákoníku: Komentář k § 1721–2893 OZ* (Leges 2017).

Prütting H and Markus G (eds), *Zivilprozessordnung: Kommentar* (10th edn, Luchterhand Verlag 2018).

Šilhán J, 'Započtení pohledávky "nejisté nebo neurčité"' (2018) 26 (22) *Prav Rozhl* 763.

Vogenauer S (ed), *Commentary on the UNIDROIT Principles of International Commercial Contracts (PICC)* (2nd edn, OUP 2015).

# 7 Restitution of use value of money in unjustified enrichment

## Some open questions in the law of Croatia, Serbia, and Slovenia

*Damjan Možina*

## 1 Introduction

In case of unjustified enrichment, the person enriched (the recipient) has to return not only the object of unjustified enrichment but must also reimburse the benefit acquired by having had or used the object of unjustified enrichment over a period of time.[1] If the object of unjustified enrichment is a thing bearing fruits, the fruits are the benefits, e.g. chicken and eggs, or property bringing rent. If the object to be returned is money (principal sum), the civil fruit is the interest.

In the former Yugoslav Obligations Act of 1978 (YZOO), which is still in force in Serbia,[2] there are some open questions and controversies regarding the duty to pay interest in claims based on unjustified enrichment. The regulation is largely based on Arts 214 and 132(5) YZOO. These provisions correspond with Arts 1115 and 368(5) of the Croatian Obligations Act of 2005 (*Zakon o obveznim odnosima*,[3] ZOO) and with Arts 193 and 111(4) of the Slovenian Obligations Code of 2002 (*Obligacijski zakonik*,[4] OblZ).

This chapter aims to address some of these questions, namely (a) about the nature of Art 214 YZOO or respective provisions in the laws of other successor states, (b) whether the *bona fide* recipient must reimburse the use value of money at all, (c) whether the reimbursement should be based on concrete or abstract use value, furthermore (d) whether the benefits arising from the business decisions of the recipient should be reimbursed too, (e) whether the duty to pay interest in claims following the termination of reciprocal contracts is

---

1 Lutman distinguishes 'primary benefit', i.e. primary object of unjustified enrichment (property which was transferred to the recipient without legal grounds), and 'secondary benefit', i.e. the benefit acquired by using the primary object, such as fruit or interest. See Karmen Lutman, 'Neupravičena obogatitev v primerjalnem in slovenskem pravu' (PhD thesis, University of Ljubljana Faculty of Law 2018) 319.

2 Obligations Act (*Zakon o obligacionim odnosima*), *SL SFRJ* 29/1978, 39/1985, 45/1989, 57/1979, *SL SRJ* 31/1993, *SL SCG* 1/2003, *SG RS* 18/2020.

3 *NN* 35/2005, 41/2008, 125/2011, 78/2015, 29/2018.

4 *UL RS* 83/2001, 28/2006, 40/2007, 64/2016. Relating to Art 193 OblZ see e.g. Damjan Možina, 'Obresti in plodovi pri neupravičeni obogatitvi' [2019] *Prav Letop* 163, 163–64.

different from the duty arising from the general rules on unjustified enrichment, and (f) about the rate of enrichment interest.

## 2 The nature of Article 214 of the Yugoslav Obligations Act

Article 214 YZOO titled 'The amount of claim' provides that when unjustified enrichment is being reimbursed, a 'dishonest' recipient shall return the fruits and pay default interest as of the date of receipt of the object of unjustified enrichment, whereas an 'honest recipient' shall only return the fruits and pay default interest as of the date the 'claim was made'. The provision was originally not included in the Draft Obligations Act of Mihailo Konstantinović, the 'Sketch' (*Skica*), and was added at a later stage of the preparation of YZOO.

By prescribing the default interest the provision aims at establishing a stricter liability of a *mala fide* recipient of a sum of money, i.e. the recipient who knows or should have known he is not entitled to keep the sum of money. A dishonest (i.e. *mala fide)* recipient is treated in the same way as a thief – he is considered to be in default (*fur semper in mora*). The punitive element of the statutory default interest is meant to discourage late payment.

The duty to return the fruits appears to be regulated in the same way as default interest in the sense that it only exists for the dishonest recipient. However, the duty to return the fruits which still exist in the property of the recipient does not as such contain a punitive element. If the dishonest recipient is to be treated more strictly, in a way as to encourage timely return, similar to the recipient of a sum of money, the duty should be understood as covering all fruits, including the fruits already consumed and the fruits which have not been harvested and have perished.[5]

The law seems to presume that a recipient is in good faith until the claim for restitution is made. Oddly, the Slovene version of the Obligations Act (*Zakon o obligacijskih razmerjih*[6]), as well as the current OblZ, even refer to the day 'the claim was filed', implying the filing of the claim at the court. Surely, the filing of the claim does not yet mean that the defendant has received it. But also, if the 'claim' should refer to the receipt of an out-of-court demand, the question remains whether the recipient can acquire knowledge of his non-entitlement in another way. The claimant must have a chance to prove that the defendant (recipient) knew or should be treated as if he knew about his non-entitlement before the moment he received the claim to return it.

In Slovenia, the High Court of Ljubljana (*Višje sodišče v Ljubljani*, VSL) has e.g. applied the provision on default interest for the dishonest recipient in case of a donation, where a man had donated a larger sum of money to a woman, expecting that they would live together in a relationship. As the expectation (functioning as an implied condition) was frustrated, he claimed the money

---

5  See also Stojan Cigoj in Borislav T Blagojević and Vrleta Krulj (eds), *Komentar Zakona o obligacionim odnosima* (Savremena administracija 1983) 817.
6  *SL SFRJ* 29/1978, 39/1985, 45/1989, 57/1989, *UL RS* 88/1999, 83/2001, 30/2002, 87/2002.

back. The VSL found that the donee had 'cultivated negative emotions' towards the donor and had kept his acquaintance solely for financial benefits; it thus considered her to be a dishonest recipient.[7]

## 3 Is an honest recipient under a duty to reimburse fruits and use value, too?

At the first glance, Art 214 YZOO appears to say that a *bona fide* recipient i.e. a recipient with justified reliance in his entitlement as to the object of the unjust enrichment, has no duty at all to return the fruits or pay interest. However, such interpretation would run contrary to the basic idea of unjustified enrichment. Namely, under the general clause of Art 210(1) YZOO or Art 1111(1) of the Croatian ZOO, the recipient has a duty to return the object or reimburse the value of benefits acquired regardless of his good or bad faith. The duty is an objective consequence of unjustified enrichment. In other words, even a recipient in good faith does not have a right to keep the benefits acquired by having used a good or a sum of money without legal ground. If, for example, the object of unjustified enrichment is a house and the house was rented out, there is no reason why the recipient should have a right to keep the rent money (a civil fruit): there is no legal ground for him to keep it.

The same idea is expressed by Arts 219 YZOO and 1120 ZOO. Here, the benefit acquired by having used a good of another person without legal ground is to be reimbursed regardless of the recipient's good faith. There is no reason for the fruits and benefits acquired by the use of money to be treated principally differently from the duty to reimburse the benefits acquired by the use of a good. The fact that the legislature had followed the basic idea that use value is to be reimbursed in any case is also apparent from the provisions on the effects of termination of contracts in Art 132(4) and (5) YZOO, or Art 368(4) and (5) ZOO.

We can thus safely conclude that the *bona fide* recipient, too, is under a duty to pay interest and return fruits. The inconsistent provision of 214 YZOO must be interpreted as a part of a coherent system. We shall return to the issue of applicable interest rate later.

A further point, although reaching beyond the scope of this chapter, needs to be briefly addressed here, namely, how to treat the situation where the recipient with justified reliance in his entitlement as to the object of the restitution (i.e. *bona fide*) consumes this object, sells it, otherwise disposes of it or the object is accidentally destroyed or lost. The recipient's good faith is protected by the defence of disenrichment.[8] If he had reasons to believe that a good or a sum of money belonged to him permanently, the fact that he consumed or otherwise disposed of it cannot be held against him. He is not obliged to reim-

---

7 See VSL judgment of 10 January 2019, I Cpg 123/2018, para 27.
8 See e.g. DCFR, Art VII-6:101 ff.

burse the goods or the money he consumed, spent, or lost (etc.) in good faith that he will never be asked to return it. If, however, he disposed of a good or money in a way that the value is still in his property, i.e. sold it in exchange for a price, he must return it.[9] The disenrichment defence covers the fruits and the benefits acquired by use, too. It counter-balances the duty of a *bona fide* recipient to reimburse fruits and use value.

## 4 What is use value?

The use value of goods or money which is to be reimbursed can be understood in more than one way. It may refer to the mere possibility to use in the sense that if the recipient had the goods or a sum of money at his disposal for a certain period of time, he is considered to have used them and benefited from use.

This is the general approach of the law of obligations to default interest. If the debtor is in default (delay) with the payment, he must pay (statutory) default interest regardless of whether the creditor suffered any loss due to his non-payment or not. Of course, the focus of the law of (contractual or delictual) damages is rather different from the law of unjustified enrichment: while the goal of the first is the recovery of the creditor's loss, the second aims at reimbursing from the debtor of what he is not entitled to. The idea behind default interest is that the creditor is considered to have suffered the loss (at least) in the amount of statutory interest rate, without having to prove it. Thus, default interest is a form of abstract damages. If we turn the idea around and consider that the recipient should reimburse the use value simply because he had the goods or money at his disposal for some time, without the other party having to prove how he benefited from them, it can be called abstract use value. This approach certainly seems practicable as the claimant does not have to prove concrete gains and can e.g. rely on market prices of use value (if such exist).

The concrete use value, on the other hand, refers to the benefits the recipient had actually gained by having used the goods or money. According to this understanding the creditor should prove the concrete benefits (concrete use value) in order to be reimbursed. In situations where the claimant does not have insight into whether and how the defendant (recipient) had used the object of unjustified enrichment and benefited from it, the concrete use concept could seem rather harsh from the point of view of claimant.

On the other hand, a duty to reimburse abstract use value could be very harsh toward the recipient who, in good faith about his entitlement to money or goods, would not gain the use value in the amount of (the market price of) abstract value or, indeed, wouldn't use the money or goods at all. From this

---

9 For disenrichment defence in Slovenian law, see Damjan Možina, 'Vsebina in obseg obogatitvenega zahtevka' in Damjan Možina (ed) *Razsežnosti zasebnega prava: Liber amicorum Ada Polajnar Pavčnik* (Univerza v Ljubljani Pravna fakulteta 2017) 159–65; VSL judgment of 25 November 2015, I Cp 2316/2015; VSL judgment of 13 December 2017, II Cp 2088/2017.

point of view, such a general duty to reimburse abstract use value would be contrary to the idea of protection of good faith in the law of unjustified enrichment. A *bona fide* recipient, not expecting that he would have to reimburse anything, should be obliged to reimburse the value he did not gain. Therefore, the duty to reimburse concrete use value should be the general approach.

However, an exception applies to a dishonest recipient. Here, the abstract use concept is not problematic as there is no good faith to protect. Thus, a *mala fide* recipient should pay for abstract use value of money or also reimburse the fruits he did not collect. It is, as was already mentioned, a case of stricter enrichment liability, similar to the liability of a debtor in delay who has to pay (abstract damages in the form of) default interest.

In some jurisdictions, abstract use value is also reimbursed in some other situations.[10] In Swiss law, for example, the concrete use value of money is the principle; however, abstract use value (interest) is awarded if the profit of the recipient can be presumed based on general life experience.[11] The presumption is rebuttable. The same applies in German law: if the object of enrichment was being used in the course of recipient's business or if the object of enrichment is a dividend-bringing bond, the average profit may be expected, without the claimant having to prove concrete gains.[12] If the recipient is a bank, the interest in the amount of reference interest rate plus 5 percentage points may be presumed.[13] If the recipient used the money to pay his debt for which he would have to pay interest, the courts presume a benefit in the amount of the interest he saved.[14]

With regard to use value, another issue needs to be briefly addressed. Namely, some benefits from use or fruits arise from the object of unjustified enrichment without much activity of the recipient. An apple growing on an apple tree or a profit-yielding property (rented out) may serve as an example. The recipient of such 'objective' benefits must reimburse them without further ado. But some benefits are different. They may arise from the object of unjustified enrichment e.g. only because of particular characteristics of the recipient, his business contacts, his work, or (more or less risky) investment. The principle is that the benefits which can be seen as 'resulting' from the particular recipient should not be reimbursed. Indeed, even a dishonest recipient should only reimburse the benefits objectively arising from the object of unjustified enrichment.[15] He may keep the benefits which can be ascribed to him.

---

10  See also Možina (n 4) 166.
11  Hermann Schulin in Heinrich Honsell, Nedim Peter Vogt, and Wolfgang Wiegand (eds), *Basler Kommentar: Obligationenrecht I: Art. 1–529 OR* (5th edn, Helbing Lichtenhahn Verlag 2011), Art 64, para 4b.
12  See Christiane Wendehorst in Heinz Georg Bamberger and Herbert Roth (eds), *Kommentar zum Bürgerlichen Gesetzbuch: Band 2* (52th edn, CH Beck 2019) § 818 para 13; Hartwig Sprau in Gerd Brudermüller and others, *Palandt: Bürgerliches Gesetzbuch* (79th edn, CH Beck 2020) § 818 para 11.
13  See e.g. BGH decision of 24 April 2007, XI ZR 17/06, *NJW* 2007, 2401.
14  See e.g. BGH decision of 19 March 1998, IX ZR 22/97, *NJW* 1998, 2592.
15  Cigoj (n 5) 817.

## 5  Restitution claims within the contractual unwinding

If a reciprocal contract is terminated due to a breach of contractual duties by one of the parties and one or both parties have already made their performances in total or in part, the first question that arises is whereas the termination has retroactive (*ex tunc*) or prospective (*ex nunc*) effect.

Article 132(2) YZOO makes clear that after termination the contract no longer represents a valid reason for the parties to keep what they have received under the contract. Thus, the termination has retroactive (*ex tunc*) effect and the parties must return to each other what they have received thus far – not only the objects of contract themselves but, as apparent from Art 132(4) YZOO, also the benefits gained by using it (use value). However, the termination has such an effect only in contracts performed in one act (one-off contracts). In long-term contracts with a recurring or continuous performance, the termination is only effective prospectively (*ex nunc*), in principle.[16] Only in one-off contracts, the law aims to set the parties in a position *que ante contractum*.[17] Of course, in both scenarios, a contract may contain clauses such as arbitration agreement which 'survive' termination. The situation where the property was transferred from one party to another under a valid reason (contract), but this reason subsequently fell away, is also covered by the general rule on unjust enrichment in Art 210(4) YZOO. However, the situation following the termination of reciprocal contracts (unwinding of contracts) is different in an important respect: here, both parties have reciprocal restitution claims. Although the contract no longer exists, these claims cannot be assessed entirely independently of each.

For the restitution claims, Art 132(2) YZOO refers to the 'rules on two-sided contracts',[18] i.e. rules on reciprocal (mutual, *synallagmatic*) contracts contained in Section 5 of Chapter II of the YZOO (Arts 121 to 147). One of the principles contained in this section is concurrent performance (Art 122 YZOO). The referral may be understood in the sense that the restitution claims are to be performed concurrently.

In this context, the first issue to be dealt with is the question of allocation of risk of subsequent deterioration or destruction, i.e. a situation where one party is unable to return what it had received under the contract. Although this issue is outside the scope of the chapter,[19] two brief remarks are in place. First, the rules on mutual contracts also include provisions on the effect of the impos-

---

16  See YZOO, Art 129(1). Only exceptionally, if the entire performance was fundamental for the contract, termination is effective *ex tunc*, see YZOO, Art 129(2). See also: Damjan Možina, 'Razdor, odpoved in odstop od pogodbe' [2011] *Prav Letop* 57.

17  Phillip Hellwege in Nils Jansen and Reinhard Zimmerman (eds), *Commentaries on European Contract Laws* (OUP 2018) 1399.

18  The title of the section preceding Art 121 YZOO, 'Two-sided contracts', is misleading as all contracts presuppose a declaration of will of (at least) two parties. A correct title would be 'reciprocal' or 'mutual' contracts, i.e. contracts where the main obligations of both parties are inter-connected in a way that one represents payment for the other (*synállagma*).

19  See e.g. Hellwege (n 17) 1401.

sibility of performance (Arts 137 and 138 YZOO) which could be used to tackle the issue. Second, in sales contracts, the YZOO principally approaches this problem in another way: according to Art 495 YZOO, the buyer loses the right to terminate the contract due to a defect if he is unable to return the goods and he may be considered responsible.

The second issue arising from the mutual restitution claims is the reimbursement of use value. As both parties are paying for the use of either money or goods or services they had received, their reimbursement claims should be treated in the same way in the sense of criteria.[20] It would seem odd if, e.g. in a terminated sales contract, the buyer was to reimburse only concrete use value whereas the seller would have to repay abstract value (interest). It would also seem rather odd if the amount of both claims for reimbursement of use value would be fundamentally different. When the contract was concluded, each of the parties considered the value of the performance of the opposing party (including its use value) was at least equal to the value of their own performance. Indeed, one could consider the mutual claims for the reimbursement claims to be – at least in principle – set-off against each other. In following this idea, some modern contract law frameworks have excluded the claims for the reimbursement of use value (benefits) altogether.[21] This was also motivated with avoiding existing difficulties with the quantification of claims.[22] Austrian courts, for example, presume that in case of termination of mutual contracts the reimbursement claims of both (*bona fide*) parties are set-off against each other.[23]

The approach of the YZOO to this problem is rather controversial: according to Art 132(4) YZOO both parties are required to reimburse the benefits acquired by use (use value); however, Art 132(5) YZOO demands the party returning the money to pay default interest as of the moment it received the money. From today's point of view, default interest does not seem appropriate here.[24] As already mentioned, the default interest contains a punitive element, providing the incentive to pay for a debtor in default. Here, the recipient can hardly be – retroactively, after the termination of the contract – considered to be in default. He had received the money under what was then a valid contract. Also, the provision stands in an odd relation to the provision on interest within the general rules on unjust enrichment (Art 214 YZOO), as the latter makes only the dishonest recipient of a sum of money pay default interest. Moreover,

---

20  Lutman (n 1) 323.

21  See e.g. UPICC, Art 7.3.6. See also Reinhard Zimmermann, 'The Unwinding of Failed Contracts in the UNIDROIT Principles 2010' (2011) 16 *Unif L Rev* 563, 582; Peter Huber in Stefan Vogenauer (ed), *Commentary on the UNIDROIT Principles of International Commercial Contracts (PICC)* (2nd edn, OUP 2015) Art 7.3.6 paras 22–24.

22  Huber (n 21).

23  See Peter Rummel in Peter Rummel (ed), *Kommentar zum Allgemeinen bürgerlichen Gesetzbuch: Band II* (3rd edn, Manz 2002) § 1437 para 9; Brigitta Lurger in Andreas Kletečka and Martin Schauer (eds), *ABGB-ON: Kommentar zum Allgemeinen bürgerlichen Gesetzbuch* (Manz 2010) § 1437 para 9.

24  See also Miha Juhart, 'Vračilo denarja kot posledica prenehanja obligacijske pogodbe' [1995] (6) *PP* 8.

the default interest implies that the interest is owed abstractly, i.e. regardless of the actual benefits acquired by the recipient while there is no such provision for the reimbursement of the use value of goods.

A possible explanation as to how this inconsistency became part of the YZOO might be the context of the provision. Article 102(5) of the academic draft of the YZOO ('Sketch'), on which the provision is based, was modelled after Arts 78 and 81 ULIS (Hague Uniform Sales Law). The seller was to pay interest as from the day of receipt of the money. The interest rate for default was defined in Art 83 as a 'rate equal to the official discount rate in the country where he has his place of business or, if he has no place of business, his habitual residence, plus 1%'. A similar approach was enacted in the first version of the YZOO: according to its Art 277(1), the interest rate for default was the interest, payable for bank deposits on demand in place of performance. However, the regulation of default interest rate soon changed. In the following years, the default interest rate – regulated outside YZOO, by government regulation – acquired a different function which became predominant in the light of remarkably high inflation (even hyper-inflation) in Yugoslavia: the preservation of value of money. The default interest rates were being changed periodically (at times monthly), reaching high and even extreme values such as 432%.[25]

In CISG – the successor of ULIS – the reference to default interest in the provision was omitted. As the agreement of the member states at the diplomatic conference regarding the interest rate could not be reached, the interest rate is not defined in the convention. Article 84(1) CISG merely states that after termination, the seller must pay 'interest' from the day the payment was received. The majority opinion considers the function of the provision not to be the recovery of damage but reimbursement of use value of money.[26] As the seller had the possibility to use the money in the country of his place of business, he is considered to have saved the interest he would otherwise have to pay for borrowing such sum; habitual interest rate in the seller's place of business is usually applied.[27] Due to the need for practicability in international trade, the basis for reimbursement is an abstract value, i.e. concrete benefits of use need not be proved.[28]

In Slovenia, the OblZ has left out the term 'default' from the provision. As in Art 84(1) CISG, the party returning the money must pay 'interest' from the moment it received the money.[29] It is for the courts to apply the interest rate they consider appropriate. Default interest is only applicable from the moment the recipient gets in default with the return of capital sum (*mora debitoris*). In Croatia and Serbia, Art 368(5) ZOO and Art 132(5) YZOO still refer to

25  See e.g. Ivanka Lekić, 'Docnja dužnika i pravo poverioca na kamatu' (1988) 38 *Pravni život* 1706.
26  Christiana Fountoulakis in Peter Schlechtriem, Ingeborg Schwenzer, and Ulrich G Schroeter (eds), *Kommentar zum UN-Kaufrecht (CISG)* (7th edn, CH Beck 2019) Art 84 para 17.
27  ibid.
28  ibid.
29  See OblZ, Art 111(4).

default interest, although the regulation and the function of default interest have changed considerably since the provision was adopted in 1978.

Apart from termination of contract due to a breach there are also other cases where a contract ends with a retroactive effect (*ex tunc*). Such is the consequence of nullity of a contract, as apparent from Art 104(1) YZOO, and of successful avoidance of a contract, e.g. due to error or threat, as described in Art 113(1) YZOO. As the legislation in these situations does not contain a reference to provisions on mutual contracts the question arises whereas analogous application of Art 132(3) YZOO is appropriate here. Despite some differences, the situation is comparable to the situation after termination: both parties are claiming back what they have performed under a contract which no longer exists; therefore, the provisions on concurrent performances and impossibility seem applicable, as well as the principle of equal treatment of parties with regard to reimbursement of use value.

This is principally true also for situations following the withdrawal from the contract; however, the EU legislation provides for some modifications as regards the effects of withdrawal in consumer contracts. Both parties have to return to each other what they have received under the contract until the consumer's withdrawal. The Consumer Rights Directive protects the contractual *synallagma* in sales contracts even after withdrawal as the trader may withhold the reimbursement of the price until he has received the goods back (or an equivalent notice) from the consumer.[30] The Directive also codifies the ruling of the ECJ in the case Messner:[31] the consumer may only be asked to pay for the direct cost of returning the goods (provided he was properly informed) and not the reimbursement of use value.[32] Nor is the trader obliged to reimburse use value of the money received. However, the consumer may be liable for the diminished value of goods, if it is a result of the handling of the goods in a manner incompatible with principles of civil law.[33]

## 6 The unwinding of credit, rent, and similar contracts

As it was said, the basic approach to use value is concrete use value. This is the result of the protection of good faith of the recipient, i.e. his reliance that he will remain the proprietor and will not be asked to reimburse the use benefits.

---

30 Directive 2011/83/EU of the European Parliament and of the Council of 25 October 2011 on consumer rights, amending Council Directive 93/13/EEC and Directive 1999/44/EC of the European Parliament and of the Council and repealing Council Directive 85/577/EEC and Directive 97/7/EC of the European Parliament and of the Council [2011] *OJ* L304/64 (Consumer Rights Directive), Art 13(3). See also Croatian Consumer Protection Act (*Zakon o zaštiti potrošača*), *NN* 41/2014, 110/2015, 14/2019, Art 76(3); Slovenian Consumer Protection Act (*Zakon o varstvu potrošnikov*), *UL RS* 25/1998, 23/1999, 110/2002, 51/2004, 114/2006, 126/2007, 86/2009, 78/2011, 38/2014, 19/2015, 31/2018, Art 43d(5).
31 Case C-489/07 *Pia Messner v Firma Stefan Krüger* [2009] ECR I-07315, ECLI:EU:C:2009:502.
32 Consumer Rights Directive, Art 14(1).
33 ibid.

The consideration is based on the (unwinding of) contracts such as sales where ownership over the goods is being exchanged for money.

However, not all contracts are like that – for instance, in credit, rent, and other contracts where it is not the ownership but the use of money or goods for certain time that is being paid for. In case of the unwinding of such contracts, the borrower's or the lessee's good faith in their continuing entitlement to use the object of contract does not need protection. They know from the outset that they must return the money or the property after the contract is over. Moreover, they know that they are paying the price (in principle, the market price) for the use. It would seem rather odd if, in case of the unwinding of contract after withdrawal or termination, they could claim that they did not gain any use value as they did not use the borrowed money or rented property.

It would appear appropriate to allow reimbursement on the basis of mere possibility to use, i.e. to presume that the benefits were gained (abstract use value). It could be considered that the recipient, by having used the money or property, gained the benefit in the amount of the market price for borrowing or renting he would otherwise (in the absence of the concrete contract) have had to pay to obtain such use.[34] In credit contracts, the average annual percentage rate[35] or the average interest rate[36] for different types of credit contracts published regularly by the national banks of Slovenia and Croatia could serve as a reference of the market price.

Another possible approach is to consider the agreed price for use as the indicator of use value, although the contract was terminated or withdrawn from. In fact, this is the approach of the EU Consumer Credit Directive[37] in case of withdrawal: if the consumer has drawn the credit, he is considered to have gained use value and is obliged to reimburse the interest, calculated on the basis of the agreed borrowing rate.[38] From this perspective, a withdrawal

---

34  See also: Možina (n 4) 171. In German law, the authors are divided regarding this question. Some consider only the concrete use value as relevant, see e.g. Martin Schwab in Mathias Habersack (ed), *Münchener Kommentar zum Bürgerlichen Gesetzbuch: BGB, Band 6: Schuldrecht – Besonderer Teil IV* (7th edn, CH Beck 2017) § 818 paras 20ff; Wendehorst (n 12) § 818 para 31. For others the abstract value is sufficient, see e.g. Stephan Lorenz in Norbert Horn (ed), *J. von Staudingers Kommentar zum Bürgerlichen Gesetzbuch: Staudinger BGB – Buch 2: Recht der Schuldverhältnisse: §§ 812–822 (Ungerechtfertigte Bereicherung)* (Sellier / de Gruyter 2007) § 818 para 13; Matthias Fervers and Beate Gsell, 'Bereicherungsrechtliche Verpflichtung zur Herausgabe von Nutzungen' (2013) 66 *NJW* 3607, 3608.

35  See Art 26 of the Slovenian Consumer Credit Act (*Zakon o potrošniških kreditih*) UL RS 77/2016 (Slovenian ZPK).

36  See Art 11b(3) of the Croatian Consumer Credit Act (*Zakon o potrošačkom kreditiranju*) NN 75/2009, 112/2012, 143/2013, 147/2013, 9/2015, 78/2015, 102/2015, 52/2016 (Croatian ZPK).

37  Directive 2008/48/EC of the European Parliament and of the Council of 23 April 2008 on credit agreements for consumers and repealing Council Directive 87/102/EEC [2008] OJ L133/66 (Consumer Credit Directive).

38  See Consumer Credit Directive, Art 14(3)(b). See also Croatian ZPK, Art 14(2)(b), and Slovenian ZPK, Art 18.

from consumer credit contract has only prospective (*ex nunc*), not retrospective (*ex tunc*) effect.

## 7  The rate of 'enrichment interest'

As already mentioned, Art 214 YZOO and the respective provisions in Croatian and Slovenian law do not prescribe the interest rate for the *bona fide* recipient of the money. It is up to the courts to apply the interest rate reflecting the benefits gained by the use of money.

In principle, only the concrete use value should be reimbursed. The interest rate to be applied can also serve as a presumption of use value, whereas the parties can prove that the benefit gained was higher or lower.

In the original version of the YZOO, Art 399(3) contained a provision on the applicable interest rate in contracts where interest was agreed but not the rate: the rate was 6%, and 8% in commercial contracts. In the Slovenian OblZ, the interest rate in such cases is 6%.[39]

The question of whether these provisions can be applied by way of analogy must be answered negatively. First, in the light of the situation on financial markets in recent years, a gain in the amount of 6% is relatively high; certainly, it is remarkably high for a consumer. Second, a fixed interest rate does not reflect the fluctuations of use value of money over time. A dynamic interest rate seems to be a more suitable approach.

In this regard the reference rate from the Late Payment Directive comes to mind, representing the price of money in inter-bank lending as determined by the central bank.[40] However, as the value of the reference rate has been zero for several years its applicability as a measure of use value is debatable. The EURIBOR and the LIBOR, too, reflect the interest rates in contracts between banks. Both values have been negative for several years. The average interest rates in credit contracts with the population, on the other hand, are far from zero, also because they reflect the credit risk. Suggestions regarding the appropriate rate of enrichment interest include a combination of one of the reference rates, such as the ECB reference rate, and an addition of a few percentage points (e.g. somewhere from 2 to 4).[41]

---

39  OblZ, Art 382(2).
40  Directive 2011/7/EU of the European Parliament and of the Council of 16 February 2011 on combating late payment in commercial transactions [2011] *OJ* L48/1 (Late Payment Directive). Under the Late Payment Directive, Art 2(6) and (7), the default interest rate (in commercial transactions) is the sum of 'reference rate', representing the price of money in inter-bank lending as determined by the central bank, and at least 8 percentage points addition.
41  Claudius Gelzer, *Verzugs-, Schadens- und Bereicherungszins: Verzinsungspflichten bei unfreiwilliger Kreditierung im schweizerischen Privatrecht mit rechtsvergleichenden Hinweisen* (Helbing Lichtenhahn Verlag 2010) 194.

A different possible approach would be to take the average interest rates in credit contracts as a basis. In Croatian law, for example, average interest rates in credit contracts with non-financial businesses for a period longer than one year, published twice a year by the National Bank, are the basis for default interest.[42]

## 8 Conclusion

Article 214 YZOO (Art 1115 ZOO, Art 193 OblZ) only regulates the strict liability of a dishonest recipient. However, the *bona fide* recipient, too, has to reimburse the use value and fruits. The basic approach to use value is concrete, i.e. the claimant must prove that the recipient gained benefits from use. A different solution – abstract use value – applies to the dishonest recipient and to the situations, where a presumption of gained use benefits or profits seems justified. In cases of unwinding of reciprocal contracts both parties must be treated equally as regards reimbursement of use value. Article 132(5) YZOO (Art 368(5) ZOO) demanding the payment of default interest as from the moment the money was received, is inappropriate and should be understood in its historical context. The interest rate of enrichment interest should reflect the benefits gained by the recipient of money.

## Bibliography

Bamberger HG and Roth H (eds), *Kommentar zum Bürgerlichen Gesetzbuch: Band 2* (4th edn, CH Beck 2019).

Blagojević BT and Krulj V (eds), *Komentar Zakona o obligacionim odnosima* (Savremena administracija 1983).

Brudermüller G and others, *Palandt: Bürgerliches Gesetzbuch* (77th edn, CH Beck 2018).

Fervers M and Gsell B, 'Bereicherungsrechtliche Verpflichtung zur Herausgabe von Nutzungen' (2013) 66 *NJW* 3607.

Gelzer C, *Verzugs-, Schadens- und Bereicherungszins: Verzinsungspflichten bei unfreiwilliger Kreditierung im schweizerischen Privatrecht mit rechtsvergleichenden Hinweisen* (Helbing Lichtenhahn Verlag 2010).

Habersack M (ed), *Münchener Kommentar zum Bürgerlichen Gesetzbuch: BGB, Band 6: Schuldrecht – Besonderer Teil IV* (7th edn, CH Beck 2017).

Honsell H, Vogt NP, and Wiegand W (eds), *Basler Kommentar: Obligationenrecht I: Art. 1–529 OR* (5th edn, Helbing Lichtenhahn Verlag 2011).

Horn N (ed), *J. von Staudingers Kommentar zum Bürgerlichen Gesetzbuch: Staudinger BGB – Buch 2: Recht der Schuldverhältnisse: §§ 812–822 (Ungerechtfertigte Bereicherung)* (Sellier/de Gruyter 2007).

Jansen N and Zimmerman R (eds), *Commentaries on European Contract Laws* (OUP 2018).

---

42  See ZOO, Art 29(2). In business-to-business relationships the average interest rate is added 5 percentage points and in other relationships 3 percentage points. The average interest rate for the first half of 2020 is 3.11%, see Announcement of the Croatian National Bank on the average interest rate, *NN* 1/2020.

Juhart M, 'Vračilo denarja kot posledica prenehanja obligacijske pogodbe' [1995] (6) *PP* 8.

Kletečka A and Schauer M (eds), *ABGB-ON: Kommentar zum Allgemeinen bürgerlichen Gesetzbuch* (Manz 2010).

Lekić I, 'Docnja dužnika i pravo poverioca na kamatu' (1988) 38 *Pravni život* 1706.

Lutman K, 'Neupravičena obogatitev v primerjalnem in slovenskem pravu' (PhD thesis, University of Ljubljana Faculty of Law 2018).

Možina D, 'Razdor, odpoved in odstop od pogodbe' [2011] *Prav Letop* 57.

——, 'Vsebina in obseg obogatitvenega zahtevka' in Možina D (ed), *Razsežnosti zasebnega prava: Liber amicorum Ada Polajnar Pavčnik* (Univerza v Ljubljani Pravna fakulteta 2017).

——, 'Obresti in plodovi pri neupravičeni obogatitvi' [2019] *Prav Letop* 163.

Rummel P (ed), *Kommentar zum Allgemeinen bürgerlichen Gesetzbuch: Band II* (3rd edn, Manz 2002).

Schlechtriem P, Schwenzer I, and Schroeter UG (eds), *Kommentar zum UN-Kaufrecht (CISG)* (7th edn, CH Beck 2019).

Vogenauer S (ed), *Commentary on the UNIDROIT Principles of International Commercial Contracts (PICC)* (2nd edn, OUP 2015).

Zimmermann R, 'The Unwinding of Failed Contracts in the UNIDROIT Principles 2010' (2011) 16 *Unif L Rev* 563 [https://doi.org/10.1093/ulr/16.3.563].

# 8 The use of negative interest rates with a special reference to banking cash deposit contracts in the law of Croatia

*Ana Vargek Stilinović and Marko Stilinović*

## 1 Introduction

Within the last six years, the European Central Bank (ECB) made a significant change in conducting its monetary policy. Traditional monetary policy measures that were consistently applied did not result in diminishing the negative consequences of the global financial crisis that seriously weakened the EU banking system. To maintain the price stability, ECB decided to expand the money supply and to stimulate banks in credits' provision. For that purpose, ECB focused on unconventional monetary policy measures and, in 2014, introduced a negative interest rate on deposits that banks are holding with ECB.[1] As a result, banks were obliged to pay the ECB 'safekeeping' fee, instead of receiving an income in virtue of positive interest.

While ECB's negative interest rate policy was considered as a justified monetary policy experiment employed in order to keep the prices stable, the legality of introducing negative interest rates was brought into the question when certain commercial banks started to impose such rates into the banking cash deposit contracts. The occurrence of negative interest rates in commercial banking triggers numerous legal questions. What would be the legal treatment of negative interest rates? Is imposing a negative interest rate on banking cash deposit contracts contrary to the nature of those contracts? Does the current Croatian legal framework support the introduction of negative interest rates on the banking cash deposit contracts? What are comparative experiences with the use of negative interest rates in the banking cash deposits contracts?

The authors of this chapter examined the legal framework of the EU member states closely related to the Croatian legal system in which negative interest

---

1 In his recent keynote speech, Philip R Lane, Member of the Executive Board of the ECB, explained:

> The ECB's current configuration is based on a broad set of non-standard tools that reinforce each other: (i) the negative policy rate; (ii) forward guidance; (iii) the asset purchase programme (APP) by which the Eurosystem buys both sovereign and private debt securities; and (iv) targeted long-term refinancing operations (TLTROs) for banks.
>
> Philip R Lane, 'Low Inflation: Macroeconomic Risks and the Monetary<br>Policy Stance' (*ECB: Media: Speeches*, 11 February 2020, Berlin) &lt;www.ecb.<br>europa.eu/press/key/html/index.en.html&gt; accessed 26 February 2020.

rates were introduced, as well as the relevant case law. Apart from using the comparative method in the analysis of the domestic law, the authors analysed the nature of negative interest rates and their possible use within the Croatian legal framework.

## 2　The reasons for introducing the negative interest rates

The financial crisis that started in 2008 with the collapse of Lehman Brothers significantly weakened the theretofore ostensibly stable EU banking system. International banking activity, which was well developed and expanded at the time the crisis broke out, inevitably created a foundation for spreading negative effects of the crisis from USA banks to EU banks and for creating the biggest global financial crisis in the recent history.[2] The collapse of Lehman Brothers revealed the flaws of the banking practice worldwide, including the EU. High-risk lending and easy credit conditions were essential characteristics of the business policies of the EU banks.[3] Because Europe's financial system is bank-centric,[4] such imprudent business policies combined with the government structural deficit[5] led to the Eurozone crisis that started in the first quarter of 2009.[6]

One of the first measurable negative effects of the Eurozone crisis was a significant decrease in the annual inflation rate in the Eurozone (from 3.3% in 2008 to 0.3% in 2009)[7] which was at a stable level until 2009.[8] Deflationary tendencies continued in the following years that represented the obstacle to economic recovery and the potential danger of deflation. It was evident that certain measures must be employed on the Eurozone level to increase inflation rates and to avoid the deepening of the crisis.

### 2.1　Negative interest rates as an unconventional monetary policy measure

Economic growth and stability are strongly dependent on the relevant monetary authority which controls the money supply by implementing monetary

---

2　Kurt Hübert, 'Eurozone: Creeping Decay, Sudden Death or Magical Solution?' in Finn Laursen (ed), *The EU and the Eurozone Crisis* (Ashgate 2013) 26–27.

3　Bryan McIntosh and Fabrizio Ferretti, 'Pandora Box: The Eurozone and the Eurozone Crisis' (2015) 3 *Cogent Econ Finance* 1.

4　Dimitrios G Tsoutsas, 'Banking Union Perspectives of Eurozone Peripheries: A Critical View' (2018) 3 (4) *Annals of Reviews and Research* 81, 82.

5　Stephen Valdez and Philip Molyneux, *An Introduction to Global Financial Markets* (6th edn, Palgrave Macmillan 2010) 364.

6　Servaas Storm and CWM Naastepad, 'Myths, Mix-Ups and Mishandlings: Understanding the Eurozone Crisis' (2016) 45 *Int J Political Econ* 46.

7　Eurostat, 'HICP: Inflation Rate' <http://appsso.eurostat.ec.europa.eü/nui/show.do?dataset=tec0011 8&lang=en> accessed 26 February 2020.

8　Paweł Smaga, 'Pre-Crisis Landscape' in Małgorzata Iwanicz-Drozdowska (ed), *European Bank Restructuring during the Global Financial Crisis* (Palgrave Macmillan 2016) 19.

policy instruments.[9] Therefore, the key role in the Eurozone economic recovery was in the hands of the ECB. According to Art 127(1) TFEU, the primary objective of the ECB's monetary policy is to maintain price stability.[10] Interestingly, the TFEU does not define 'price stability' neither does it give criteria for determining when it would be considered that the prices are stable. Only Art 140(1) TFEU indicates that the price stability is apparent from an inflation rate.[11] On 13 October 1998, the ECB Governing Council defined 'price stability' as the inflation rate for the euro area of 'below 2%',[12] while on 8 May 2003 it specified that the 'price stability' stands for the inflation rate that is 'below', but 'close to 2%'.[13]

ECB can influence the Eurozone inflation rate by setting the so-called key interest rates on its transactions with the Eurozone banks: marginal lending facility, main refinancing operation, and deposit facility.[14] When ECB wants to counter high inflation, it increases the key interest rates and, vice versa, if ECB wants to counter low inflation it decreases them.[15] As already mentioned, at the beginning of the Eurozone crisis the inflation rate was at its lowest level and remained low in the following years. For this reason, from 2011, ECB started to continuously decrease the key interest rates on loans provided to banks and on their funds deposited with ECB.[16] The rationale of this policy was to increase the money supply in the banking system by encouraging banks to lend more money from ECB and to channel that money to their clients through loans. Eventually, clients would spend borrowed money and invest more, which would ultimately lead to economic growth.[17]

However, the described policy did not yield the expected results. After several years of countering deflationary tendencies by traditional monetary policy instruments, the statistic was devastating: the Eurozone inflation rate

9  Tonći Svilokos, 'Monetary Policy Effectiveness in the Period of Economic Crisis' (2013) 1 *Dubrovnik International Economic Meeting* <https://hrcak.srce.hr/161441> accessed 29 February 2020.
10  Consolidated version of the Treaty on the Functioning of the European Union [2012] *OJ* C326/47.
11  Art 140(1) of the TFEU: 'the achievement of a high degree of price stability; this will be apparent from a rate of inflation'.
12  ECB, 'A Stability-Oriented Monetary Policy Strategy for the ESCB' (*ECB: Media: Press Releases*, 13 October 1998) <www.ecb.europa.eu/press/pr/date/1998/html/pr981013_1.en.html> accessed 26 February 2020.
13  ECB, 'The ECB's Monetary Policy Strategy' (*ECB: Media: Press Releases*, 8 May 2003) <www.ecb.europa.eu/press/pr/date/2003/html/pr030508_2.en.html> accessed 26 February 2020.
14  See Guideline (EU) 2015/510 of the European Central Bank of 19 December 2014 on the implementation of the Eurosystem monetary policy framework (ECB/2014/60) [2015] *OJ* L91/3, Arts 2(56), 2(52) and 2(21).
15  ECB, 'The ECB's Negative Interest Rate' (*ECB: Explainers*, 12 June 2014) <www.ecb.europa.eu/explainers/tell-me-more/html/why-negative-interest-rate.en.html> accessed 26 February 2020.
16  ECB, 'Key ECB Interest Rates' (*ECB: Statistics*) <www.ecb.europa.eu/stats/policy_and_exchange_rates/key_ecb_interest_rates/html/index.en.html> accessed 26 February 2020.
17  Jovan Đurašković, Milivoje Radović, and Žarko Božović, 'Circularity of Economic Theories' (2016) 49 *Informatologia* 9, 12.

remained far below the targeted inflation rate of below but close to 2%,[18] and the economy continued to stagnate. Namely, even though ECB was continuously decreasing the key interest rates, banks were still holding large amounts of funds deposited with ECB instead of channelling those funds to their clients through loans. This outcome was understandable since, during the period of crisis, banks are often unwilling to grant loans due to increased credit risk connected with rising unemployment.[19]

For this reason, ECB focused on unconventional measures and in 2014 it introduced a negative interest rate by setting the interest rate on deposit facility below zero (−0.10%).[20] This monetary policy measure was unconventional as it changed usual and commonly accepted interest payment flows in the monetary economy.[21] Namely, since the introduction of negative interest rates on the deposit facility, banks were obliged to pay ECB a 'safekeeping fee' in a form of negative interest for keeping their funds, instead of receiving an interest yield. The amount of this 'safekeeping fee' increased as ECB lowered key interest rates on deposit facility four more times: in September 2014 (−0.20%), December 2015 (−0.30%), March 2016 (−0.40%), and in September 2019 (−0.50%).[22] ECB did not specify for how long it will keep key interest rates on deposit facility negative or whether it will go further into negative territory. However, according to ECB's press release given on 12 September 2019, ECB expects the key interest rates 'to remain at their present or lower levels until it has seen the inflation outlook robustly converge to a level sufficiently close to, but below, 2%'.[23]

### 2.2 Transmission of negative interest rate monetary policy to banking commercial business

ECB's negative interest rate policy indeed discouraged banks in depositing large amounts of funds with ECB. The total amount of banks' deposits that in 2017 amounted to 682.5 billion euros was significantly reduced, especially after the negative interest rate on the deposit facility was finally lowered at the level of −0.50% in September 2019.[24] The latest statistic data shows that in

18  Eurostat (n 7).
19  Svilokos (n 9).
20  ECB, 'ECB Introduces a Negative Deposit Facility Interest Rate' (*ECB: Media: Press Releases*, 5 June 2014) <www.ecb.europa.eu/press/pr/date/2014/html/pr140605_3.en.html> accessed 26 February 2020.
21  Committee on the Global Financial System, *CGFS Papers No 63: Unconventional Monetary Policy Tools: A Cross-Country Analysis* (Bank for International Settlements 2019) 8, 10.
22  ECB, 'Key ECB Interest Rates' (n 16).
23  ECB, 'Monetary Policy Decisions' (*ECB: Media: Press Releases*, 12 September 2019) <www.ecb.europa.eu/press/pr/date/2019/html/ecb.mp190912~08de50b4d2.en.html> accessed 25 February 2020.
24  ECB, 'Minimum Reserve and Liquidity Statistics' (*ECB: Statistical Data Warehouse: Monetary Policy Statistics*) <http://sdw.ecb.europa.eu/reports.do?node=10000027> accessed 25 February 2020.

January 2020 banks held only 254.6 billion euros with ECB.[25] The objective of ECB, however, was not to simply reduce the volume of the banks' deposits, but rather to stimulate the banks to loan those funds to their clients, instead of keeping them with ECB. The statistics show that simultaneously with reducing the value of deposits held with ECB, banks increased their lending activity[26] and the Eurozone annual inflation rate started to rise.[27] Therefore, it can be concluded that ECB's negative interest rate policy had a positive impact on the Eurozone economy in general.

However, this policy directly reduced, or it is expected to reduce, the profitability of most of the Eurozone banks.[28] Obligation to pay negative interest rates to ECB on the deposit facility incurred significant direct costs for the Eurozone banks. German banks bore the highest costs that in 2017 amounted to 2.4 billion euros, which represented 23.8% of their profit.[29] But profit-oriented banks are finding their way to pass those costs on their clients. While some banks are increasing their lending rates[30] and setting higher fees[31] as an answer to negative interest rate policy, some German banks started to impose negative interest rates on retail and corporate deposits[32] and several Dutch banks announced that they would start to charge their clients with the negative deposit interest rates as of 2020. Therefore, it is evident that ECB's negative interest rate policy is starting to indirectly affect the customers and it is unknown whether the other Eurozone banks will follow the German and the Dutch example. Nevertheless, unlike the ECB and other monetary policy authorities whose objective is to keep the prices stable and do whatever it takes to fulfil their goal, banks must conduct their business within the legal framework in which they operate. This means that the banks would be able to introduce negative interest rates on clients' deposits only if such a policy is legally allowed.

---

25  ibid.

26  Selva Demiralp, Jens Eisenschmidt, and Thomas Vlassopoulos, 'Negative Interest Rates, Excess Liquidity and Retail Deposits: Banks' Reaction to Unconventional Monetary Policy in the Euro Area' (2019) *ECB Working Paper No 2283* 34–35 <https://ssrn.com/abstract=3391745> accessed 25 February 2020.

27  Eurostat (n 7).

28  Jan Stráský and Hyunjeong Hwang, 'Negative Interest Rates in the Euro Area: Does It Hurt Banks?' (2019) *OECD Economics Department Working Papers No 1574* 6. See also Linas Jurkšas, 'An Impact Assessment of Negative Interest Rate Policy of Central Banks' (2017) 96 *Ekonomika* 25, 29, 35.

29  Zsolt Darvas and David Pichler, 'Excess Liquidity and Bank Lending Risks in the Euro Area' (*Policy Contribution, Bruegel*, September 2018) 11 <www.bruegel.org/2018/09/excess-liquidity-and-bank-lending-risks-in-the-euro-area/> accessed 26 February 2020.

30  Christoph Basten and Mike Mariathasan, 'How Banks Respond to Negative Interest Rates: Evidence from the Swiss Exemption Threshold' (2018) *CESifo Working Paper Series No 6901* 23–27. <https://ssrn.com/abstract=3164780> accessed 26 February 2020.

31  Oscar Arce and others, 'Adapting Lending Policies When Negative Interest Rates Hit Banks' Profits' (2018) *Banco de Espana Working Paper No 1832* 7 <https://ssrn.com/abstract=3255441> accessed 26 February 2020.

32  Stephan Kahl, 'German Lenders Pass Pain of Negative Interest Rates to Retail Clients' (*Bloomberg*, 7 October 2019) <www.bloomberg.com/news/articles/2019-10-07/german-lenders-drag-retail-clients-into-fray-of-negative-rates> accessed 26 February 2020.

# 3 The concept of negative interest

## 3.1 The legal nature and definition of interest

The concept of interest[33] has a unique position amongst the concepts of private law, due to its distinctive development. Much like the concept of money, in the legal context, the concept of interest represented an economic reality that had to be regulated.[34] Therefore, the normative intervention to the concept of interest seemed to be purely functional.[35] This distinctive approach resulted in a piecemeal regulation of various specific issues related to the concept since private law codifications usually do not even provide a definition of interest.[36]

The Croatian Obligations Act (*Zakon o obveznim odnosima*,[37] ZOO), which regulates the law of obligations, provides the normative framework for the use of interest, and sets the interest rates in the Croatian legal system, does not provide the legal definition of the notion of interest. In the legal doctrine, an almost universally accepted definition of interest is that it represents a 'compensation for the use of someone else's money or other fungible things'.[38] However, this definition is not entirely complete. Several authors correctly define the interest as a compensation 'to be paid for the possibility of using temporarily lent capital, which is calculated on the time-dependent basis but is at the same time independent of profit and turnover'[39] or as a compensation 'for the temporary possibility of use of capital (primarily money, then other fungible things, including fungible financial instruments) whereas the amount of the compensation depends on the duration of such possibility, without regard to the actual debtor's turnover created from such possibility'.[40] At first glance, this may seem like an insignificant detail added to the first definition, but especially in current market circumstances, it should be clear that the payment of interest does not depend on actual use of the lent capital.

---

33 For a thorough analysis of the concept and the related case law in Croatia see Ivica Crnić, *Kamate zatezne i ugovorne: pravni aspekti* (Organizator 2002); Miljenko Giunio and others, *Kamate: jučer i danas* (TEB 2008).

34 Petar Miladin, 'Novčane obveze i kamate – izabrana pitanja (zabrana anatocizma i uračunavanje djelomičnog plaćanja)' (2019) 58 *Pravo u gospodarstvu* 757, 761.

35 This is evident from the fact that the first regulation of interest did not thoroughly regulate the concept but sought to limit its use in cases when it was viewed as harmful to the society (e.g. Code of Hammurabi set the maximum interest rate at 33% for grain and 20% for silver in order to protect the debtors). See Crnić (n 33) 15.

36 cf BGB, § 288; CCiv, Art 1343; Cod Civ, Art 1224; CCQ, Art 1565.

37 *NN* 35/2005, 41/2008, 125/2011, 78/2015, 29/2018.

38 Crnić (n 33) 13; Miljenko Giunio, 'Ugovorne i zatezne kamate – zakonsko uređenje i praksa' in Miljenko Giunio and others, *Ugovorne i zatezne kamate* (Novi informator 2005) 15; Mladen Pavlović, 'Kamate u novijoj sudskoj praksi' (2005) 5 (5) *Hrv Prav Rev* 8, 17; Hrvoje Momčinović, 'Ugovorne i zatezne kamate – pravna viđenja nakon 1. siječnja 2008' (2008) 8 (11) *Hrv Prav Rev* 32; Petar Klarić and Martin Vedriš, *Građansko pravo* (Narodne novine 2014) 398.

39 Zvonimir Slakoper in Vilim Gorenc (ed), *Komentar Zakona o obveznim odnosima* (Narodne novine 2014) 68.

40 Miladin (n 34) 762.

As the interest represents a price for the possibility of use of the capital,[41] it is, like other prices, subject to the market mechanism (primarily, the forces of supply and demand).[42] The use of interest was also (and, in some cases still is) a subject of much philosophical debate[43] which significantly influenced the regulation of interest. In the legal context, the payment of interest represents an obligation that has to be performed by the party receiving the capital and hereto related right to use such capital. For example, in the classic (non-gratuitous) loan contract, the lender undertakes to provide to the borrower a certain amount of capital (lender's specific obligation), whereas the borrower undertakes to return this capital increased for the amount of contractual interest (borrower's specific obligation).[44]

Apart from the notion of interest, a notion of effective interest is often used in legal jargon. However, those two terms do not have the same meaning: interest represents compensation for the (temporary possibility of) use of capital, while effective interest represents the compounded value of the actual interest and various payable fees related to the transaction (such as e.g. transaction costs). Some authors claim that the function of effective interest is a mere mathematical elaboration which represents all the costs payable on the basis of various contractual provisions and therefore effective interest is not interest, *stricto sensu*.[45] Furthermore, it is stressed that some of the costs could be carved out of interest and fixed independently only to avoid certain regulatory limitations related to the interest (such as maximum allowed interest rate).[46] Costs and fees represent interest if they 'occur periodically and if they are tied to the loan term, whereby one-off borrowing costs are considered as fees' and not interest.[47]

### 3.2 The legal nature and definition of negative interest

Considering previous conclusions, it is necessary to determine what negative interest is. Currently, there are no references to negative interest in the Croatian

---

41 Giunio and others, *Kamate* (n 33) 17, 21.
42 For intriguing insight into the development of economic theories related to the role of interest and its historical development, see Gustav Cassel, *The Nature and Necessity of Interest* (Kelley & Millman 1957).
43 The Catholic Church, aiming to protect uneducated masses, prohibited the use of interest claiming that it is immoral. However, economic reality quickly created the need for its re-introduction. Therefore, various forms of advance payments were tolerated. As this was not sufficient, a form of interest (*usura*) was also allowed. See ibid, 2–6. Due to Islamic prohibition of the use of interest, the parties to the CISG could not agree on the specific limit for the interest rates in Art 78. See Kai-Michael Hingst and Karl-Alexander Neumann, 'Negative Zinsen – Die zivilrechtliche Einordnung eines nur scheinbar neuen geldpolitischen Phänomens' [2016] *BKR* 95.
44 Klarić and Vedriš (n 38) 530.
45 Hingst and Neumann (n 43) 95.
46 Slakoper in Gorenc (n 39) 71.
47 Hans-Michael Krepold and Constanze Herrle, 'Negative Zinsen – rechtliches Neuland' [2018] *BKR* 89, 90.

laws. The legal nature of interest is only occasionally analysed,[48] whereas negative interest rates were not a subject of deeper scrutiny yet, although they emerged already in the 1970s in Switzerland.[49] Even in economic science, the emergence of negative interest in the first half of the twentieth century was considered unrealistic, even impossible.[50] The central question in the legal analysis of the negative interest is whether the negative interest could even be considered as interest at all?[51] This question is of particular importance, as it determines the next step in the analysis: if the negative interest is not regarded as interest at all, then the legal framework related to the interest cannot be applied to the compensation in the form of negative interest.[52]

On one side – having in mind what was previously said on the legal nature of interest – once the interest becomes negative, the obligation of its payment passes to the other side. Considering the example in which lender provides a loan to the borrower and the borrower has to repay this loan alongside with the interest, once the interest becomes negative, the borrower only repays the principal and can even claim payment of negative interest from the lender. If the interest is negative, this practically leads to reversal of parties' obligations.[53] Interest, in this sense, once it has a negative value, is no longer a compensation payable by one party to the other party for the temporary possibility of use of capital. Thus, this can lead to the conclusion that negative interest is not interest at all and that interest must necessarily be positive.[54]

Authors defending the 'interest-like' nature of negative interest admit that they no longer correspond to the definition of interest; however, in order to maintain the 'unity of legal system',[55] negative interest must be considered interest. This especially in cases when ECB already in reality charges commercial banks negative interest for the safekeeping of their deposits, but at the same time the commercial banks would be prevented from charging negative interest in relation to deposits of their clients since negative interest (according to the previous interpretation) is not considered interest.[56] Also, the same authors claim that certain legal systems have a mathematical formula for calculation of interest rates, which may very well fall into negative[57] and thus negative interest

---

48  E.g. Giunio and others, *Kamate* (n 33) 17–88.

49  Hingst and Neumann (n 43) 95.

50  Cassel (n 42) 109; Hingst and Neumann (n 43) 96.

51  cf Hingst and Neumann (n 43) 97.

52  E.g. prohibition of anatocism then does not apply to negative interest.

53  Tobias Tröger, 'Vertragsrechtliche Fragen negativer Zinsen auf Einlagen' (2015) 68 *NJW* 657, 658; Ulrike Suendorf-Bischof, 'Negative Zinsen bei Sicht-, Termin- und Spareinlagen im Geschäft der Kreditinstitute mit Verbrauchern' [2019] *BKR* 279, 281. See also LG Tübingen decision of 26 January 2018, 4 O 187/17, *ZIP* 2018, 315.

54  Suendorf-Bischof (n 53) 281; Tröger (n 53) 659–60.

55  Hingst and Neumann (n 43) 97.

56  ibid. In Croatian legal system this argument cannot be put forward, as it will be explained further on, due to explicit regulation of cash deposit contracts.

57  ibid. The example here was given for BGB, § 247. A comparable example in Croatian law would be ZOO, Art 29, although such a scenario is extremely unlikely.

rates are *de facto* permitted by such laws. Here, it must also be borne in mind, that it is highly likely that the legislature, at the time of setting those rules (and, for that matter, the interest as a private law concept) did not have in mind the possibility of a potential fall of such interest rates into a negative value,[58] as such scenario was inconceivable.

### 3.3 The effect of the introduction of negative interest on the parties' relationship

The natural next question is, does the introduction of negative interest rates into an existing contract lead to the transformation of a contract into another type of contract? If the parties agree to provide a loan with negative interest, does it not mean that this is now a mixed contract composed of features of two different contract types? One of them being a form of gratuitous loan for consumption[59] in relation to the principal that shall be repaid by the borrower, while the other being a gift in relation to the principal that shall never be repaid as it is compensated with the amount of outstanding negative interest payable by the lender to the borrower. In case of a cash deposit, would the introduction of negative interest rate transform such a contract into irregular deposit where depositor now pays for safekeeping? This has important implications since the correct qualification of the legal relationship is necessary to determine the applicable legal framework.

To give one possible answer to the previous question, the nature of the contract shall primarily depend on the intention of the parties. If the parties were initially aware that the negative interest shall be paid by one party to the other and if they expressly agreed on the payment of negative interest, the parties' will was not to arrange remuneration for the possible use of capital but to compensate a different form of service. In this scenario, it is the least likely that such a form of compensation could be considered as interest in the legal sense of the concept, as the parties never intended to include the payment of interest-like compensation in their contract.[60] Stressing the importance of the will of the parties, which was in this case explicitly expressed, some authors conclude that in such situations there is no problem of introduction of negative interest (unless such disposition is expressly prohibited).[61]

---

58  ibid 96; Krepold and Herrle (n 47) 90, 99.

59  Sometimes also called simple loan, e.g. CCQ, Art 2314.

60  This seems to be a central point for analysis in Austrian court practice. As it is evident from the OGH decision of 21 March 2017, 10 Ob 13/17k, the Austrian jurisprudence tentatively allows claims for the payment of the negative interest in cases where the claimant could prove that this was original parties' will, however this is regularly not the case in the consumer loan contracts. See Suendorf-Bischof (n 53) 280. Also, for German court practice which stresses the importance of the parties' original will, see BGH decision of 13 April 2010, ZR 197/09, *NJW* 2010, 1742; Suendorf-Bischof (n 53) 283.

61  Sebastian Omlor, 'Negativzinsen im Einlagengeschäft' [2018] *BKR* 109, 110–11; Hingst and Neumann (n 43) 98. This is not the case with the banking cash deposit contracts in Croatian law, see further in 4.2.

The second situation is when the parties agreed on the payment of the interest but agreed that the interest amount shall be calculated on the basis of the floating (variable) interest rate. This mechanism proved to be flexible and adaptable to the market conditions thus fulfilling the same task which was once done by unilateral determination of the interest rate by financial institutions. It is common in such arrangements that the amount of interest is determined as the sum of a variable parameter (such as EURIBOR) and the fixed margin of the borrower. In certain cases, however, due to the fact that the variable parameter of a floating (variable) interest rate sinks so low, it tends to 'eat-up' the fixed margin and the interest becomes negative. Whether in such cases negative interest could be charged created a lot of debate among scholars.

One possible interpretation of the situation in which negative interest emerged as a result of the application of a variable interest rate is that no negative interest can be charged since the intention of the parties was not to reverse the obligations at any point.[62] It was through the pure mathematical operation that the interest has fallen into negative. Therefore, the parties' initial will did not encompass such a change of circumstances and the reversal of their roles. Also, by using the concept of interest in their contract language, without making additional clarifications, parties obviously ascribed to this term a widely accepted meaning of the concept of interest, which, as argued earlier in part 3.2, does not encompass the compensation in the form of negative interest. Therefore, negative interest, under these views, is not payable in case of such contracts.

On the other hand, some authors claim that due to the fact that the parties were free to arrange their relationship according to their needs (and they could have introduced a 'floor clause' which would prevent fall of interest rate into negative value), according to the rule *pacta sunt servanda*, negative interest is nonetheless payable.[63] Furthermore, if the fall of the contractual interest rate into negative value could have been foreseen at the moment of the conclusion of the contract, the negative interest could be charged as well.[64]

Therefore, in conclusion, it is possible to claim that interest loses its function and leads to a reversal of parties' obligations if it has a negative value. However, in certain exceptional cases, as it is seen from comparative jurisprudence,[65] the same legal framework foreseen for the positive interest could be applicable to protect the parties' original intention and roles. This seems to be a satisfactory functional approach, needed to fill the existing legal void.[66] However, in cer-

---

62  Suendorf-Bischof (n 53) 283, 285.

63  Hingst and Neumann (n 43) 100–1.

64  The clause could stay in force if the parties were aware that the interest thus calculated could fall into negative values. Omlor considers this to be the same case as when the parties expressly agreed to use negative interest, see Omlor (n 61) 110–11. Certain court decisions seem to leave room for such an interpretation as well, e.g. OGH decision of 21 March 2017, 10 Ob 13/17k.

65  E.g. OGH decision of 21 March 2017, 10 Ob 13/17k.

66  Authors call for the regulatory intervention, to protect the legal certainty and foreseeability of legal consequences. See Klaus Wagner, 'Zur rechtliche Wirksamkeit von Negativzinsen' [2017] *BKR* 315, 320.

tain cases in Croatian law, negative interest cannot be claimed since it is *ex lege* excluded.

### 3.4 Negative interest in the Croatian court practice

In Croatian court practice, the use of the term 'negative interest' is rare and usually not attributable to the same concept described in this chapter. Older court practice in the early 1990s used the term 'negative interest' as an interest that had to be paid by the depositor in the banking cash deposit contracts, in cases when depositor withdrew an amount of money that exceeded the amount of available deposit.[67] In such cases, by performing the payment over the available amount, the bank actually tacitly concluded a loan contract with the depositor and paid the amount from the available overdraft. Therefore, the 'negative interest' that was paid by the depositor was actually 'classic' positive interest that had to be paid by the depositor for the approved loan alongside the principal. Newer court practice, however, uses the term 'negative interest' to denote the compensation payable by the lender in cases when the variable interest rate sinks into a negative value. However, although banks claim that such strict adherence to the *pacta sunt servanda* principle in loan contracts would lead to 'ridiculous' results in which the bank would actually pay the borrower a compensation,[68] so far, we have not detected a court decision dealing with this problem in detail and it is yet to be seen how negative interest is going to be treated in the Croatian jurisprudence.

## 4 Banking cash deposit contract

### 4.1 Concept and regulation

In the Croatian legal system, the banking cash deposit contract is a nominate contract regulated by Arts 990 to 1001 of the ZOO.[69] It is defined as a consensual contract under which the bank undertakes to receive and the depositor undertakes to deposit at the bank a certain amount of money.[70] ZOO can thus be counted among the few general codifications of the law of obligations that provide specific provisions on banking cash deposit contracts.[71]

---

67 VSRH decision of 10 January 1991, Rev-2105/1990, and VSRH decision of 27 February 1992, Rev-2677/1991.
68 See e.g. argumentation in the County Court in Rijeka (*Županijski sud u Rijeci*) decision of 6 February 2017, Gž-2637/2016.
69 For a detailed analysis and perspective into banking cash deposit contracts, see Zvonimir Slakoper, 'Ugovor o bankovnom pologu (depozitu)' (2005) 5 (6) *Hrv Prav Rev* 51.
70 ZOO, Art 990.
71 Slakoper in Gorenc (n 39) 1616. Another example is the Italian Cod Civ, Arts 1834 to 1838. These contracts are usually regulated by special laws with specific provisions regulating certain issues, which do not have the character of general legal framework for such contract (e.g. Austrian *Bankwesengesetz*).

The banking cash deposit contract is, as its name indicates, a type of deposit contract and a sub-type of irregular deposit. In legal theory, a contract whereby one side (the depositor) undertakes to deposit a certain amount of fungible things, simultaneously transferring ownership to the other side (the depositary) giving it the right to use the object of deposit and the other side (the depositary) undertakes to return the same amount of fungible things after the end of a certain period is usually classified as an irregular deposit.[72] Due to its specific character in comparison with the regular deposit contract, the ZOO prescribes that provisions regulating the loan contract shall apply to the irregular deposit.[73] In comparative legal practice and literature, this is often a construction used to bridge the existing legal void, in cases when the banking cash deposit contracts are not generally regulated.[74] Therefore, once the customer deposits money with the bank, the bank becomes its owner and the customer retains an obligatory claim towards the bank.[75]

Furthermore, ZOO differentiates current (*a vista*) deposits (whereby the depositor may withdraw the balance at any time) and time deposits (whereby the deposit may not be withdrawn by the depositor during a certain period of time).[76] It is clear that depositor's motivation to conclude one or the other type of deposit contract differs. If the depositor wants to have quick access to the funds, the safekeeping characteristics of the contract are prevalent (such as in current deposits), whereas if the depositor wants to accumulate interest and temporarily relinquishes the right to use the money enabling the bank to freely use the money during a certain period, the loan characteristics prevail (such as in time deposits).[77]

An important factor in the definition of the banking deposit contract is that the depositary is always and exclusively 'the bank', whereas the other party may be a consumer, as well as any other party (such as e.g. another bank). Furthermore, the bank's duty to pay the interest[78] (and therefore, positive interest) arises *eo ipso*, even if the parties did not specifically regulate this issue, or despite their wish to exclude such obligation.[79] This provision was introduced already in the previous Yugoslav Obligations Act of 1978,[80] clearly in order to protect the depositors who were seen as the weaker parties in dealing with the banks.

---

72  Klarić and Vedriš (n 38) 548; Slakoper in Gorenc (n 39) 1620.

73  ZOO, Art 735. This provision would, of course, only apply to banking cash deposit contracts in case of the legal void in the provisions regulating banking cash deposit contracts (ZOO, Arts 990 to 1006). The same provision can be found in BGB, § 700.

74  E.g. in Germany, see Tröger (n 53) 657–58; Suendorf-Bischof (n 53) 281–82.

75  Slakoper in Gorenc (n 39) 1618–19.

76  Slakoper (n 69) 53–54. There are further types of the contract, but these are irrelevant for the legal analysis in this chapter.

77  Suendorf-Bischof (n 53) 280; cf Slakoper (n 69) 51.

78  Often called 'passive interest', see Giunio and others, *Kamate* (n 33) 20.

79  Slakoper in Gorenc (n 39) 1618; Slakoper (n 69) 57–58. This has been confirmed in the Croatian court practice as well, see e.g. VTSRH decision of 23 January 2007, Pž-3823/05, and the USRH decision of 4 October 2000, U-III-297/2000, NN 101/2000.

80  YZOO, Art 1042.

### 4.2 Negative interest rates in the banking cash deposit contracts

Arrangement in which the bank gains ownership over the customer's money deposited through a cash deposit contract was always seen as beneficial for the bank as the bank could use this money to provide loans to customers and earn interest that could later be reinvested on the cash deposit. Such a mechanism worked perfectly in the environment in which there is no liquidity surplus on the market. However, today it is becoming difficult for the banks to handle the liquidity surplus because they are forced to deposit excess money with the ECB and pay safekeeping fees. To minimize the costs they have to pay to ECB and to discourage more deposits, banks are strongly influenced to introduce negative interest rates in the cash deposit contracts.[81]

In Croatian jurisprudence, due to unambiguous regulation, there is no doubt: ZOO strictly excludes negative interest as the provision on payment of interest on banking cash deposit contracts prescribes that the bank is obligated to pay interest, 'unless otherwise prescribed by the law'.[82] Therefore, any party disposition is expressly excluded, as only the law can derogate the aforementioned bank's obligation. However, if in the future, the legislature would use this exception, it would be necessary to analyse the comparative legal solutions of jurisdictions that do not so expressively exclude the possibility of negative interest.

In case of existing cash deposit contracts, due to the fact that these contracts are usually concluded through adhesion of one party (customer) to the bank's contract templates supplemented by terms and conditions, banks first sought to introduce negative interest rate through a change in the terms and conditions. However, this method of change of one of the essential parts of the contract is not deemed legally acceptable.[83]

In cases where the variable interest rate is agreed in the contract, it is questionable whether interest could fall into negative value. In cases where such an event was predicted or predictable and parties thus tacitly approved negative interest, parties' will is often cited as the most important factor (or, in case of absence of certainty that parties discussed such issues, the hypothetical parties' will as construed from the contract).[84] As the approach in which the construction of hypothetical parties' will is often criticized,[85] an alternative approach

---

81  Some authors even warn that there is an existential risk for the banks if they continue using current business models, e.g. Hingst and Neumann (n 43) 100. Banks are introducing more fees and compensations to cover the perceived losses incurred through the payment of interest on customers' deposits, see Krepold and Herrle (n 49) 97–98.

82  ZOO, Art 997.

83  Achim Tiffe, 'Unzulässigkeit von Negativzinsen' [2019] *VuR* 339, 340–41, related to the OLG Stuttgart decision of 27 March 2019, 4 U 184/18.

84  For German law, if this was clear and unambiguous from the contract. See Suendorf-Bischof (n 53) 285. For Swiss law, see BGer decision of 7 May 2019, BGE 4A 596/2018.

85  For the critic of 'natural consensus' theory in Austrian law, see Andreas Vonkilch, 'Negativzinsen beim Kreditvertrag?' in Francesco Schurr and Manfred Umlauft (eds), *Festschrift für Bernhard Eccher* (Verlag Österreich 2017) 1237. Vonkilch explains that it cannot be argued that the parties 'naturally

is to analyse the purpose of the contract to see if negative interest would be permissible. As previously stated, certain types of cash deposit contracts have an asset accumulation purpose (e.g. time deposits), whereas certain contracts have more elements of safekeeping (e.g. current deposits).[86] If the safekeeping element prevails, payment of a safekeeping fee (i.e. negative interest) could be allowed.

Furthermore, it is possible that depositaries carve out some of the costs usually charged within the interest and charge them as separate fees. If such fees would be higher than the payable positive interest, this would actually mean that depositors must pay the difference, which leads to the same consequences as contracting negative interest. Any recurring costs normally accounted for in the calculation of interest cannot be separated in the form of a special fee, and they would have to be included in the calculation of interest.[87]

Thus, the results of interpretation wary. Austrian jurisprudence rejects the possibility of the introduction of negative interest rates on banking cash deposit contracts.[88] German BGH thus far has not considered whether negative interest in the banking cash deposit contracts is in accordance with the German law, but the practice is already widespread,[89] while several lower courts have found that the introduction of negative interest in the existing contracts through a change in terms and conditions is impermissible.[90]

### 4.3 'Spill-over' effect: possible mitigatory measures

An increasing number of authors warn of potential threats in the extreme cases to the banking business when banks cannot pass the costs of ECB's negative interest rate policy to the customers on their deposits, some even calling them

---

consented' on something that they did not even discuss or ponder, and that the contract should primarily be interpreted in accordance with the law (§ 914 ABGB). See also OGH decision of 3 May 2017, 4 Ob 60/17b.

86  Hans-Gert Vogel, 'Negativzinsen im Einlagengeschäft der Kreditinstitute' [2018] *BKR* 45, 47–49. German theorists also point to the fact that the application of the loan agreement rules to the irregular deposit creates an imbalance to the detriment of the depositors, as the loan agreement rules of the BGB (specifically §§ 488–489 applicable with the § 700 BGB) set considerable constraints on the lender seeing the borrower as the weaker party. See Tiffe (n 83) 342.

87  Suendorf-Bischof (n 53) 281, 283. cf OGH decision of 3 May 2017, 4 Ob 60/17b. Otherwise, this practice can be used to avoid legal framework applicable to interest. See 3.1 in relation to the effective interest rate.

88  See OGH decision of 13 October 2009, 5 Ob 138/09v. However, OGH seems to be more reluctant in relation to negative interest rates in loan contracts, but also confirms that the payment of negative interest leads to reversal of parties' roles and is therefore contrary to the purpose of contract. See OGH decision of 21 March 2017, 10 Ob 13/17k, and OGH decision of 3 May 2017, 4 Ob 60/17b.

89  Suendorf-Bischof (n 53) 279, 281; Wagner (n 66) 317–18.

90  See OLG Stuttgart decision of 27 March 2017, 4 U 184/18, *ZIP* 2019, 910; LG Tübingen decision of 26 January 2018, 4 O 187/17, *ZIP* 2018, 315; LG Tübingen decision of 25 May 2018, 4 O 225/17, *juris*.

'existential threats'.[91] Croatia is currently not in the Eurozone, but if in the future, when Croatia becomes a part of Eurozone, ECB still charges negative interest rates, this problem may appear in Croatia as well. However, due to the somewhat unique Croatian regulation of deposit contract interest, these costs shall not be passed on to the customers. Furthermore, foreign depositors may use this legal peculiarity and relocate their deposits to the Croatian banks. Such cross-border 'spill-over' of deposits would multiply the earlier-described difficulties for the Croatian banks.

The logical solution for banks would be to terminate the deposit contracts (if such possibility is foreseen in the contract or if the other party agrees to the termination). There is also a possibility to suggest a change to contractual terms or introduce new fees. However, this is also a limited option as consumer protection rules could prevent such changes.[92]

Another possible way to redefine obligations arising from certain deposit contracts, often mentioned in the comparative literature, is to use the *rebus sic stantibus* clause due to material changes in circumstances.[93] Under Art 369 ZOO, if in case of extraordinary circumstances arising after the conclusion of the contract, which were not foreseeable at the moments of its conclusion, the performance of the obligation for one party becomes excessively burdensome or would cause excessive losses to it, such party may request alteration or even termination of the contract. This provision (and concept of extraordinary circumstances) is, however, very narrowly interpreted in Croatian court practice.[94] Also, it would be difficult to prove that such circumstances were not foreseeable (having in mind the trends related to the introduction of negative interest rates in neighbouring jurisdiction). This would depend on whether the party applied sufficient attention (i.e. whether the party is at fault for the

---

91  Hingst and Neumann (n 45) 100.

92  See German cases in n 90. See also ECJ case C-143/13 *Bogdan Matei, Ioana Ofelia Matei v SC Volksbank România SA* [2015] ECLI:EU:C:2015:127. For a detailed analysis of the consumer protection ECJ case law see Tatjana Josipović, *Zaštita potrošača od nepoštenih ugovornih odredbi* (Narodne novine 2018).

93  For a thorough analysis of this remedy, regulated by Arts 369 to 372 ZOO, see Saša Nikšić, 'Clausula rebus sic stantibus i ekonomska kriza' in Jakša Barbić and Miljenko Giunio (eds), *Zbornik 54. susreta pravnika* (Hrvatski savez udruga pravnika u gospodarstvu 2016). In German civil law, the comparable remedy is '*Störung der Geschäftsgrundlage*'; ibid 164. German theorists often analyse the use of this remedy to overcome difficulties related to the introduction of negative interest rates; see Krepold and Herrle (n 47) 97, Wagner (n 66) 319. Comparatively, hardship clause is also used in this context; see Nikšić (n 93) 163; Giuseppe Settanni, 'Loans and Negative Interest Rates' (2016) 27 *EBLR* 697, 701.

94  Nikšić points out that a recent trend in court practice seems to *a priori* exclude any economic difficulties from the definition of extraordinary circumstances, which is worrisome since it excessively restricts the application of the remedy; see Nikšić (n 93) 167. German theorists support the idea that the flooding of the market with money and introduction of the negative interest rates by the ECB may represent the extraordinary circumstances for the application of the remedy; see Krepold and Herrle (n 47) 97. Some, however, consider that the lack of profitable investment of deposits received from the customers falls exclusively in the bank's business risk; see Tröger (n 53) 660.

lack of attention).[95] Thus, when it comes to more recent contracts, this would be more difficult and it is less likely that the party invoking *rebus sic stantibus* would succeed. Furthermore, it would be very difficult to demonstrate that the performance of one party has become 'excessively burdensome' or that it 'would cause excessive losses to it'.[96] It is also claimed that the losses of banks related to the impossibility of investing of deposits fall within the bank's sole business risk, so the successful application of the aforementioned remedy may only take place if the banks mirror the policy of ECB (i.e. when they pay negative interest to the ECB as well).[97] Therefore, it seems that the application of this remedy could be considered only in case of systematic and widespread losses caused by sudden pressure on the banking system and this only for older contracts (under the condition that the Croatian courts change their excessively restrictive approach to the application of remedy).

Any change to the interest rate itself is, due to the obligation of payment of positive interest, legally impossible. However, Art 997 ZOO leaves room for an exception provided through legal intervention. If the pressure on the banks continues to rise, this exception could be exercised, at least in the limited form (e.g. for interbank deposits), which could ensure the protection of both the customers and the banks.[98]

## 5 Conclusion

In order to counter the low inflation rates, ECB introduced negative interest rates to discourage the creation of new deposits and encourage investments. As a consequence of such an unorthodox monetary policy tool, several banks started to mirror this policy by introducing negative interest to the deposits in their business. However, once negative interest is transferred into the private law context, it is doubtful whether it could fit into the existing legal framework. Although there is no consensus on this issue, there are more arguments that support the conclusion that negative interest is legally not interest. Therefore, if there will be a growing need to introduce its use in the economy, instead of trying to fit them into 'existing boxes' a functional approach should be taken and negative interest should be regulated, much like in the past the phenomenon of interest represented an economic reality that had to be regulated.[99]

In relation to the banking cash deposit contracts, the current Croatian legal framework does not permit the introduction of negative interest rates. There are, however, converging views in the comparative literature in regard to the

---

95  Nikšić (n 93) 170.
96  ibid 171–72. Although this varies greatly, losses from anywhere between 50% and 100% (and even up to 300% in speculative transactions) were, pursuant to legal theory, necessary for the successful application of this remedy.
97  Wagner (n 66) 319.
98  For other potential solutions, see Settanni (n 93) 702–6.
99  Wagner (n 66) 320.

question of whether negative interest rates are permissible in cash deposit contracts. It is likely that legislature did not predict current economic developments and if the consequences of ECB's policy and circumstances in neighbouring jurisdictions start to threaten the business of the domestic banks, there may be a need for separate regulation of the issues, as current remedies are difficult to apply (e.g. *rebus sic stantibus*) and any change to the contract depends on the will of both parties.

## Bibliography

Arce O and others, 'Adapting Lending Policies When Negative Interest Rates Hit Banks' Profits' (2018) *Banco de Espana Working Paper No 1832* <https://ssrn.com/abstract=3255441> accessed 26 February 2020 [https://doi.org/10.2139/ssrn.3255441].

Basten C and Mariathasan M, 'How Banks Respond to Negative Interest Rates: Evidence from the Swiss Exemption Threshold' (2018) *CESifo Working Paper Series No 6901* <https://ssrn.com/abstract=3164780> accessed 26 February 2020.

Cassel G, *The Nature and Necessity of Interest* (Kelley & Millman 1957).

Committee on the Global Financial System, *CGFS Papers No 63: Unconventional Monetary Policy Tools: A Cross-Country Analysis* (Bank for International Settlements 2019).

Crnić I, *Kamate zatezne i ugovorne: pravni aspekti* (Organizator 2002).

Darvas Z and Pichler D, 'Excess Liquidity and Bank Lending Risks in the Euro Area' (*Policy Contribution, Bruegel*, September 2018) <www.bruegel.org/2018/09/excess-liquidity-and-bank-lending-risks-in-the-euro-area/> accessed 26 February 2020.

Demiralp S, Eisenschmidt J, and Thomas Vlassopoulos T, 'Negative Interest Rates, Excess Liquidity and Retail Deposits: Banks' Reaction to Unconventional Monetary Policy in the Euro Area' (2019) *ECB Working Paper No 2283* <https://ssrn.com/abstract=3391745> accessed 25 February 2020 [https://doi.org/10.2139/ssrn.2941377].

Đurašković J, Radović M, and Božović Ž, 'Circularity of Economic Theories' (2016) 49 *Informatologia* 9.

European Central Bank, 'A Stability-Oriented Monetary Policy Strategy for the ESCB' (*ECB: Media: Press Releases*, 13 October 1998) <www.ecb.europa.eu/press/pr/date/1998/html/pr981013_1.en.html> accessed 26 February 2020.

——, 'The ECB's Monetary Policy Strategy' (*ECB: Media: Press Releases*, 8 May 2003) <www.ecb.europa.eu/press/pr/date/2003/html/pr030508_2.en.html> accessed 26 February 2020.

——, 'ECB Introduces a Negative Deposit Facility Interest Rate' (*ECB: Media: Press Releases*, 5 June 2014) <www.ecb.europa.eu/press/pr/date/2014/html/pr140605_3.en.html> accessed 26 February 2020.

——, 'The ECB's Negative Interest Rate' (*ECB: Explainers*, 12 June 2014) <www.ecb.europa.eu/explainers/tell-me-more/html/why-negative-interest-rate.en.html> accessed 26 February 2020.

——, 'Monetary Policy Decisions' (*ECB: Media: Press Releases*, 12 September 2019) <www.ecb.europa.eu/press/pr/date/2019/html/ecb.mp190912~08de50b4d2.en.html> accessed 25 February 2020.

——, 'Key ECB Interest Rates' (*ECB: Statistics*) <www.ecb.europa.eu/stats/policy_and_exchange_rates/key_ecb_interest_rates/html/index.en.html> accessed 26 February 2020.

——, 'Minimum Reserve and Liquidity Statistics' (*ECB: Statistical Data Warehouse: Monetary Policy Statistics*) <http://sdw.ecb.europa.eu/reports.do?node=10000027> accessed 25 February 2020.

Giunio M, 'Ugovorne i zatezne kamate – zakonsko uređenje i praksa' in Giunio M and others, *Ugovorne i zatezne kamate* (Novi informator 2005).

—— and others, *Kamate: jučer i danas* (TEB 2008).

Gorenc V (ed), *Komentar Zakona o obveznim odnosima* (Narodne novine 2014).

Hingst KM and Neumann KA, 'Negative Zinsen – Die zivilrechtliche Einordnung eines nur
scheinbar neuen geldpolitischen Phänomens' [2016] *BKR* 95.

Hübert K, 'Eurozone: Creeping Decay, Sudden Death or Magical Solution?' in Laursen F (ed),
*The EU and the Eurozone Crisis* (Ashgate 2013) [https://doi.org/10.4324/9781315616278].

Josipović T, *Zaštita potrošača od nepoštenih ugovornih odredbi* (Narodne novine 2018).

Jurkšas L, 'An Impact Assessment of Negative Interest Rate Policy of Central Banks' (2017)
96 *Ekonomika* 25 [https://doi.org/10.15388/Ekon.2017.1.10662].

Kahl S, 'German Lenders Pass Pain of Negative Interest Rates to Retail Clients' (*Bloomberg*,
7 October 2019) <www.bloomberg.com/news/articles/2019-10-07/german-lenders-
drag-retail-clients-into-fray-of-negative-rates> accessed 26 February 2020.

Klarić P and Vedriš M, *Građansko pravo* (Narodne novine 2014).

Krepold HM and Herrle C, 'Negative Zinsen – rechtliches Neuland' [2018] *BKR* 89.

Lane PR, 'Low Inflation: Macroeconomic Risks and the Monetary Policy Stance' (*ECB: Media:
Speeches*, 11 February 2020) <www.ecb.europa.eu/press/key/html/index.en.html> accessed
26 February 2020.

McIntosh B and Ferretti F, 'Pandora Box: The Eurozone and the Eurozone Crisis' (2015) 3
*Cogent Econ Finance* 1 [https://doi.org/10.1080/23322039.2015.1124741].

Miladin P, 'Novčane obveze i kamate – izabrana pitanja (zabrana anatocizma i uračunavanje
djelomičnog plaćanja)' (2019) 58 *Pravo u gospodarstvu* 757.

Momčinović H, 'Ugovorne i zatezne kamate – pravna viđenja nakon 1. siječnja 2008.'
(2008) 8 (11) *Hrv Prav Rev* 32.

Nikšić S, 'Clausula rebus sic stantibus i ekonomska kriza' in Barbić J and Giunio M (eds),
*Zbornik 54. susreta pravnika* (Hrvatski savez udruga pravnika u gospodarstvu 2016).

Omlor S, 'Negativzinsen im Einlagengeschäft' [2018] *BKR* 109.

Pavlović M, 'Kamate u novijoj sudskoj praksi' (2005) 5 (5) *Hrv Prav Rev* 8.

Settanni G, 'Loans and Negative Interest Rates' (2016) 27 *EBLR* 697.

Slakoper Z, 'Ugovor o bankovnom pologu (depozitu)' (2005) 5 (6) *Hrv Prav Rev* 51.

Smaga P, 'Pre-Crisis Landscape' in Iwanicz-Drozdowska M (ed), *European Bank Restructuring
during the Global Financial Crisis* (Palgrave Macmillan 2016) [https://doi.org/10.1057/
9781137560247_2].

Storm S and Naastepad CWM, 'Myths, Mix-Ups and Mishandlings: Understanding the
Eurozone Crisis' (2016) 45 *Int J Political Econ* 46 [https://doi.org/10.1080/08911916.20
16.1159084].

Stráský J and Hwang H, 'Negative Interest Rates in the Euro Area: Does It Hurt Banks?'
(2019) *OECD Economics Department Working Papers No 1574* [https://doi.org/10.1787/
d3227540-en].

Suendorf-Bischof U, 'Negative Zinsen bei Sicht-, Termin- und Spareinlagen im Geschäft
der Kreditinstitute mit Verbrauchern' [2019] *BKR* 279.

Svilokos T, 'Monetary Policy Effectiveness in the Period of Economic Crisis' (2013) 1
*Dubrovnik International Economic Meeting* <https://hrcak.srce.hr/161441> accessed 29
February 2020.

Tiffe A, 'Unzulässigkeit von Negativzinsen' [2019] *VuR* 339.

Tröger T, 'Vertragsrechtliche Fragen negativer Zinsen auf Einlagen' (2015) 68 *NJW* 657.

Tsoutsas DG, 'Banking Union Perspectives of Eurozone Peripheries: A Critical View'
(2018) 3 (4) *Annals of Reviews and Research* 81.

Valdez S and Molyneux P, *An Introduction to Global Financial Markets* (6th edn, Palgrave Macmillan 2010).

Vogel HG, 'Negativzinsen im Einlagengeschäft der Kreditinstitute' [2018] *BKR* 45.

Vonkilch A, 'Negativzinsen beim Kreditvertrag?' in Schurr F and Umlauft M (eds), *Festschrift für Bernhard Eccher* (Verlag Österreich 2017).

Wagner K, 'Zur rechtliche Wirksamkeit von Negativzinsen' [2017] *BKR* 315.

# 9 The formality of real estate transactions in the law of Slovenia and Croatia in the light of new technologies

*David Borlinič Gačnik and Jure Jakšić*

## 1 Introduction

The chapter deals with the impact of new technologies on the formality rules, particularly the written form of the contract regarding real estate transactions, based on the sales agreement. We aim to analyse the formality rules in the light of new technologies, mainly blockchain-based smart contracts. The chapter aims to address the legal problems, raised by the potential implementation of the smart contracts to the real estate transaction regarding the formality pre-requisites, namely, the prerequisite of a written form under the Slovenian and Croatian law.

The content of Slovenian and Croatian law in the field of real estate transactions is remarkably similar due to historical resemblance of legal development in the two countries. Therefore, the chapter is primarily focused on the Slovenian law, with emphasizing only the differences between the two jurisdictions, if any compelling difference even exists. Both countries have similar land cadastre and land register systems, which are based practically on the same principles; the notary public is involved in the legal transaction of real property in both countries, etc.[1] As further explained next, the two countries also share comparable rules concerning the written form of the contracts when dealing with real estate transactions.

The topic is interesting for research because of the importance of ownership as an essential property right, which is protected by law at the constitutional,[2]

---

1 The two countries have practically the same national and historical background from even before the seventh century, and both countries were later a part of the Austro-Hungarian tradition of land registration. They established practically the same land legislation and land registration system until 1991. After that the real estate law of named countries developed simultaneously. See Marija Repanić, 'Real Property Transactions in the Republic of Croatia: Procedures of Property Transfer, Change of Real Property Rights and Property Formation' (MSc thesis, KTH Royal Institute of Technology Stockholm 2005) 70–103.

2 Constitution of the Republic of Slovenia (*Ustava Republike Slovenije*), UL RS 33/1991, 42/1997, 66/2000, 24/2003, 69/2004, 68/2006, 47/2013, 75/2016, Arts 33 and 67; Constitution of the Republic of Croatia (*Ustav Republike Hrvatske*), NN 56/1990, 135/1997, 8/1998, 113/2000, 124/2000, 28/2001, 41/2001, 55/2001, 76/2010, 85/2010, 5/2014, Art 48.

international,[3] and supranational level.[4] The acquisition or sale of property is one of the most important events for most people. Further, the real estate market represents an important field for investments. Considering the uncontested importance of real estate property rights, on the one hand, and the risk and potential hazards connected to the transfer of property, on the other hand, the law developed special (formality) rules to protect both public interest and the interest of the parties to the transaction (private interest), as it is discussed later on. The legislature should always make an effort to detect potential weaknesses of the regulation in order to adapt the legislation according to the changes in the society and technological development, to provide legal certainty and make sure that the rules are still 'up to date'. New challenges are raised by new technology development in the field of real estate transactions, with a long tradition of paper-based transactions.[5] Moreover, it is worthwhile to explore the impact of new technologies on the formality rules of the transfer of ownership. The transfer of ownership represents a typical example of the transfer of property rights. Therefore, the findings regarding the impact of the new technologies to the formality rules regarding real estate transactions might be applicable (by analogy) also to transfer of other property rights.[6]

In the first part of the chapter, we aim to analyse the legal framework of the formality rules regarding real estate transactions, especially the written form of the agreement under Slovenian and Croatian law, including legal consequences of the non-compliance to the formality prerequisites. The second part of the chapter shows the emerging new technology trends in the field of real estate transactions around the world, together with its functionalities, which are then compared to the purpose behind the current formality prerequisite of a written form. Finally, we shall deal with the necessity of the legislative amendments in the case of implementing the blockchain-based smart contracts to the field of real estate transactions.

## 2  Legal framework (formality rules, written form): general overview of the Slovenian and Croatian law

To address and properly understand the topic of new technologies' impact on the formality of real estate transactions, we should briefly look to the legal

---

3  Universal Declaration of Human Rights (adopted 10 December 1948) UNGA Res 217 A(III), Art 17.
4  Charter of Fundamental Rights of the European Union [2012] OJ C326/391, Art 17.
5  The long tradition of paper-based transactions facing the difficulties when implementing new technologies can be illustrated by the statement of an employee of the Swedish start-up ChromaWay, Henrik Hjelte, who expressed the logistical delays when implementing smart contracts to the field of real estate transactions, stating: 'We are replacing paper that has been around for several thousands of years . . . it will take some time.' Griffin P Heil, 'Blockchain's Impact on Real Estate and the Future' (2019) 18 *J Intl Bus & L* 237, 249.
6  The detailed arrangement of the transfer of ownership fulfils an exemplary role for transfer of other property rights in civil law, e.g. assignment of claim by contract. See Miha Juhart, Matjaž Tratnik, and Renato Vrenčur, *Stvarnopravni zakonik (SPZ) s komentarjem* (Uradni list Republike Slovenije 2016) 259–60.

framework regarding the formality prerequisites of the real estate transactions under the Slovenian and Croatian law and its origin.

## 2.1 Optional nature of the form and the form of contract regarding real estate transactions

According to positive Slovenian and Croatian law, contracts can be concluded in written form, orally, or even implicitly. According to Slovenian Obligations Code (*Obligacijski zakonik*,[7] OblZ) and Croatian Obligations Act (*Zakon o obveznim odnosima*,[8] ZOO), no particular form for the conclusion of a contract is prescribed, unless stipulated otherwise by law. Under the general principle of freedom of contract, the nature of a form is optional.[9] Under the general rule, there are no formal obstacles to enter into any form of contract, even into a blockchain-based smart contract in electronic form.

Under Slovenian and Croatian law, a contract that creates a legal basis for the transfer of ownership (sales agreement) must be concluded in written form. This requirement is derived from the literal interpretation of Art 52 OblZ, which states that 'a contract under which the title to real estate is transferred . . . must be concluded in written form'. The regulation expressly settles the form of the contracts, which represents the legal foundation of the transfer of ownership. The legal foundation for the transfer of ownership is a legal transaction of obligation, for example, a sales agreement.[10] Croatian ZOO is more specified on the topic and expressly settles the contract of sale of immovable property, which shall be entered into in writing.[11] The written form of the other legal basis for the transfer of ownership of the real estate (deed of gift, a contract of exchange, etc.) is stipulated by Croatian Act on Ownership and Other Real Rights (*Zakon o vlasništvu i drugim stvarnim pravima*,[12] ZVDSP).

Both Slovenian and Croatian law is based on German tradition[13] that distinguishes between a legal transaction of obligation (*Verpflichtungsgeschäft*) and a legal transaction of disposition (*Verfügungsgeschäft*). The divergence between the contract of sale and the transfer of ownership is deeply rooted in Roman law, which distinguished between the contract of sale (transaction of obligation) and

7  *UL RS* 83/2001, 28/2006, 40/2007, 64/2016, Art 51.

8  *NN* 35/2005, 41/2008, 125/2011, 78/2015, 29/2018, Art 268.

9  Ada Polajnar Pavčnik in Miha Juhart and Nina Plavšak (eds), *Obligacijski zakonik (OZ): (splošni del): s komentarjem: 1. knjiga* (GV Založba 2003) 365.

10  The real estate sales agreement is merely one of the possible legal grounds for the transfer of ownership. Besides that, the legal foundation of the transfer of ownership can represent a deed of gift, a contract of exchange, a contract on delivery and distribution of property, etc. This chapter addresses only the questions related to the real estate purchase agreement.

11  ZOO, Art 377.

12  *NN* 91/1996, 68/1998, 137/1999, 22/2000, 73/2000, 12/2000, 114/2001, 79/2006, 141/2006, 146/2008, 38/2009, 153/2009, 143/2012, 152/2014, Art 115.

13  For more about the common tradition of Slovenian and Croatian law in the field of real estate transactions see in Repanić (n 1) 70–103.

the act of conveyance: *mancipatio* (transaction of disposition).[14] Therefore, the conclusion of the sales agreement does not transfer the ownership but merely creates an obligation of the seller to transfer the ownership to the buyer and the buyer's obligation to pay the price. The content of seller's obligation is to issue a land register permission (registration clause, *clausula intabulandi*),[15] with a notarized signature,[16] which allows for the entry into the land register and the transfer of the ownership. The land register permission represents the expression of the formality of legal transaction of disposition with direct effects to the transfer of rights *in rem*.[17]

Legal transaction regarding the real estate property is completed only if the transaction is entered into land register, based on notarized registration clause, that shall by the nature of the notarization be concluded in a form of written document.[18] The transaction of obligation and the transaction of disposition could be both included in a single document or separated into two documents. It is therefore unavoidable to create at least one written document to transfer the ownership of real estate under the positive law of Slovenia and Croatia. The question we are dealing with is, shall this paper-based written document be replaced by the blockchain-based smart contract? Is it allowed to enter into a blockchain-based smart contract concerning the real estate transaction under present regulation?

### 2.2 Legal consequences of the breach of the formality rules

If the conclusion of a smart contract contravenes the formality rules, the contract would be invalid according to theory[19] and case law.[20] It is argued that written form in the case of real estate transaction is provided as a condition of validity *(forma ad valorem)*. If the parties failed to comply with the formality prerequisites, the contract is considered invalid. The invalidity of the contract

---

14  See Reinhard Zimmermann, *The Law of Obligations: Roman Foundations of the Civilian Tradition* (Juta & Co 1990) 271.

15  According to Art 49 of the Slovenian Property Law Code (*Stvarnopravni zakonik*), *UL RS* 87/2002, 91/2013, 23/2020 (SPZ), an entry in the land register is required for the acquisition of an ownership right over immovable property through a legal transaction. Entry in the land register shall be made based on a document containing the land register permission. A land register permission (registration clause) is an explicit and unconditional statement by a person whose right is being transferred, altered, encumbered, or extinguished, permitting an entry in the land register (Art 23 SPZ). Croatian law encompasses practically the same rule in Art 88 ZVDSP.

16  Croatian Land Register Act (*Zakon o zemljišnim knjigama*), *NN* 63/2019, Art 57; Slovenian Land Register Act (*Zakon o zemljiški knjigi*), *UL RS* 58/2003, 37/2008, 45/2008, 28/2009, 25/2011, 14/2015, 69/2017, 11/2018, 16/2019 (ZZK), Art 41.

17  Juhart, Tratnik, and Vrenčur (n 6) 346.

18  Polajnar Pavčnik in Juhart and Plavšak (n 9) 367.

19  Nina Plavšak in Juhart and Plavšak (n 9) 183; Ivica Crnić, *Zakon o obveznim odnosima: opsežna sudska praksa, napomene i komentari, detaljno abecedno kazalo pojmova* (Organizator 2016) 879.

20  VSL decision of 4 November 2009, I Cp 3717/2009; VSRH decision of 3 May 2007, Rev-304/07–2; VSRH decision of 16 December 2003, Rev-2593/00.

is a term that includes voidness (nullity) and voidability (challengeability) of the contract.[21] The correct sanction for the case of non-compliance with the formality prerequisites is usually not implicitly prescribed by the law but should be determined through the interpretation.

The general rule under Slovenian OblZ states that a contract not concluded in the prescribed form shall be null and void unless otherwise proceeding from the purpose of the regulation by which the form is specified.[22] Croatian ZOO contains a similar rule, which stipulates that a contract not entered in the prescribed form has no legal effect unless the purpose of the regulation determining the form indicates otherwise.[23] Hence, to determine the correct sanction for the breach of the formality rules, further interpretation of the purpose of the regulation is needed, which includes recourse to the interest (public interest, private interest) that the regulation aims to protect. Knowing the purpose behind the current regulation is crucial to determine the sanctions of potential non-compliance with the formality prerequisites (voidness, voidability). On the other hand, the purpose behind the current regulation shall be useful as a guideline for the future legislature when adopting the legislation in an event of the implementation of new technologies.

The purpose of the prescribed form when dealing with the real estate sales agreement is to protect both public and private interest. The prescribed written form enables the parties to the transaction to carefully rethink the content and the consequences of the commitment they are acquiring, which represents private interest behind the regulation. The interest of the parties is also the function of a written document, which could serve the parties as proof of the transaction in an eventual later dispute. On the one hand, the written form protects the parties from potential fraud and misunderstanding, which clearly shows the private interest behind the regulation. On the other hand, the public interest can also be found in the intent to reduce the number of disputes in society by preventing fraud. The written form also undoubtedly empowers the *pacta sunt servanda* principle, since the parties will be prone to fulfil their obligation if it was written on the paper.[24] Moreover, the prescribed written form aims to ensure the payment of property transfer tax and to enable the notary public to check the compliance with the restrictions associated with the transfer of farmland and forests (e.g. pre-emptive rights), the nationality of the buyer, etc.[25] It can be concluded that the prescribed written form of the real estate sales agreement aims to bring legal certainty and transparency to the real estate's market, which undoubtedly represents a public interest and interest of the parties behind the regulation.

---

21  OblZ, Arts 86 to 99; ZOO, Arts 322 to 325.

22  OblZ, Art 55.

23  ZOO, Art 290.

24  Nina Plavšak, Miha Juhart, and Renato Vrenčur, *Obligacijsko pravo: splošni del* (GV Založba 2009) 247.

25  Slovenian ZZK, Arts 37 and 38.

The decision between nullity and challengeability sanction should be based on the conclusion of whether the regulation protects broader public interests or merely the interests of the parties to the transaction. If only the interest of the parties is protected, there is no need to apply the severe nullity sanction in order to keep the contract in force (*favor contractus*). In such a case, the law grants the parties the ability to challenge the contract. In another case, when broader public interests are violated, such a contract could be considered void and null.[26] Knowing the fact that the formality rules considering the real estate contracts aim to protect both public and private interest, the consequence for not complying with the formalities would most probably represent a nullity sanction.

The consequences for the parties not complying with formality rules are severe. Each contracting party must return to the other party everything that was received based on the contract.[27] The court shall attend to the nullity as an official duty, and any person concerned may refer to it.[28] When entering into contracts to acquire and dispose of immovable property it is therefore of great importance for the parties to respect the formal prerequisites prescribed by law.

Aforementioned strict rules are slightly lightened by the realization rule.[29] Under Slovenian law, the realization rule states that in the case when parties fully or at large extent performed the contract, the contract shall be valid, even if the parties failed to comply with the formality prerequisites.[30] Croatian law encompasses the complementary rule for the case where a contract is required to be in writing,[31] which is exactly the case for the real estate transactions. The realization rule under Slovenian and Croatian law could only be invoked where the parties performed their obligations fully or at a large extent. For the case of real estate ownership transfer, it is necessary for the buyer to pay the price and the seller to deliver the possession of the real property to the buyer.

The rule of realization is a result of the principle of good faith and fair dealing but also represents an exception and should, therefore, be interpreted strictly. The realization rule applies only where the factual situation of the performed contract demands a legal recognition of the facts according to the principle of good faith.[32] It is consequently not appropriate to implement the new technical solutions, knowingly not complying with the formality prerequisites,

---

26 cf Polajnar Pavčnik in Juhart and Plavšak (n 9) 505–6.
27 OblZ, Art 87; ZOO, Art 323.
28 OblZ, Art 92; ZOO, Art 327.
29 Polajnar Pavčnik in Juhart and Plavšak (n 9) 372.
30 Article 58 of the OblZ states: 'A contract for which the written form is required shall be valid even if not concluded in this form if the contracting parties fully or partly perform the obligations arising therefrom, unless clearly indicated otherwise in the purpose for which the form was prescribed.'
31 Article 294 of the ZOO states: 'Where a contract that is required to be in writing is not entered in written form, it is considered to be valid, if the contracting parties have executed, fully or in large part, the obligations that arise from the contract, unless it results otherwise from the purpose for which the form is prescribed.'
32 Polajnar Pavčnik in Juhart and Plavšak (n 9) 374.

and at the same time calculating to the realization rule as a possible solution to avoid the nullity sanction. Avoiding the strict formality rules, calculating to the realization rule, could represent the breach of the principle of good faith, which would disable the parties to invoke the realization rule.

To conclude, the consequences for the parties not complying with the formality prerequisites when dealing with real estate ownership under Slovenian and Croatian law are severe. Therefore, entering into new kinds of legal contracts, such as blockchain-based smart contract in electronic form, before the sufficient legal grounds are provided, represents a serious risk for the parties. When implementing new technologies to the real estate transactions, the legislature needs to take into account the functionalities and protected interests behind the positive regulation of formality prerequisites, in order to grant at least equal level of legal certainty and transparency as provided by the present regulation.

## 3 Smart contracts in the field of real estate transactions

Knowing the legal concepts of formality rules under the positive regulation, let us take a closer look at the concept of emerging new technologies in the field of real estate transactions – blockchain-based smart contracts.

Informatization of every possible process and economic activity is becoming an upward trend amongst economists, even in the field of real estate transactions.[33] The notion of smart contract was firstly explained by Nick Szabo in 1997 as a set of promises, including protocols within which the parties perform other promises. The aim of the system was to make a breach of the contract expensive for the breacher. The initial idea was described with the elementary example of vending machines and hypothetical lock-key systems for the automobiles.[34] The breaking point for the smart contracts was the development of the cryptocurrency Bitcoin,[35] primarily mentioned by Satoshi Nakamoto in 2008.[36] Afterwards, smart contracts were discussed amongst many authors and implemented in different fields of law.[37] One of the interesting fields for the implementation of new technology is the field of real estate transactions.[38]

---

33 Fernando P Méndez, 'Smart Contracts, Blockchain and Land Registry' (European Land Registry Association General Assembly, Brussels, 30 November 2018) 2 <www.elra.eu/wp-content/uploads/2018/12/Smart-Contracts-Blockchain-and-Land-Registry-by-F-Mendez.pdf> accessed 24 February 2020.

34 Nick Szabo, 'The Idea of Smart Contracts' (1997) (*Satoshi Nakamoto Institute: Literature*) <https://nakamotoinstitute.org/the-idea-of-smart-contracts/> accessed 24 February 2020.

35 See Kevin Werbach and Nicolas Cornell, 'Contracts *ex machina*' (2017) 67 *Duke LJ* 313, 330.

36 Satoshi Nakamoto, 'Bitcoin: A Peer-to-Peer Electronic Cash System' (2008) (*Bitcoin Project: Introduction: White Paper*) <https://bitcoin.org/bitcoin.pdf > accessed 24 February 2020.

37 See Jerry I-H Hsiao, '"Smart" Contract on the Blockchain-Paradigm Shift for Contract Law?' (2017) 14 *US-China L Rev* 685, 688–89; Bryce Suzuki, Todd Taylor, and Garry Marchant, 'Blockchain: How It Will Change Your Legal Practice' (2018) 35 (7) *CILW* 5.

38 See Heil (n 5) 237; Gale M Hyman and Mathew P Digesti, 'New Nevada Legislation Recognizes Blockchain and Smart Contract Technologies' (2017) 25 (8) *Nevada Lawyer* 13; Nataša Samec

In this chapter, we will focus on the basic idea behind the transfer of real estate property based on the smart contract, which aims to include the seller's obligation to provide unencumbered property and the buyer's obligation to pay the price in the smart contract. It is expected that the contract would automatically execute the transaction at the time when the conditions of the unenumerated property at the land register and sufficient resources at the buyer's bank meet. The initial idea is to exclude the role of intermediaries (real estate agent, notary public), additional entries in the land register, and all the other 'analogues' proceedings connected to the real estate conveyance.[39]

To the best of our knowledge, we can list some upward trends of the real estate informatization blockchain technology and smart contracts. According to Griffin P. Heil, Georgia was one of the first countries that turned its land registry into blockchain as a precondition to implementing the smart contract technology to the real estate transaction. They are using blockchain technology as a separate, additional technology layer that provides safety and security for digital certificates stored in the National Agency of Public Registry's land title database.[40] Their next target is to support smart contracts, which will enable real estate transactions themselves to be executed digitally.[41] In 2018 first execution of the comprehensive blockchain-recorded property deal took place in California, USA, by setting of the whole conveyance of real estate online.[42] Australia also implements the smart contract to the field of real estate transactions, already in the phase of the conclusion of the contract and completing the whole conveyance online.[43] Sweden has been developing a property purchase using blockchain and smart contract technology in cooperation with ChromaWay start-up company since 2016.[44] In 2018, they already presented

---

Berghaus and Klemen Drnovšek, 'Iluzija pojma pametne pogodbe' in Martina Repaš (ed), *X. posvet Pravo in ekonomija: Digitalno gospodarstvo: Konferenčni zbornik* (Univerza v Mariboru Pravna fakulteta 2018) 25; Nataša Samec Berghaus and Klemen Drnovšek, 'Domet uporabne vrednosti pametnih pogodb na področju pogodbenega prava' [2018] *Prav Letop* 41, 46.

39  Aljaž Jadek and Peter Merc, 'Pametne pogodbe v verigi podatkovnih blokov' (*Portal FinD-INFO*, 19 March 2018) <www.findinfo.si/medijsko-sredisce/v-srediscu/216777> accessed 24 February 2020.

40  According to Griffin P Heil, 'Blockchain's efficiency allows Georgian citizens to complete an entire real estate transaction in ten minutes instead of three days.' Heil (n 5) 248.

41  'Georgia to use smart contracts in real estate registrations' (*Agenda*, 22 February 2018) <https://agenda.ge/en/news/2018/396> accessed 24 February 2020.

42  'Propy Announces the First California Property Sale on the Blockchain' (*Business Wire*, 23 July 2018) <www.businesswire.com/news/home/20180723005199/en/Propy-Announces-California-Property-Sale-Blockchain> accessed 24 February 2020.

43  'Corrs and OpenLaw Have Successfully Developed and Simulated an End-to-End Real Estate Transaction on the Ethereum Blockchain' (*Legal Practice Intelligence*, 16 June 2018) <www.legalpracticeintelligence.com.au/corrs-and-openlaw-have-successfully-developed-and-simulated-an-end-to-end-real-estate-transaction-on-the-ethereum-blockchain/> accessed 24 February 2020.

44  According to Griffin P Heil, 'It is projected that a Blockchain land registry could save the Swedish taxpayers over E100 million ($106 million) a year by eliminating paperwork, reducing fraud, and speeding up transactions.' Heil (n 5) 249.

the live demonstration which included client-side verification of government-approved digital signatures and the final exporting of necessary legal contracts.[45]

There are also many private companies in the world, for example, Block-square in Slovenia, which runs a private system of real estate tokenization that enables the investor to buy tokens[46] as an investment into real estate rights.[47] This is the system that allows investors to buy tokens that entitle them to take part in the economic benefits of the real estate but does not entitle them as the actual owners (the ideal part) of the real estate (co-ownership). The owner of real estate is still the company, which issued 'tokens', therefore no further consideration of the real estate tokenization is addressed in this chapter.[48]

There are still many opened questions related to the implementation of the blockchain-based smart contracts, related to the ability of the technology to exclude intermediaries, questions related to the possibility to implement the smart contracts in different land registration systems,[49] questions connected to the true meeting of the minds, the legal capacity of the parties,[50] etc. Nevertheless, when reviewing relevant literature and resources one cannot unsee the emerging trends and benefits of new technologies implementation to the field of real estate transactions. Although most of the before-mentioned countries' real estate transaction systems are not directly comparable to the Slovenian and Croatian regime of real estate transactions, the bottom line remains that it is very likely that the technological development of smart contracts also will impact the real estate law of Slovenia and Croatia in the future. The development of new technologies in the field of real estate transactions has already initiated theoretical discussions, taking place in Germany[51] and Austria,[52] whose legal systems regarding real estate transactions are much closer to the Slovenian and Croatian systems. Considering the technology development and theoretical discussions taking place abroad, it is reasonable to analyse the possible implementation of new technologies also to Slovenian and Croatian law.

---

45  Christine Kim, 'Sweden's Land Registry Demos Live Transaction on a Blockchain' (*CoinDesk*, 15 June 2018) <www.coindesk.com/sweden-demos-live-land-registry-transaction-on-a-blockchain> accessed 26 February 2020.

46  According to Oleksii Konashevych, 'Tokens are blockchain-based records that represent the title and other property rights.' Oleksii Konashevych, 'General Concept of Real Estate Tokenization on Blockchain: The Right to Choose' (2020) 9 *Eur Prop LJ* (forthcoming).

47  Denis Petrovčič, 'The World's First Tokenized Garage' (*Hacker Noon*, 2 October 2018) <https://hackernoon.com/the-worlds-first-tokenized-real-estate-property-is-a-garage-bb0c1364fbc1> accessed 29 February 2020.

48  The questions of tokenization are not directly connected with the transfer of rights *in rem*, especially not in the legal systems where the entry into land register is necessary as the precondition for the transfer of such rights.

49  Méndez (n 33) 13.

50  See Werbach and Cornell (n 35) 368–72.

51  See Harald Wilsch, 'Die Blockchain-Technologie aus der Sicht des deutschen Grundbuchrechts' [2018] *DNotZ* 761.

52  See Thomaas Seeber, Manuel Schweiger, and Martin Schachner, 'Immobilientransaktionen über die Blockchain' [2018] (2) *Immolex* 38.

While analysing the potential implementation of smart contracts to real estate transactions one should take into consideration the potential benefits of the blockchain and smart contract technology that are widely mentioned amongst the causes to implement such technology to the real estate transactions. At first, we should mention the minimalization of potential fraud and data security, since the ledger is distributed amongst many computers, so a potential hacker would need to simultaneously attack at least 51% of the network in order to change records, which is practically impossible or at least unprofitable to gain. The arguments in favour of blockchain-based smart contracts are also transparency, accuracy, and efficiency of the new technology's solutions.[53] Since the ledger is practically impossible to change, the transactions are trackable, and the technology could ease the eventual proving of the chain of transfers.

Implementing blockchain technologies and smart contracts undoubtedly aims to eliminate paperwork, speed up transactions, minimalize the role of intermediaries, and therefore reduce costs.[54] However, it is not reasonable to expect that the technology would completely exclude the intermediaries from the real estate transactions.[55] Taking into account the nature of the land register proceedings, it is to be expected that the only official registry in the countries which implement the smart contract-supported conveyance of real estate transfers remains the one under the power of the state.[56] At this point, it is expected that blockchain could be applied only if properly adapted to the existing land registration architecture, which implies the existence of the central authority.[57] It can be argued that the new technology is able to maintain an adequate level of harmonization of the land register and *de facto* situation in the field since the system is implemented to support land registries mainly in the states that lack a registry, or in the countries where the land registry is inefficient.[58]

One of the frequently mentioned prevailing functionalities of the smart contract is automatization and self-execution function, mostly in connection to the *pacta sunt servanda* principle,[59] since the smart contract could automatically execute the terms of a deal. The smart contract's self-execution function empowers the contract to 'self-execute' the obligations when the conditions are met and it does so without 'human input' or human will, therefore strengthening the *pacta sunt servanda* principle.[60]

A common characteristic of the listed benefits of the smart contract's implementation in the real estate transaction is to increase efficiency, legal safety, and transparency in the field. On the general scale, we can conclude that at least some

53  See Heil (n 5) 241–50.
54  ibid 249.
55  Text to n 84.
56  Méndez (n 33) 4.
57  Maria Kaczorowska, 'Blockchain-Based Land Registration: Possibilities and Challenges' (2019) 13 *Masaryk U JL & Tech* 339, 355.
58  Méndez (n 33) 4.
59  Klemen Drnovšek, 'Tehnologija veriženja podatkovnih blokov in pravni vidiki sklepanja pametnih pogodb' [2018] *Podjetje in delo* 721, 729.
60  Hsiao (n 37) 686.

of the functionalities are remarkably close to the purpose and functionalities of the rules which demand written form for the real estate transactions. To illustrate, it is possible to compare the functionality of the written form as proof of the transaction to the security and transparency of blockchain data. If the agreement is written on paper it indisputably serves as the proof of the transaction and at the same time prevents potential frauds by disabling the potential fraudulent party to unilaterally change the terms of the contract. The written document as a proof of the transaction can be used in many occasions, not only in the case of an eventual dispute between the parties but also for the purpose of land register proceedings, paying the transfer tax, etc.[61] Knowing the fact that the blockchain data is practically impossible to change,[62] it can be concluded that in the light of the functionality of the new technologies of proving the transaction, preventing fraud, and ensuring data security, the blockchain-based smart contract follows practically the same objective.

A similar conclusion can be drawn for the tendency to empower the *pacta sunt servanda* principle. If contract terms are written on the paper, the parties are generally more likely to perform their obligations.[63] The blockchain-based smart contract provides the performance of the contract by the aforementioned self-execution function.[64] Hence, in the light of the self-execution function, the smart contract can bring an even higher level of certainty that the contract will be executed than the present paper-based transactions since the contract will execute the contract terms of the contract automatically.

However, technology can not eliminate all the risk connected to the transfer of real estate ownership. Namely, the self-execution function is argued to potentially cause problems since the execution of the contract is autonomous and performs the obligation in any case, even in the case of a potential mistake, fallacy, or even fraud in the phase of forming the contract or changed circumstances in the phase of performing the contract.[65] A smart contract does not assure a true meeting of the minds in the contracting phase of an agreement.[66]

All the mentioned advantages and disadvantages of the new technologies should be considered in the event of amending the legislation. Still, the question remains, whether a need to amend the applicable legislation when implementing the smart contracts to the field of real estate transactions even exists.

## 4  The necessity of legislative amendments in the case of smart contract implementation to real estate transactions under Slovenian and Croatian law

The earlier-mentioned question is connected to the question of whether the smart contracts are going to cause a drastic change in the 'paradigm' of contract

61  Text to nn 24 and 25.
62  Text to nn 54 and 55.
63  Text to n 60.
64  Hsiao (n 37) 686.
65  See Suzuki, Taylor, and Marchant (n 37) 8.
66  Werbach and Cornell (n 35) 368.

law or should the smart contracts be recognized under the positive law. The answer to that question exceeds the scope of this chapter, however, it is possible to agree on this point with Hsiao's conclusion that smart contracts will probably not bring the paradigm shift to contract law in the near future, and 'we will see more traditional contract and smart contract coexisting to supplement each other but not to replace the other'.[67] A similar conclusion was drawn by Fernando P. Méndez stating that 'blockchain can perform a supporting function to immovables secure transaction systems' rather than an independent, autonomous, decentralized, and indelible system when dealing with real estate transactions and blockchain-based land registers.[68]

### 4.1 The electronic form of the contract under Slovenian and Croatian law and smart contracts in the field of real estate transactions

Given the fact that neither Slovenian nor Croatian law expressly settles the notion of smart contract, we shall use the rules and principles which govern the traditional contracts at this point. Since the bottom line of any smart contract is that such a contract is concluded in electronic form[69] the question emerges whether the applicable law allows the conclusion of the contract regarding real estate transactions in electronic form.

Under the Slovenian OblZ, 'any method or form of communication that retains the official wording intact and allows the origin of the wording to be checked using generally accepted means is generally equalized with the contract in written form and has the same effects as a document.'[70] Croatian law expressly addresses the electronic formation of a contract, stipulating that such contract is formed 'when the parties have agreed on the essential elements of the agreement'.[71] The regulation represents a legal ground for the contracts to be valid, even if concluded by email or other means of electronic communication. Both Croatian ZOO and Slovenian OblZ at general level equalize the form of a written document and electronic form of documents. The regulation complies with the UNCITRAL Model Law on Electronic Commerce (MLEC)[72] and its principles of non-discrimination, functional equivalence, and technological neutrality of the electronic documents.

According to the Slovenian Electronic Business and Electronic Signature Act (*Zakon o elektronskom poslovanju in elektronskem podpisu*,[73] ZEPEP), 'data in

---

67   Hsiao (n 37) 694.
68   Méndez (n 33) 21.
69   cf Werbach and Cornell (n 35) 320–24.
70   Slovenian OZ, Art 57.
71   Croatian ZOO, Art 293.
72   United Nations Commission on International Trade Law (UNCITRAL), *UNCITRAL Model Law on Electronic Commerce with Guide to Enactment 1996: With Additional Article 5 Bis as Adopted in 1998* (United Nations 1999) <https://uncitral.un.org/en/texts/ecommerce/modellaw/electronic_commerce> accessed 26 February 2020.
73   *UR LS* 98/2004, 61/2006, 46/2014.

electronic form shall not be denied legal effect or admissibility as evidence solely on the grounds that they are in electronic form.'[74] A similar rule is encompassed under Croatian Electronic Commerce Act (*Zakon o elektroničkoj trgovini*,[75] ZET) for the case when an electronic message or electronic form is used to conclude a contract.[76] At first glance, someone could argue that the conclusion of the binding legal agreement regarding the real estate transaction in electronic form (in the form of the smart contract) is therefore admissible and valid. But this is not the case. The regulation under Slovenian and Croatian law expressly excludes legal acts by which property rights to real estate are transferred.[77] The regulation is harmonized with the Directive on Electronic Commerce[78] which allows the EU Member States to exclude the real estate transactions from its scope,[79] as well as with the MLEC which is not intended for real estate transactions.[80]

Knowing the fact that non-compliance with formality prerequisites when entering into contracts regarding real estate transfer results in voidness of the contract, it is to be concluded that the eventual conclusion of the smart contract in electronic form under current regulation would be void and null.

The voidness as the sanction for a real estate transaction concluded in electronic form was confirmed in the Slovenian case law. The High Court of Ljubljana (*Višje sodišče v Ljubljani*, VSL) dealt with the question of whether the binding legal agreement (sales contract) concerning the ownership of real estate is valid. In this case, the claimant claimed the payment of 52.655,79 euros based on the respondent's non-payment for delivered goods. The respondent built its defence by offsetting the claim based on alleged counterclaim towards the claimant. Respondent claimed that it holds an obligation towards the claimant, based on another binding legal agreement (sales contract) for the purchase of the apartment, supposedly concluded by email. Respondent's argument was

---

74  ZEPEP, Art 4.

75  *NN* 173/2003, 67/2008, 36/2009, 130/2011, 30/2014, 32/2019.

76  Article 9(3) of the ZET provides that such contract shall not be denied legal effect solely on the grounds that it is in electronic form.

77  ZEPEP, Art 4; ZET, Art 9.

78  Directive 2000/31/EC of the European Parliament and of the Council of 8 June 2000 on certain legal aspects of information society services, in particular electronic commerce, in the Internal Market [2000] *OJ* L178/1 (Directive on Electronic Commerce).

79  Article 9(1) of the Directive on Electronic Commerce provides:

> Member States shall ensure that their legal system allows contracts to be concluded by electronic means. Member States shall in particular ensure that the legal requirements applicable to the contractual process neither create obstacles for the use of electronic contracts nor result in such contracts being deprived of legal effectiveness and validity on account of their having been made by electronic means.
>
> Article 9(2) of the Directive on Electronic Commerce stipulates that Member States may lay down that Art 9(1) shall not apply to all or certain contracts falling into one of the categories defined in Art 9(2), including '(a) contracts that create or transfer rights in real estate, except for rental rights'.

80  UNCITRAL (n 72) 41.

not accepted by the VSL. The VSL decided that the conditions for the offset of the claims were not met since the alleged obligation to pay the price for the apartment on the side of claimant did not exist. The court clearly stated that the electronic form, hence email, is not equal to written form in the case of transfer of the ownership of the real estate, therefore no binding legal agreement was concluded in the case.[81]

If the conclusion of the real estate agreement by the email is null and void, then the conclusion of the agreement in the form of a smart contract would also be null and void. But in the light of the emerging trends in the world and especially the legal certainty and transparency that aims to be brought to the field of real estate transactions by implementing new technologies, it may be the time for the legislature to rethink the purpose and legitimacy of the regulation that prevents conclusion of binding agreement in the electronic form under applicable law.

### 4.2  The role of the notary public in the light of smart contracts functionalities

The question of the role of the notary public in the process of real estate conveyance emerges as a field for further research, posed by the prevailing idea of excluding the intermediaries in the real estate transaction using smart contracts. Even though the potential technical solutions exist (e.g. electronic notarization of the signature), the problem remains that blockchain technology itself cannot ascertain the identity or capacity of the parties to a transaction at the moment of signing the deal.[82]

Another prevailing problem is also the smart contract's self-execution function, which can, on the one hand, bring legal certainty to the real estate transactions, empowering the *pacta sunt servanda* principle, but on the other hand, represents the danger for the parties, especially in the case of changed circumstances (*rebus sic stantibus*), mistakes in the phase of the conclusion of the contract, etc.[83] Being aware of the importance of real estate ownership and its value, the legislature should protect the parties to the transaction before such risks. When resolving these issues, the smart contract's emphasized function to resolve the contractual questions *ex ante*[84] should be taken into consideration. Hence, the legislature should be concerned to grant proper legal security to the parties in the case of implementing new technologies, mainly in the phase of the conclusion of the smart contract.

Rather than being fully excluded from the real estate transactions, notaries and other intermediaries' function may change to consulting the parties when forming the smart contract. The specific technical and legal nature of the smart

---

81  VSL judgment of 28 January 2014, I Cpg 905/2012.
82  Méndez (n 33) 2.
83  ibid 13.
84  Hsiao (n 37) 690.

contract requires specific technical and legal knowledge. It is therefore very likely to expect that the parties would need the assistance of the intermediaries in the phase of forming a smart contract.[85] Only that way would it be possible to assure the parties sufficient legal certainty and precaution when entering into a new kind of legal agreement.

The question of the notary public role in the real estate transactions under the emerging trends of blockchain-based real estate transactions would undoubt-edly exceed the scope of this chapter which mainly deals with the prerequi-site of a written form. Namely, the positive law of Slovenia and Croatia does not even allow the parties to enter into a binding legal transaction of real estate property by using electronic communication. Engagement of the notary public is not even necessary in the phase of entering into a legal transaction of obligation (sales contract) under applicable law. Therefore, the legislature will inevitably have to deal with the legitimacy of the regulation that prevents conclusion of the sales contract for the purchase of real estate property in the electronic form, probably even before dealing with questions related to the role of the notary public and the notarization of the registration clause (*clausula intabulandi*).

## 5 Conclusion

To summarize, it is highly likely to expect further informatization in the field of real estate transactions in the future, which is confirmed by the emerging trends abroad.

As explained in the chapter, the conclusion of the real estate legal transaction of obligation (e.g. sales agreement) in electronic form is considered void and null under present Slovenian and Croatian law. The same conclusion is derived for real estate transaction in the form of smart contract since the blockchain-based smart contracts are concluded in electronic form. If the parties entered into a smart contract regarding a real estate transaction, such contract would most probably be considered void and null under applicable law (*de lege lata*). If the parties willingly avoided the rule of the written form, calculating to the realization rule, it would be difficult or even impossible to invoke the realiza-tion rule to turn the invalid contract into a valid agreement.

Under present regulation, the parties will not be prone to take the risk to enter into electronic agreements regarding real estate because of the danger (and the severity) of the nullity sanctions. The regulation which disables the parties to enter into an electronic agreement regarding real estate transactions, therefore, represents the obstacle for the use of the smart contract in the field. Considering the emerging trends abroad and the functionality of new tech-nologies, it may be the time for the legislature to rethink the current regulation which prevents the parties to enter into a contract in electronic form when

---

85  Drnovšek (n 59) 729.

dealing with real estate transfer of ownership. In the case of the implementation of the smart contract, one of the inevitable steps is to slightly amend the formality rules regarding real estate transactions, particularly where the law provides unequal treatment of electronic form and form of a written document as in the case of legal transactions under which property rights to real estate are transferred.

When adopting the legislation in order to implement the smart contracts to the field of real estate transactions, the purpose of the current formality rules – to protect both private and public interest – should be taken into consideration. The purpose of legal rules regarding the formality of real estate transactions (written form) of the real estate transactions can be compared to the functionalities of blockchain-based smart contracts. Both written form of the agreement and blockchain-based smart contracts at a general level seek to ensure legal certainty and transparency of the real estate transactions. The legislature should consider advantages and weaknesses of current regulation and new technologies functions in order to grant at least equal level of legal certainty and transparency of the real estate transactions, as provided by the present regulation.

## Bibliography

——, 'Corrs and OpenLaw Have Successfully Developed and Simulated an End-to-End Real Estate Transaction on the Ethereum Blockchain' (*Legal Practice Intelligence*, 16 June 2018) <www.legalpracticeintelligence.com.au/corrs-and-openlaw-have-successfully-developed-and-simulated-an-end-to-end-real-estate-transaction-on-the-ethereum-blockchain/> accessed 24 February 2020.

——, 'Georgia to Use Smart Contracts in Real Estate Registrations' (*Agenda*, 22 February 2018) <https://agenda.ge/en/news/2018/396> accessed 24 February 2020.

——, 'Propy Announces the First California Property Sale on the Blockchain' (*Business Wire*, 23 July 2018) <www.businesswire.com/news/home/20180723005199/en/Propy-Announces-California-Property-Sale-Blockchain> accessed 24 February 2020.

Crnić I, *Zakon o obveznim odnosima: opsežna sudska praksa, napomene i komentari, detaljno abecedno kazalo pojmova* (Organizator 2016).

Drnovšek K, 'Tehnologija veriženja podatkovnih blokov in pravni vidiki sklepanja pametnih pogodb' [2018] *Podjetje in delo* 721.

Heil GP, 'Blockchain's Impact on Real Estate and the Future' (2019) 18 *J Intl Bus & L* 237.

Hsiao JIH, '"Smart" Contract on the Blockchain-Paradigm Shift for Contract Law?' (2017) 14 *US-China Law Review* 685 [https://doi.org/10.17265/1548-6605/2017.10.002].

Hyman GM and Digesti MP, 'New Nevada Legislation Recognizes Blockchain and Smart Contract Technologies' (2017) 25 (8) *Nevada Lawyer* 13.

Jadek A and Merc P, 'Pametne pogodbe v verigi podatkovnih blokov' (*Portal FinD-INFO*, 19 March 2018) <www.findinfo.si/medijsko-sredisce/v-srediscu/216777> accessed 24 February 2020.

Juhart M and Plavšak N (eds), *Obligacijski zakonik (OZ): (splošni del): s komentarjem: 1. knjiga* (GV Založba 2003).

——, Tratnik M, and Vrenčur R, *Stvarnopravni zakonik (SPZ) s komentarjem* (Uradni list Republike Slovenije 2016).

Kaczorowska M, 'Blockchain-Based Land Registration: Possibilities and Challenges' (2019) 13 *Masaryk U JL & Tech* 339.

Kim C, 'Sweden's Land Registry Demos Live Transaction on a Blockchain' (*CoinDesk*, 15 June 2018) <www.coindesk.com/sweden-demos-live-land-registry-transaction-on-a-blockchain> accessed 26 February 2020.

Konashevych O, 'General Concept of Real Estate Tokenization on Blockchain: The Right to Choose' (2020) 9 *Eur Prop LJ* (forthcoming) [https://doi.org/10.1515/eplj-2020-0003].

Méndez FP, 'Smart Contracts, Blockchain and Land Registry' (*European Land Registry Association General Assembly*, Brussels, 30 November 2018) <www.elra.eu/wp-content/uploads/2018/12/Smart-Contracts-Blockchain-and-Land-Registry-by-F-Mendez.pdf> accessed 12 June 2020.

Nakamoto S, 'Bitcoin: A Peer-to-Peer Electronic Cash System' (2008) (*Bitcoin Project: Introduction: White Paper*) <https://bitcoin.org/bitcoin.pdf> accessed 24 February 2020.

Petrovčič D, 'The World's First Tokenized Garage' (*Hacker Noon*, 2 October 2018) <https://hackernoon.com/the-worlds-first-tokenized-real-estate-property-is-a-garage-bb0c1364fbc1> accessed 29 February 2020.

Plavšak N, Juhart M, and Vrenčur R, *Obligacijsko pravo: splošni del* (GV Založba 2009).

Repanić M, 'Real Property Transactions in the Republic of Croatia: Procedures of Property Transfer, Change of Real Property Rights and Property Formation' (MSc thesis, KTH Royal Institute of Technology Stockholm 2005).

Samec Berghaus N and Drnovšek K, 'Iluzija pojma pametne pogodbe' in Repaš M (ed), *X. posvet Pravo in ekonomija: Digitalno gospodarstvo: Konferenčni zbornik* (Univerza v Mariboru Pravna fakulteta 2018) [https://doi.org/10.18690/978-961-286-169-8.2].

—— and Drnovšek K, 'Domet uporabne vrednosti pametnih pogodb na področju pogodbenega prava' [2018] *Prav Letop* 41.

Seeber T, Schweiger M, and Schachner M, 'Immobilientransaktionen über die Blockchain' [2018] (2) *Immolex* 38.

Suzuki B, Taylor T, and Marchant G, 'Blockchain: How It Will Change Your Legal Practice' (2018) 35 (7) *CILW* 5.

Szabo N, 'The Idea of Smart Contracts' (1997) (*Satoshi Nakamoto Institute: Literature*) <https://nakamotoinstitute.org/the-idea-of-smart-contracts/> accessed 24 February 2020.

United Nations Commission on International Trade Law (UNCITRAL), *UNCITRAL Model Law on Electronic Commerce with Guide to Enactment 1996: With Additional Article 5 Bis as Adopted in 1998* (United Nations 1999) <https://uncitral.un.org/en/texts/ecommerce/modellaw/electronic_commerce> accessed 26 February 2020.

Werbach K and Cornell N, 'Contracts *ex machina*' (2017) 67 *Duke LJ* 313.

Wilsch H, 'Die Blockchain-Technologie aus der Sicht des deutschen Grundbuchrechts' [2018] *DNotZ* 761.

Zimmermann R, *The Law of Obligations: Roman Foundations of the Civilian Tradition* (Juta & Co 1990).

# 10 A contradiction arising from an annulment decision of the Turkish Constitutional Court

The unique problem of a unique provision of the new Code of Obligations

*Orhan Emre Konuralp*

## 1 Introduction

During the establishment of the modern republic, Turkey amended all leg-islation. As part of the process of the modernization of the Turkish law, the Code of Obligations was enacted in 1926, as an adoption of the Swiss Code of Obligations (*Obligationenrecht*, OR) without the commercial law section.[1] The former Turkish Code of Civil Procedure entered into force also in 1926 and it was an adoption of the Code of Civil Procedure of the Swiss canton Neuchâ-tel.[2] Many modifications were made in the following eighty years to both of these codes, while in 2011 both the new Turkish Code of Obligations (*Türk Borçlar Kanunu*,[3] TBK) and the new Code of Civil Procedure (*Hukuk Muhake-meleri Kanunu*,[4] HMK) were enacted. The new HMK entered into force on 1 October 2011, and the new TBK entered into force on 1 July 2012. It was a historical coincidence that the federal Swiss Civil Procedure Code, which has abrogated the civil procedure codes of the Swiss cantons, entered into force in 2011 as well. However, unlike other main codes of Turkish private law, the new Turkish HMK is not based on the Swiss Civil Procedure Code, nor any specific foreign law. The new TBK has retained the same structure as the previ-ous Code of Obligations, as well as the Swiss influence, and like the previous Code of Obligations and the Swiss OR, the new TBK also constitutes the Fifth Book of the new Turkish Civil Code (*Türk Medenî Kanunu*,[5] TMK). It should be added that the former Turkish Civil Code of 1926 was also an adoption of

---

1 Erhan Adal, *Fundamentals of Turkish Private Law* (7th edn, Legal 2004) 50; Osman Berat Gürzumar, 'İsviçre Medeni Kanunu'nun Türkiye'de İktibası' in A Lale Sirmen, Çiğdem Kırca, and Vedat Buz (eds), *Symposium anlässlich des 80. Jahrestages des Inkrafttretens des Türkischen Zivilgesetzbuches: Türk Medenî Kanununun Yürürlüğe Girişinin 80. Yılı Münasebetiyle Düzenlenen Sempozyum* (Ankara Üniver-sitesi 2007) 17, 26.
2 Adal (n 1) 50.
3 Act 6098: Turkish Code of Obligations (6098 *sayılı Türk Borçlar Kanunu*), RG 27836/2011, as later amended.
4 Act 6100: Code of Civil Procedure (6100 *sayılı Hukuk Muhakemeleri Kanunu*), RG 27836/2011, as later amended.
5 Act 4721: Turkish Civil Code (4721 *sayılı Türk Medenî Kanunu*), RG 24607/2001, as later amended.

the Swiss Civil Code (*Zivilgesetzbuch*, ZGB)[6] and that the new TMK of 2001 is still based on the Swiss ZGB.[7] Following these facts, it is easy to say that the Turkish private law originates from the Swiss private law.

As a result of the coordination between the committees that drafted the new TBK and the new HMK, there are some cumulative provisions in these codes. One such cumulative provision relates to the liability of the state for its acts.[8] Before the new codes were enacted, the disputes arising from the liability of the state for its acts, as well as the disputes arising from administrative contracts and transactions, were under the jurisdiction of the administrative courts as one of the major branches of the Turkish judicial system. However, according to the new Art 3 HMK, in the cases related to the harm of the physical integrity of persons as a result of an act of state, the civil courts would have jurisdiction instead of administrative courts. Additionally, according to Art 55 TBK, the applicable law for these cases would be the TBK, which means that civil law would be applied in administrative issues. It should be added that the Swiss OR does not have such a provision and that it was also unfamiliar to the former Turkish Code of Obligations.[9] These two provisions are considered as cumulative provisions[10] since one provision regulates the jurisdiction and the other one the applicable law.

## 2 Judiciary of Turkey

The Turkish judiciary system is a highly separated judicial system and the substantive jurisdiction of courts is defined by different codes and laws. The main classification of Turkish judiciary is based on the six supreme courts: Constitutional Court of Turkey, the High Court of Appeals, the Council of State, the Court of Jurisdictional Disputes, the Court of Accounts, and the Supreme Board of Election.

Turkish Constitutional Court (*Anayasa Mahkemesi*, AYM) mainly has two duties: one is to examine 'the constitutionality in respect of both form and substance of laws, presidential decrees and the Rules of Procedure of the Grand National Assembly of Turkey',[11] and the other one is to decide on individual applications. The High Court of Appeals (*Yargıtay*) is the supreme court above

---

6  Gürzumar (n 1) 26.
7  ibid 29; Adal (n 1) 50.
8  M Murat İnceoğlu and Meliha Sermin Paksoy, 'Bedensel Zararlarda Ve Ölüm Halinde Zararın Belirlenmesi (TBK. m. 55)' (2013) 8 (Special Issue) *Yaşar Üniversitesi E-Dergisi* 1383, 1398; Fatma Nur Tekçe, 'Manevi Tazminat Davalarında Görevli ve Yetkili Mahkeme' (2016) 22 *Marmara Üniversitesi Hukuk Fakültesi Hukuk Araştırmaları Dergisi* 2623, 2633.
9  Mustafa Ünlütepe, 'TBK'nın 55/I. Maddesi Çerçevesinde Ölüm Hâlinde Uğranılan Zararların ve Bedensel Zararların Belirlenmesi' (2018) 13 (141) *Terazi Hukuk Dergisi* 68, 70.
10  Nedim Akkurt, '6098 Sayılı Türk Borçlar Kanunu'nda Uygulayıcı Gözüyle Hâksiz Fiiller ve Tazminat' in Emel Badur (ed), *6098 Sayılı Türk Borçlar Kanunu Sempozyumu: 12–13 Mayis 2011* (Ankara Barosu 2012) 41, 46.
11  Act 2709: Constitution of the Republic of Turkey (2709 *sayılı Türkiye Cumhuriyeti Anayasası*), RG 17844/1982 and 17863/1982, as later amended (Constitution), Art 148.

the criminal and civil courts, whereas the Council of State (*Danıştay*) is the supreme court above the administrative and tax courts. The reason for the existence of the Court of Jurisdictional Disputes (*Uyuşmazlık Mahkemesi*) is the dualist system of separation between administrative law and civil law courts. Its main function is 'to deliver final judgments in disputes between civil and administrative courts concerning their jurisdiction and judgments'.[12]

The qualification of both the Court of Accounts and the Supreme Board of Elections as a supreme court and even a court is a controversial issue in Turkish law. This is because these institutions function a bit differently than a court. The Court of Accounts (*Sayıştay*) is charged with 'auditing, on behalf of the Grand National Assembly of Turkey, revenues, expenditures, and assets of the public administrations financed by central government budget and social security institutions', with 'taking final decisions on the accounts and acts of the responsible officials', and with 'exercising the functions prescribed by the law in matters of inquiry, auditing and judgment'.[13] On the other hand, the tasks of the Supreme Board of Elections (*Yüksek Seçim Kurulu*) are to execute 'all the functions to ensure the fair and orderly conduct of elections from the beginning to the end', to carry out 'investigations and take final decisions, during and after the elections, on all irregularities, complaints and objections concerning the electoral matters', and to receive 'the electoral records of the members of the Grand National Assembly of Turkey and presidential election'.[14] Article 79 of the Constitution states that no appeal could be made against the decisions of the Supreme Board of Elections, and similarly, Art 160 of the Constitution states that no applications for judicial review of the decisions of the Court of Accounts are to be filed in any other court. It should be added that the members of the Court of Accounts and the Supreme Board of Elections are appointed from the judges and they are subject to judicial liability during their duties. For these reasons, these two institutions are defined as courts, even though their functioning is not similar to regular courts that individuals could directly apply.

The main problem relating to the jurisdiction of these different courts concerns determining the jurisdiction of civil courts and administrative courts since other courts do have distinctive substantive jurisdictions. The amendments made in the new HMK and TBK in 2011 also relate to the separation between the civil and administrative courts.

## 3  Justification for Article 3 of the new Code of Civil Procedure

As will be explained further in the chapter, there are several legal provisions in Turkish law which have changed the competent authority for certain cases. Thus, Art 3 HMK was not a radical novelty, however, its scope was significantly

---

12  Constitution, Art 158.
13  Constitution, Art 160.
14  Constitution, Art 79.

wider than the scope of other provisions that have modified the judicial juris-diction. The main legal ground for the change of the competent courts for cer-tain disputes in these provisions was that the nature of the disputes is closer to the jurisdiction of civil courts than to the jurisdiction of administrative courts. The justification for Art 3 HMK relied on a similar reason. In the pre-amble of the HMK, the rationale behind Art 3 HMK was explained as follows:

> The basic approach to the solution of the problem of determining the competence for personal injury is to use a criterion based on the subject of injury (human), instead of the nature of the cause of personal injury and the nature of the area to which the cause belongs. Comparing 'the crite-rion of the area and the criterion of injury', when the subject of injury is human, of course 'the criterion of injury' should be called upon.[15]

## 4 The Constitutional Court's decision on annulment of Article 3 of the Code of Civil Procedure

In 2011, Art 3 HMK was challenged before the Turkish Constitutional Court (AYM) by the main opposing party (Republican People's Party) and was annulled as a result of this application. The AYM confirmed that the adminis-trative judiciary shall have its jurisdiction over the cases related to the adminis-trative law, finding the legal ground for the annulment decision in Arts 155 and 157 of the Constitution. In its decision on the annulment of Art 3 HMK, the AYM has reasoned as follows:

> With this rule, only the injuries to the person's bodily integrity and the related material and moral losses due to death are covered, and the jurisdic-tion for these damages is given to the civil courts. Accordingly, since the other losses arising from the same administrative actions, transactions and other situations the administration is liable, are not covered, the claims for compensation of these losses will continue to be filed in the administra tive judiciary, even if the reason of the liability is the same; in this case, it would be harmful to the integrity of the trial that claims arising from the same administrative action or transaction are partly heard in the adminis-trative judiciary, and partly in the civil courts. Also, through hearing cases before two separate judicial bodies, different conclusions could be reached regarding the liability of the administration, the scope of this liability, and the compensation obligation of the administration. Essentially, the con-cepts of neglect of duty and strict liability existing in administrative law are concepts used to compensate individuals for losses and to extend the scope of protection of individuals against the administration. In administrative

15 Adalet Komisyonu, *Hukuk Muhakemeleri Kanunu Tasarısı ve Adalet Komisyonu Raporu* (TC, Başbakanlık, Kanunlar ve Kararla, 16 April 2008) <www.kgm.adalet.gov.tr/Tasariasamalari/Kanunlasan/2011Yili/kanmetni/6100ss.pdf > accessed 17 June 2020.

law, even if there was no fault of administration, it is possible to compensate the losses that individuals have suffered, based on the concepts of social risk, terrorist acts, and the balancing of sacrifices. The strict liability in private law is applied only for certain issues and is limited. Undoubtedly, administrative judiciary shall have jurisdiction over the cases relating to administrative actions and transactions and other situations that the administration is liable on the basis of administrative law. For this reason, it cannot be said that it serves the public interest and that there is a justified reason for the cases related to the compensation of losses arising from the same administrative action, transaction or liability to be heard in different jurisdictions as stated above.[16]

Interestingly, Art 3 HMK is not the only example from the Turkish legal system of a provision that requires jurisdiction of the civil courts in administrative matters. Similar examples can be found relating to expropriation; correction of the civil registry; land registry; liability of judges, prosecutors, and enforcement officers; traffic fines; cases against the Social Security Institution (except fines); damages caused by state's vehicles; some cases arising from misdemeanour law; and arbitration. Therefore, it is clear that defining civil courts as competent for administrative law issues is not a novelty. Moreover, in its former decisions, AYM stated that it is in the legislature's discretion to define the jurisdiction of civil courts as long as the legislative solution is in favour of public interest and has a legitimate reason.[17]

It should be added that Art 155 of the Constitution, which served as one of the legal grounds for the annulment decision, does not state that administrative courts shall have jurisdiction over the administrative cases. Instead, it states:

> The Council of State is the last instance for reviewing decisions and judgments given by administrative courts and not referred by law to other administrative courts. It shall also be the first and last instance for dealing with specific cases prescribed by law.

Therefore, the change of the jurisdiction from administrative to civil courts should not be assessed as a breach of this article,[18] as the Constitution does not provide a clear scope of jurisdiction of the administrative judiciary.[19] Only if a

---

16 AYM decision of 16 February 2012, E 2011/35, K 2012/23, *RG* 28297/2012.
17 See AYM decision of 26 December 2013, E 2013/68, K 2013/165, *RG* 28954/2014. See also Kemal Gözler and Gürsel Kaplan, 'İdari Eylemlerden Kaynaklanan Zararlara İlişkin Davalar Adlî Yargının Görev Alanına Sokulabilir Mi? (HMK m. 3 ve TBK m. 55/2 Hakkında Eleştiriler)' (2011) 6 (63) *Terazi Hukuk Dergisi* 36, 40; Nesibe Kurt Konca, 'İnsan Zararları Mahkemelerinin Kuruluş ve Görevlerine Dair Kanun Teklifi Hakkında Kısa Bir Değerlendirme' (2016) 1 (2) *Çankaya Üniversitesi Hukuk Fakültesi Dergisi* 293, 299.
18 Gözler and Kaplan (n 17) 40; Sedat Çal, 'İdare Hukukunda Bedensel Zararların Tazminine Yönelik Gelişmeler: Aym'nin HMK 3. Maddesini İptal Kararı ve Çağrışımları' (2016) in Sema Uçakhan Güleç and Necdet Basa (eds), *Yeni Gelişmeler Işığında: Bedensel Zararların Tazmini: Uluslararası Kongre*, vol 1 (Türkiye Barolar Birliği 2016) 319, 324.
19 Kurt Konca (n 17) 298; Çal (n 18) 321.

competent appeal authority for the administrative judiciary would be changed to an authority other than Council of State, such provision might constitute a breach of Art 155 of the Constitution.

For this reason, AYM needed an additional justification for the annulment decision. The AYM found that Art 3 HMK also breached Art 157 of the Constitution[20] which regulates the jurisdiction of the High Military Administrative Court.[21] In its annulment decision, the AYM stated:

> Disputes arising from actions and transactions concerning military staff and related to military service are not civil cases; they belong to the jurisdiction of the military administrative judiciary, the High Military Administrative Court. Under the rule subject to examination, even if the action or transaction that causes the loss of bodily integrity is partially or completely related to military service and concerns military staff, the disputes arising from such event are included within the scope of the jurisdiction of the civil courts. It is also contrary to Article 157 of the Constitution to make civil courts as jurisdictive authorities for disputes arising from actions and transactions concerning military staff and related to the military.[22]

Although Art 3 HMK and Art 55 TBK were two harmonized provisions, the constitutionality of the 55 TBK could not be examined by the AYM in the same decision by which Art 3 HMK was annulled since the issue of the constitutionality of Art 55 TBK was not raised by the applicant. However, it was asserted by scholars that Art 55 TBK does not breach the Constitution.[23] The unconstitutionality of Art 55 TBK was claimed later in a separate case, but AYM did not find the provision to be unconstitutional. However, in that decision, AYM clearly stated that the provision is applicable only for the calculation of damages, not for the determination of the conditions of liability.[24] This issue will be discussed further in the chapter.

Since Art 55 TBK was not annulled, unlike Art 3 HMK, nor was it later repealed, the 55 TBK still orders that civil law should be applied to the cases arising from the harm of the physical integrity of persons as a result of an act of state. Thus, it could be argued that administrative courts have jurisdiction over these cases, but that they should apply civil law to such cases. However, the main principles of administrative law for the liability of the state differ from the civil law principles, and on the basis of these differences, it also could be argued that administrative courts should apply administrative law to such cases.

---

20  Bahtiyar Akyılmaz and others, 'İnsan Zararları Mahkemelerinin Kuruluş ve Görevlerine Dair Kanun Teklifine Eleştirel Bakış' (2015) 19 (2) *Gazi Üniversitesi Hukuk Fakültesi Dergisi* 167, 183; Gözler and Kaplan (n 17) 41; Kurt Konca (n 17) 307.

21  The Article 157 of the Constitution was repealed after the Referendum on Amendments of Constitution, held on 16 April 2017, and High Military Administrative Court was abolished.

22  AYM decision of 16 February 2012, E 2011/35, K 2012/23, *RG* 28297/2012.

23  Gözler and Kaplan (n 17) 40.

24  AYM decision of 22 October 2014, E 2014/94, K 2014/160, *RG* 29285/2015.

## 5 Differences between administrative and civil procedure

Under Turkish law, there are several differences between the administrative and civil procedure. One of the reasons behind the unique solutions of Art 3 HMK and Art 55 TBK was to eliminate these differences concerning personal injury claims and establish a harmonized dispute resolution procedure for claims arising from loss of bodily integrity or death, regardless of the nature of the parties and the tort. It would be useful to add that the reasons behind these differences are neither clear nor convincing. They could only be explained as the result of the evolution of the law.

### 5.1 Applicable law

The major difference between administrative and civil judiciary is the applicable law. Turkish administrative law does not have a major substantive written law regarding the liability of the state.[25] Instead, administrative law consists of the Constitution and many different laws, by-laws, and regulations.[26] Also, one of the major resources of the Turkish administrative law is the jurisprudence.[27] Jurisprudence is essential for the civil judiciary as well; however, the importance of it for the administrative judiciary is much higher. Therefore, jurisprudence is cited as the second most important resource for Turkish administrative law after the Constitution.[28]

### 5.2 Prescription periods

According to TBK, claims arising from torts are subject to the two-year prescription period which starts from the date of claimant's knowledge of the tort and the damage, and to the general prescription period of ten years which starts from the date of tort.[29] The initial point of the prescription period is criticized.[30] It is stated that the date of knowledge of the damage is not a specific point as the damage might be higher or different than at the date of tort.[31]

---

25  Akyılmaz and others (n 20) 175.
26  Metin Günday, *İdare Hukuku* (7th edn, İmaj Yayınevi 2003) 32; Şeref Gözübüyük, *Yönetim Hukuku* (27th edn, Turhan Kitabevi 2008) 45–47.
27  Taner Ayanoğlu, 'İnsan Zararlarına İlişkin Tam Yargı Davalarını Çözme Görevini Asliye Hukuku Mahkemelerine Vermek Reform mu Yoksa Fantezi mi?' (2012) 86 (2) *İstanbul Barosu Dergisi* 71, 73; Gözübüyük (n 26) 67.
28  Günday (n 26) 32.
29  TBK, Art 72.
30  Ayça Akkayan Yıldırım, 'Geç Ortaya Çıkan Bedensel Zararların Tazmini Taleplerinde Uygulanacak Zamanaşımının Yeni Eğilimler Çerçevesinde Değerlendirilmesi' (2016) 74 (1) *İstanbul Üniversitesi Hukuk Fakültesi Mecmuası* 185, 186.
31  Çelik Ahmet Çelik, 'Can Zararları Tüketici Yasası'nın Konusu Değildir' in Hakan Tokbaş and Fehim Üçışık (eds), *4. Tüketici Hukuku Kongresi Makale, Bildiri ve Ses Çözümleri: Sektörel Bazda Tüketici Hukuku ve Uygulamaları* (Bilge Yayınevi 2015) 300, 310.

The regulation for the administrative procedure is entirely different. According to the Law on Administrative Procedure (*İdari Yargılama Usulleri Kanunu*,[32] IYUK), tort claims should be raised directly against the public entity within one year from learning of the tort and damage, and in any case within the five years from the date of tort.[33] However, these are not prescription periods but preclusion periods.[34] The conformity to the preclusion periods is observed *ex officio* by the court under Turkish law,[35] whereas objection of the defendant is required for the observation of the prescription periods. The main reason for this difference lies in the legal nature of these time periods. After the application to the state, if the public entity refuses the application or does not respond to the application, another preclusion period is applied which runs only for sixty days.[36]

### 5.3 Evidence

The HMK has detailed provisions about evidence, whereas IYUK only refers to the HMK in terms of evidence with some exceptions.[37] The HMK provides for a different kind of evidence such as a bill of debt, oath of the party, testimony of a witness, expert evidence, and local inspection. However, Art 31 of the IYUK states that in administrative judiciary only the provisions of HMK relating to experts and local inspection are applicable. Whereas the testimony of a witness is one of the most important types of evidence in the civil procedure, IYUK does not allow parties to bring witnesses to the court.

Additionally, hearing is exceptional in administrative procedure. According to Art 17 IYUK, the hearing may be requested by one of the parties of an annulment case or a dispute of a value exceeding 53 000 Turkish liras.[38] Cases about damages cannot be described as annulment cases, thus they are subject to this monetary limit.

On the contrary, hearing is an absolute requirement for the civil procedure, as lack of a hearing constitutes a reason for the reversal of the decision of the first instance court. According to Art 140 HMK, a preliminary hearing is an absolute requirement for all civil courts. Additionally, after the preliminary hearing parties shall be invited to the investigation hearing. Finally, under the provision of Art 186 HMK, after the completion of the investigation phase, the court has to invite both parties to the oral proceedings. The only exception from these requirements is for the courts that are subject to the simple trial

---

32 Act 2577: Administrative Jurisdiction Procedures Law (2577 *sayılı İdari Yargılama Usulleri Kanunu*), *RG* 17580/1982, as later amended.
33 Gözübüyük (n 26) 424.
34 ibid 447.
35 ibid.
36 ibid 424.
37 IYUK, Art 31.
38 Gözübüyük (n 26) 461.

procedure. According to Art 320 HMK, these courts may conduct preliminary examination without a preliminary hearing. It should be added that almost none of the cases about damages are subject to a simple trial procedure.

### 5.4  Conditions of liability

The main principle of Turkish law of obligations is the fault-based liability.[39] A claim of damages should include the proof of fault of the opposing party.[40] Strict liability is applied only in exceptional cases.[41] For instance, to claim damages against owners of vehicles,[42] buildings,[43] and animals,[44] or enterprises with hazardous activities,[45] no proof of fault is necessary. This is because the liability arising from these kinds of risks is regulated specifically by the TBK as strict liability.

On the other hand, the liability of the public entities under Turkish administrative law is subject to principles of the neglect of duty[46] and strict liability.[47] It is safe to say that strict liability has a wider scope of application in Turkish administrative law than in Turkish civil law.[48] As it is stated in the AYM annulment decision, the main justifications for this system are the concepts of social risk[49] and balancing of sacrifices.[50] The main aim is to protect persons against the state,[51] as these two parties are not equal on a legal basis.[52] This difference between the two law systems requires a very different approach to liability cases.

### 5.5  Requirements for judicial appointment

Under Turkish law, being a law graduate is a requirement for civil judges without any exception. However, for judges of administrative courts, it is not. According to Art 8(c) of the Law on Judges and Prosecutors,[53] candidates to

---

39  Adal (n 1) 286.
40  ibid.
41  ibid 290.
42  ibid 297.
43  ibid 295.
44  ibid.
45  ibid 290.
46  Gözübüyük (n 26) 350.
47  Aysema Pelin Şaşmaz, 'İdarenin Sorumluluğu ve Danıştay Kararlarındaki Görünümüne Genel Bakış' (2016) 2 *Ekonomi İşletme Siyaset ve Uluslararası İlişkiler Dergisi* 211, 215; Müzeyyen Eroğlu Durkal, 'İdarenin Sorumluluğunun Ortaya Çıkışı ve Temeli' (2019) 23 (1) *Ankara Hacı Bayram Veli Üniversitesi Hukuk Fakültesi Dergisi* 159, 160; Gözübüyük (n 26) 354–55; Günday (n 26) 329; Kurt Konca (n 17) 298; Çal (n 18) 322.
48  Akyılmaz and others (n 20) 175.
49  Eroğlu Durkal (n 47) 180; Günday (n 26) 332.
50  Günday (n 26) 333.
51  Eroğlu Durkal (n 47) 184; Kurt Konca (n 17) 298.
52  Şaşmaz (n 47) 213.
53  Act 2802: Law on Judges and Prosecutors (2802 *sayılı Hakimler ve Savcılar Kanunu*), RG 17971/1983, as later amended.

be appointed as a judge or prosecutor in civil and criminal courts need to be law graduates. However, the same paragraph states that graduates of political sciences, administrative sciences, economics, or finance are also eligible to be appointed as judges in administrative judiciary. This is a controversial issue for Turkish judiciary, but the difference in requirements for a judicial appointment is explained with a different character and legal nature of the civil law and administrative law disputes.

## 6 The aftermath of the annulment decision of the Turkish Constitutional Court

### 6.1 The reaction of the legislature to the annulment decision

One year after the annulment decision of the AYM, a bill of law was submitted to the General Assembly of Turkey: Law Proposal on Establishment and Duties of the Human Damages Courts. The aim was to establish specialized courts only for the cases relating to compensation arising from personal injuries and death, defined as the 'human damage'. These courts were to be established as civil courts, just like commercial, family, or consumer courts. Their jurisdiction was supposed to cover all claims arising from the 'human damage', including the administrative law ones.

The proposal was supported by some scholars.[54] Their main argument in favour of the proposal was the existing differences between the civil and administrative judicial system. They argued that due to the nature of the 'human damage', the related claims are more suitable to be decided by specialized courts, rather than by courts with general jurisdiction,[55] especially because 'human damage' is a violation of the fundamental human right to life.[56]

However, the majority of the scholars have heavily criticized both the annulled Art 3 HMK and the new legislative proposal.[57] The criticism was mainly grounded in the *ratio* of the legislative proposal. They argued that jurisdiction should be defined on the basis of the tort with all its legal consequences, and not only on the basis of the damage caused.[58] They insisted that, relating to the issue of jurisdiction, the damage itself should not be differentiated as material and human damage, and that different types of damage do not require a different kind of trial.[59]

This bill never passed through the Assembly and has not become a part of the legislation. However, if it were all claims including both human and

---

54 Çelik (n 31) 311.

55 ibid.

56 ibid.

57 Ayanoğlu (n 27) 77; İsmail Birsen and Emre Yavaş, '6100 Sayılı Hukuk Muhakemeleri Kanunu'nun 3. Maddesi ile Getirilen Düzenlemenin Hukuk Aleminde Doğuracağı Sorunlar ve Bu Maddenin Anayasa'ya Aykırılığı Sorunu' (2011) 6 (63) *Terazi Hukuk Dergisi* 14, 15.

58 Akyılmaz and others (n 20) 169–70; Birsen and Yavaş (n 57) 15.

59 Akyılmaz and others (n 20) 172.

material damages would need to be filed separately. The material damages would be claimed either through ordinary civil courts or administrative courts depending on the legal nature of the dispute, while the 'human damages' would be claimed in front of the specialized 'human damages' courts. This would require at least two simultaneous lawsuits. It is obvious that the workload of these courts might differ from each other and that one of these proceedings might be finalized before the other one. It should be added that the legislative proposal also included a provision which restricted the prejudicial question: the 'human damages' courts would have to continue with the proceedings irrespective of the claims filed in front of other courts, while the other courts would have to wait for the decision of a 'human damages' court to avoid giving any contradictory decisions. This solution would lengthen the average time of proceedings and would result in a breach of the right to due process.

Interestingly, in the light of the AYM annulment decision, the legislative proposal was *per se* unconstitutional,[60] since it had a wider scope of application than the annulled Art 3 HMK. Also, the special procedural provisions and requirement of simultaneous lawsuits included in the proposal would be very problematic in the practice.

### 6.2 Application of Article 55 of the Code of Obligations by administrative courts

As a result of the AYM annulment decision, Art 55 TBK remained in effect without the corresponding Art 3 HBK. This situation raised the question of whether the administrative courts should apply Art 55 TBK or not, and to what extent.

As it was explained, the applicable law and general principles in Turkish administrative law are slightly different than in Turkish civil law. Thus, if the question is answered as yes without any annotation, that would be very problematic for administrative courts as they would be required to apply civil law to the cases related with 'human damages', whereas they would apply administrative law to all other cases. Moreover, the application of both bodies of law could also occur in the same case, if there is a combination of human and material damage as a result of the same act of the state, as also addressed by AYM in its decision. The main reason for these issues is the unclear drafting of Art 55 TBK.[61]

The general assessment of the doctrine is as follows. Article 55 TBK would be applied by civil courts that have jurisdiction over all claims about loss of body integrity and death, including the ones related to administrative law, as a result of Art 3 HMK. Article 55 TBK mostly concerns the question of the calculation of the damages, and although it states that 'provisions of this Code' will be applied even if the personal injury or death is caused with an act of administration, this should be interpreted as meaning that the civil law is to be applied in the administrative law related cases only in respect of the calculation

---

60  Kurt Konca (n 17) 301.
61  İnceoğlu and Paksoy (n 8) 1399; Ayanoğlu (n 27) 73.

of damages.[62] After the annulment of Art 3 HMK, the civil courts have lost their jurisdiction over the administrative law related cases and administrative courts gained its jurisdiction. Consequently, based on a teleological reduction of Art 55 TBK,[63] Art 55 TBK should be applied by administrative courts only for the calculation of the damages,[64] and not for the determination of the conditions of liability. This assessment is also in compliance with the application of the previous Code of Obligations by administrative courts, which was also applied only in respect of the calculation of damages.[65]

The application of Art 55 TBK by administrative courts was dealt with in several recent decisions of the Council of State. In one of the decisions, the Council of State only referred to the Art 55 TBK and stated that the calculation of damages complied with Art 55 TBK.[66] In another decision, the Council of State stated that the calculation of damages is supposed to comply with Art 55 TBK.[67] On the other hand, in one decision Council of State reasoned that the strict liability should be applied for the liability of the state,[68] although strict liability is exceptional under TBK. In another decision, the Council of State decided that neglect of duty should be determined in light of administrative jurisprudence but as a result of Art 55 TBK, the damages should be calculated according to TBK.[69]

## 7 Proposition and conclusion

Apart from the question of the need for a separated judiciary system, it is clear that different disputes with different backgrounds require a variety of courts, at least trial procedures. It is acceptable for the legislature to give priority to compensation of 'human damage'. However, as it is explained, it is so rare that a tort only leads to human damage; instead, it generally leads both to human and material damages. Thus, the system that was proposed by the legislature would require two different trials in the same case,[70] even though there was only one

---

62 However, it is also argued that the provisions of Art 55 TBK dealing with the calculation of damages represent a breach of the Constitution as well, because they intervene in the judicial discretion. See Adnan Deynekli, 'Türk Borçlar Kanunu'nda Yer Alan Önemli Usul Hükümleri' (2011) 2 (2) *İnönü Üniversitesi Hukuk Fakültesi Dergisi* 45, 70. See also İnceoğlu and Paksoy (n 8) 1394; Ünlütepe (n 9) 87.

63 Hasan Seçkin Ozanoğlu, 'Türk Borçlar Hukuku ve Sorumluluk Hukuku Açısından TBK 55. Madde ve Bedensel Zararlar' (2016) in Sema Uçakhan Güleç and Necdet Basa (eds), *Yeni Gelişmeler Işığında: Bedensel Zararların Tazmini: Uluslararası Kongre*, vol 1 (Türkiye Barolar Birliği 2016) 121, 126.

64 İnceoğlu and Paksoy (n 8) 1407.

65 ibid 1400.

66 Council of State, 10th Chamber decision of 21 March 2016, E 2013/8065, K 2016/1554,

67 Council of State, 15th Chamber decision of 3 April 2018, E 2013/13459, K 2018/3300.

68 Council of State, 10th Chamber decision of 8 March 2016, E 2013/4297, K 2016/1198.

69 Council of State, 15th Chamber decision of 18 April 2016, E 2015/7589, K 2016/2661.

70 Hülya Taş Korkmaz, '6100 Sayılı Hukuk Muhakemeleri Kanunu'nun Görev, Yetki ve Yargı Yeri Belirlenmesine İlişkin Hükümlerinin Değerlendirilmesi' (2013) 8 (Special Issue) *Yaşar Üniversitesi E-Dergisi* 1753, 1765; Birsen and Yavaş (n 57) 15; Kurt Konca (n 17) 305.

tort. The main purpose of procedural rules is to simplify the procedure, not to make it more complicated.

The differences between civil and administrative courts may constitute a logical ground for a provision such as Art 55 TBK. However, a different solution could be offered, such as amending the procedural rules of administrative judiciary or correcting inconsistencies.

The provisions of Art 3 HMK and Art 55 TBK were legislated to complete each other and harmonize the dispute resolution system for claims arising from loss of body integrity and death. However, the annulment of Art 3 HMK leads to a controversial application of Art 55 TBK. Because of the differences between civil and administrative procedures, the application of principles of the law of obligations in the administrative cases may lead to some contradictions.

As AYM decided that the provision of Art 3 HMK is contrary to the Constitution, legislating such a provision again should not be an option. On the other hand, the main *ratio* of Art 55 TBK was that it is to be applied by the civil courts, as Art 3 HMK stated. However, the current situation makes it impossible. It is argued that Art 55 TBK has a limited applicability in administrative courts while Turkish administrative law has its own principles for compensation of damages. Thus, abrogation of the second paragraph of Art 55 TBK could be helpful to avoid any further arguments and misconceptions.

## Bibliography

Adal E, *Fundamentals of Turkish Private Law* (7th edn, Legal 2004).

Adalet Komisyonu, *Hukuk Muhakemeleri Kanunu Tasarısı ve Adalet Komisyonu Raporu* (TC, Başbakanlık, Kanunlar ve Kararla, 16 April 2008) <www.kgm.adalet.gov.tr/Tasariasama lari/Kanunlasan/2011Yili/kanmetni/6100ss.pdf> accessed 17 June 2020.

Akkayan Yıldırım A, 'Geç Ortaya Çıkan Bedensel Zararların Tazmini Taleplerinde Uygulanacak Zamanaşımının Yeni Eğilimler Çerçevesinde Değerlendirilmesi' (2016) 74 (1) *İstanbul Üniversitesi Hukuk Fakültesi Mecmuası* 185.

Akkurt N, '6098 Sayılı Türk Borçlar Kanunu'nda Uygulayıcı Gözüyle Hâksiz Fiiller ve Tazminat' in Badur E (ed), *6098 Sayılı Türk Borçlar Kanunu Sempozyumu: 12–13 Mayis 2011* (Ankara Barosu 2012).

Akyılmaz B and others, 'İnsan Zararları Mahkemelerinin Kuruluş ve Görevlerine Dair Kanun Teklifine Eleştirel Bakış' (2015) 19 (2) *Gazi Üniversitesi Hukuk Fakültesi Dergisi* 167.

Ayanoğlu T, 'İnsan Zararlarına İlişkin Tam Yargı Davalarını Çözme Görevini Asliye Hukuku Mahkemelerine Vermek Reform mu Yoksa Fantezi mi?' (2012) 86 (2) *İstanbul Barosu Dergisi* 71.

Birsen İ and Yavaş E, '6100 Sayılı Hukuk Muhakemeleri Kanunu'nun 3. Maddesi ile Getirilen Düzenlemenin Hukuk Aleminde Doğuracağı Sorunlar ve Bu Maddenin Anayasa'ya Aykırılığı Sorunu' (2011) 6 (63) *Terazi Hukuk Dergisi* 14.

Çal S, 'İdare Hukukunda Bedensel Zararların Tazminine Yönelik Gelişmeler: Aym'nin HMK 3. Maddesini İptal Kararı ve Çağrışımları' in Uçakhan Güleç S and Basa N (eds), *Yeni Gelişmeler Işığında: Bedensel Zararların Tazmini: Uluslararası Kongre*, vol 1 (Türkiye Barolar Birliği 2016) 319.

Çelik ÇA, 'Can Zararları Tüketici Yasası'nın Konusu Değildir' in Tokbaş H and Üçışık F (eds), *4. Tüketici Hukuku Kongresi Makale, Bildiri ve Ses Çözümleri: Sektörel Bazda Tüketici Hukuku ve Uygulamaları* (Bilge Yayınevi 2015).

Deynekli A, 'Türk Borçlar Kanunu'nda Yer Alan Önemli Usul Hükümleri' (2011) 2 (2) *İnönü Üniversitesi Hukuk Fakültesi Dergisi* 45.

Eroğlu Durkal M, 'İdarenin Sorumluluğunun Ortaya Çıkışı ve Temeli' (2019) 23 (1) *Ankara Hacı Bayram Veli Üniversitesi Hukuk Fakültesi Dergisi* 159 [https://doi.org/10.34246/ahbvuhfd.548483].

Gözler K and Kaplan G, 'İdari Eylemlerden Kaynaklanan Zararlara İlişkin Davalar Adlî Yargının Görev Alanına Sokulabilir Mi? (HMK m. 3 ve TBK m. 55/2 Hakkında Eleştiriler)' (2011) 6 (63) *Terazi Hukuk Dergisi* 36.

Gözübüyük Ş, *Yönetim Hukuku* (27th edn, Turhan Kitabevi 2008).

Günday M, *İdare Hukuku* (7th edn, İmaj Yayınevi 2003).

Gürzumar OB, 'İsviçre Medeni Kanunu'nun Türkiye'de İktibası' in Sirmen AL, Kırca C, and Buz V (eds), *Symposium anlässlich des 80. Jahrestages des Inkrafttretens des Türkischen Zivilgesetzbuches: Türk Medenî Kanununun Yürürlüğe Girişinin 80. Yılı Münasebetiyle Düzenlenen Sempozyum* (Ankara Üniversitesi 2007).

İnceoğlu MM and Paksoy MS, 'Bedensel Zararlarda Ve Ölüm Halinde Zararın Belirlenmesi (TBK. m. 55)' (2013) 8 (Special Issue) *Yaşar Üniversitesi E-Dergisi* 1383.

Kurt Konca N, 'İnsan Zararları Mahkemelerinin Kuruluş ve Görevlerine Dair Kanun Teklifi Hakkında Kısa Bir Değerlendirme' (2016) 1 (2) *Çankaya Üniversitesi Hukuk Fakültesi Dergisi* 293.

Ozanoğlu HS, 'Türk Borçlar Hukuku ve Sorumluluk Hukuku Açısından TBK 55. Madde ve Bedensel Zararlar' (2016) in Uçakhan Güleç S and Basa N (eds), *Yeni Gelişmeler Işığında: Bedensel Zararların Tazmini: Uluslararası Kongre*, vol 1 (Türkiye Barolar Birliği 2016).

Şaşmaz AP, 'İdarenin Sorumluluğu ve Danıştay Kararlarındaki Görünümüne Genel Bakış' (2016) 2 *Ekonomi İşletme Siyaset ve Uluslararası İlişkiler Dergisi* 211.

Taş Korkmaz H, '6100 Sayılı Hukuk Muhakemeleri Kanunu'nun Görev, Yetki ve Yargı Yeri Belirlenmesine İlişkin Hükümlerinin Değerlendirilmesi' (2013) 8 (Special Issue) *Yaşar Üniversitesi E-Dergisi* 1753.

Tekçe FN, 'Manevi Tazminat Davalarında Görevli ve Yetkili Mahkeme' (2016) 22 *Marmara Üniversitesi Hukuk Fakültesi Hukuk Araştırmaları Dergisi* 2623.

Ünlütepe M, 'TBK'nın 55/I. Maddesi Çerçevesinde Ölüm Hâlinde Uğranılan Zararların ve Bedensel Zararların Belirlenmesi' (2018) 13 (141) *Terazi Hukuk Dergisi* 68.

# Index